Praise for
LinkedIn for Busi

"It took me years of trial and error to figure out how to truly leverage ~~LinkedIn to drive~~ ales and revenue for my company. If only Brian Carter had written this book in 2007, I could have fast-forwarded to success. Fortunately, you can. Buy it. Learn it. Do it. You'll be glad you did."

—**Jason Falls**, CEO, Social Media Explorer, and author, *No Bullshit Social Media*

"For business-to-business marketers, a million followers isn't what's cool in social media. A thousand qualified leads, now that's what's cool. Brian Carter explains, convincingly and colorfully, why year-making deals most often trace back to LinkedIn, and he shares what companies need to do to carve off their own chunk of LinkedIn's revenue opportunity."

—**Joe Chernov**, VP of content marketing, Eloqua

"Managing LinkedIn detached from your overall strategy is as effective as an arm detached from a body. Zombies can survive this ~~without a head~~. Carter supplies a brilliant LinkedIn survival guide."

—**Erik Qualman**, international bestselling author and speaker

"If you want to generate leads for your business, then you have to read Brian's new book. It will show you how to best use all the tools that LinkedIn has to offer to grow your business."

—**Dan Schawbel**, founder, Millennial Branding, and author, *Me 2.0*

"*LinkedIn for Business* is a book that every B2B marketer should read. It shows how B2B businesses can engage communities effectively, generate leads (not just any leads, better leads), and ignite advocacy."

—**Ekaterina Walter**, global social innovation strategist, Intel

"One thing is certain: Today's successful sales, advertising, and marketing executives need to acknowledge LinkedIn is more than a modern Rolodex. This book is filled with strategies to generate more leads and sales with LinkedIn. How will social media positively impact your organizational goals? Uncover the answer to this question and more once you read Carter's definitive guide for generating real business on LinkedIn."

—**Patrick Dorsey**, vice president of marketing, Avectra

"From strategy to tactics, Brian breaks down LinkedIn so you can finally determine how to best leverage the platform for your business. This book will help you clearly develop a robust plan where LinkedIn fits into your strategy. Developing digital plans around this ever-evolving industry is a challenge, and Brian ensures that you are leveraging LinkedIn to meet your marketing and advertising objectives with best practices in mind."

—**Brandon Prebynski**, digital and social business strategist (@prebynski)

LinkedIn for Business

How Advertisers, Marketers, and Salespeople Get Leads, Sales, and Profits from LinkedIn

BRIAN CARTER

800 East 96th Street,
Indianapolis, Indiana 46240 USA

LinkedIn for Business: How Advertisers, Marketers, and Salespeople Get Leads, Sales, and Profits from LinkedIn

Copyright © 2013 by Pearson Education

All rights reserved. No part of this book shall be reproduced, stored in a retrieval system, or transmitted by any means, electronic, mechanical, photocopying, recording, or otherwise, without written permission from the publisher. No patent liability is assumed with respect to the use of the information contained herein. Although every precaution has been taken in the preparation of this book, the publisher and author assume no responsibility for errors or omissions. Nor is any liability assumed for damages resulting from the use of the information contained herein.

ISBN-13: 978-0-7897-4968-0
ISBN-10: 0-7897-4968-8

Library of Congress Cataloging-in-Publication Data
Carter, Brian, 1973-
   LinkedIn for business : how advertisers, marketers, and salespeople get leads, sales, and profits from LinkedIn / Brian Carter.
       p. cm.
   Includes index.
   ISBN 978-0-7897-4968-0
   1. LinkedIn (Electronic resource) 2. Business networks. 3. Internet marketing. I. Title.
   HD69.S8C366 2013
   658.800285'53--dc23

                                     2012021628
Printed in the United States of America
First Printing: August 2012

Trademarks

All terms mentioned in this book that are known to be trademarks or service marks have been appropriately capitalized. Que Publishing cannot attest to the accuracy of this information. Use of a term in this book should not be regarded as affecting the validity of any trademark or service mark.

Warning and Disclaimer

Every effort has been made to make this book as complete and as accurate as possible, but no warranty or fitness is implied. The information provided is on an "as is" basis. The author and the publisher shall have neither liability nor responsibility to any person or entity with respect to any loss or damages arising from the information contained in this book or from the use of programs accompanying it.

Bulk Sales

Que Publishing offers excellent discounts on this book when ordered in quantity for bulk purchases or special sales. For more information, please contact

> U.S. Corporate and Government Sales
> 1-800-382-3419
> corpsales@pearsontechgroup.com

For sales outside of the U.S., please contact
> International Sales
> international@pearsoned.com

CONTENTS AT A GLANCE

TABLE OF CONTENTS

4 Amazing Brands: Company Pages That Grow Business   65

5 Generating Leads with Content Marketing and LinkedIn Answers, Events, & Groups   77

6 Get It All Done: Your Weekly LinkedIn Marketing Routine   107

PART III LINKEDIN ADVERTISING

7 Best Practices: Online Advertising and LinkedIn Advertising   115

About the Author

Brian Carter is regarded as one of the elite Internet marketing experts in the world. He is the author of the book *The Like Economy* and co-author of *Facebook Marketing (Third Edition)*. He has 13 years of experience, including Google, Twitter, and Facebook marketing, both as a consultant and marketing agency director.

Brian develops strategies and builds search and social media programs for companies of all sizes, including well-known entities such as Universal Studios, The U.S. Army, Hardee's, and Carl's Jr. He has been quoted and profiled by *The Wall Street Journal*, ABC News, Mashable, *Forbes*, *Information Week*, *U.S. News & World Report*, and *Entrepreneur Magazine*.

Brian writes for several of the most popular marketing blogs, including Search Engine Journal, AllFacebook, and Mashable (which boasts 20 million monthly readers). He has more than 50,000 online fans—and growing—and his content is viewed over 8 million times a month.

Brian is a professional speaker who delivers entertaining, motivational talks on Internet marketing and social media. He has presented to corporations and associations. Audience members include CEOs, business owners, and expert marketers. His hands-on business experience, cutting-edge insights, and background in improv and stand-up comedy culminate in a speaker and trainer who leaves every audience not only entertained, but armed with powerful strategies and tactics.

He is a regular presenter for top marketing conferences such as SEOmoz, SMX, Pubcon, The AllFacebook Expo, Socialize, The South Carolina Society of Association Executives, and The American Marketing Association.

Dedication

Often I see authors dedicate their books to the people who've supported them the most through the writing process, and this is no exception. You don't know how hard writing a book is until you've done it. And writing three in a year is like running a marathon a week, both mentally and emotionally. The people near you have to put up with you, so they deserve your gratitude. I've already acknowledged a couple of them, but the people who helped me the most in the process were my wife, Lynda Harvey-Carter, and my acquisitions editor, Katherine Bull. If I could also dedicate this book to the calming influence of the wind in the trees in my backyard, I would do that, too. Our dogs, Brad Pitt and Serotonin, and our cats, Larry and Little B, were of great personal support in the process. My great friends in the improv and comedy community in Charleston, South Carolina, have been an excellent outlet to balance my stress. Am I allowed to dedicate a book to thirty people, four animals, and nature? Let's do that.

Acknowledgments

I love writing books that teach cutting-edge, repeatable, resulted-oriented marketing systems. This is another such book, and that means it required input and feedback from an army of people who are implementing these ideas on the frontlines, as well as the hard-fought wisdom of other authors and bloggers.

I want to thank Joe Chernov and Elle Woulfe of Eloqua for their infinite generosity explaining their approach to LinkedIn advertising lead generation, lead nurturing, and advanced marketing automation. Joe also connected me with Eloqua's Melissa Madian and Alex Shootman, who answered my questions about "brand armies" and their salespeople's use of LinkedIn.

Super-duper heartfelt gratitude to my editors: Katherine Bull, Romny French, Betsy Harris, Ginny Munroe, Bart Reed, and Marty Weintraub. You guys rock! Oh, yes, and my wife, Lynda Harvey-Carter, who gave invaluable input on everything I wrote before sending it to Pearson!

A third of this book relates LinkedIn to modern sales strategies and processes. Thanks to everyone at Miller-Heiman for your books, whitepapers, and research. This book benefited from modern sales classics by Jeff Thull, Neil Rackham, Mack Hanan, and Michael Bosworth. Garrison Wynn and Jeff Thacker of Wynn Solutions also contributed unique and powerful perspectives on sales in the Internet lead-generation era.

I held this book to a high standard of referencing, often relying on the outstanding work of organizations such as MarketingProfs, MECLABS, The Content Marketing Institute, LeadFormix, Mashable, Techcrunch, Accenture, SEOmoz, The Bureau of Labor Statistics, ZDNet, eMarketer, comScore, SEER Interactive, Eloqua, Marketo, The Interactive Advertising Bureau, CNET, Marketing Sherpa, The Harvard

Business Review, Miller-Heiman, Cisco, and Search Engine Land. One more thing: I know we don't reference Wikipedia, and I always looked for the primary reference beyond it, but I believe the anonymous, hard-working, misunderstood, under-appreciated civilians who edit Wikipedia deserve a shout-out: Thanks!

Thanks to those who generously shared their sales, marketing, and advertising experiences in response to my questions on LinkedIn Answers, including Jason Croyle of MECLABS, Jeff Lee, Han Mo of Teleperformance, Chris Griffin of Salesforce, William Cooper of ChristiaNet, John Scranton of StartUpSelling, Inc., Dave Maskin, Sahar Andrade, Melissa Galt, Justin Miller, Veiko Herne, Pablo Ruiz of InfinixSoft, Julia Stege, Michael Manthey, Babette Ten Haken, Dallas Moore, Nery Leal, Patrick Hollister, James Gingerich of Sybase, Judy Freeman, Sarah Houston, Beth Avery, Robert Madison of Spiral16, Pat McGraw, Russ Hayman, and Jeff Lee of Optimize Sales.

We Want to Hear from You!

As the reader of this book, *you* are our most important critic and commentator. We value your opinion and want to know what we're doing right, what we could do better, what areas you'd like to see us publish in, and any other words of wisdom you're willing to pass our way.

We welcome your comments. You can email or write to let us know what you did or didn't like about this book—as well as what we can do to make our books better.

Please note that we cannot help you with technical problems related to the topic of this book.

When you write, please be sure to include this book's title and author as well as your name, email address, and phone number. I will carefully review your comments and share them with the author and editors who worked on the book.

Email: feedback@quepublishing.com

Mail: Que Publishing
ATTN: Reader Feedback
800 East 96th Street
Indianapolis, IN 46240 USA

Reader Services

Visit our website and register this book at quepublishing.com/register for convenient access to any updates, downloads, or errata that might be available for this book.

Twenty-first Century Sales and Marketing: LinkedIn Meets Marketing, Advertising, and Sales

This book describes a marketing system whereby advertisers, marketers, and salespeople can leverage LinkedIn to get more leads and sales for their company. The book is divided into five parts:

1. *This first section and chapter is an overview and introduction to the book.*

2. *The second section (Chapters 2 through 6) talks about how marketing people can help their companies on LinkedIn. It covers LinkedIn employee profiles, LinkedIn company pages, content marketing, LinkedIn Answers, LinkedIn Events, and LinkedIn Groups, all from the perspective of the marketing department.*

3. *The third section (Chapters 7 through 10) is focused on helping people in an advertising role. We talk about best practices from the last decade of Internet advertising, how to set up LinkedIn ads, and how to get excellent results from them.*

4. The fourth section (Chapters 11 through 13) is for salespeople. It covers the history of sales, how sales has changed, and what role LinkedIn plays in sales—most specifically, how salespeople can find new prospects and build relationships on LinkedIn.

5. The fifth section (Chapters 14 through 16) is for everyone, including advertisers, marketers, salespeople, executives, and managers. It discusses how the three major roles (advertising, marketing, and sales) must work together to go beyond mediocre social media results and the kind of support these teams will require from company leadership.

How have business and marketing changed in the twenty-first century? What has the Internet changed about the sales process? In the rest of this chapter, we'll look at online versus offline sales, and how introverts and extroverts can work together. Then we'll examine the social media revenue and the history of LinkedIn. We close with a few LinkedIn case studies for inspiration.

Networking and Business: Face-to-Face and Online

LinkedIn is an online social network. Online social networks (especially Facebook, Twitter, and LinkedIn) have become extremely popular and frequently talked about over the last few years. But using LinkedIn to get more business is not fundamentally new, because human beings have been meeting new people and socializing for thousands of years. Social networks have always existed. Business people network to build relationships and generate new opportunities. New friends, partners, and customers come from simply getting to know people on a professional and personal basis.

Historically, much new business has been driven by extroverted salespeople who thrive on social contact, love talking on the phone, and create interaction by talking to clients in person. The cliché, which surely contains some truth, is that sales come from golf outings, Kiwanis meetings, and Chamber of Commerce gatherings. Many purchases involve some sort of social contact, even if it's just the store employee who asks, "Can I help you with something?"

Social networks like LinkedIn and Twitter remove barriers and accelerate the networking process. You can escape the physical boundaries of face-to-face networking and meet people across the globe. You can share white papers, information about your company, pictures, and blog posts instantly without needing to be in the same place or send a letter. These online networks also offer social advertising, with which you can raise awareness about yourself and your company.

Many Internet marketing and social media experts, who do the majority of their work alone with computers, are introverts. I am one. We aren't the type to go out and socialize with new people constantly. While writing this book, I was also reading *The New York Times* bestseller *Quiet: The Power of Introverts in a World That Can't Stop Talking*.[1] It quotes many studies and repeats one of the best definitions of introversion I've heard: Introverts are people who can be intentionally extroverted but need to recharge afterward. Gandhi, Einstein, Rosa Parks, and Van Gogh were introverts. We get our energy from performing solo activities such as computer work that the extroverted salesperson might find tedious and exhausting.

My personal observation is that many of "geeks" like me who speak at Internet-oriented conferences do a much higher percentage of our socializing via Twitter, Facebook, LinkedIn, blogging, email, and Skype. Socializing online can be incredibly enjoyable, because it's a Mihaly Csikszentmihalyi–style "flow" experience.[2] We make an art out of multitasking our content consumption, content creation, and networking. We share business opportunities, give each other online media exposure, and create search engine and social media authority that brings us new business. It's not uncommon for us to email, tweet, Facebook, chat, and work all at the same time, interacting with and influencing hundreds or thousands of people per day.

When we meet our online friends in person at conferences or local gatherings, we solidify our bonds further. Some use acronyms for these "face-to-face" meetings (F2F) and real-life experiences (IRL, in real life). When I first started speaking at conferences, I found the extroversion so anxiety-producing that I would use Twitter to schedule meetings with peers because otherwise I would have hid in my hotel room every second I wasn't speaking!

When you combine introverted social marketers with extroverted salespeople, you can achieve online reach and influence *plus* sales-closing ability (see Figure 1.1). Each operates in his or her strengths and complements the other. Think of it the way you'd put two all-stars on the same sports team: a quarterback throwing to a receiver for a touchdown, or a point guard throwing an alley-oop to a power forward. The combination of these two different skill sets leads to championships for sports teams and competitive dominance for companies.

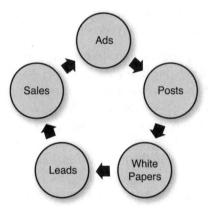

Figure 1.1   *How business is created with LinkedIn, from advertising to marketing to sales.*

This book teaches your team and its role players the following:

- How to improve teamwork among the employees responsible for LinkedIn ads, marketing, and sales
- How to improve and use their skills at advertising, marketing, networking, relationship-building, and sales
- How marketers and salespeople can build relationships that result in more business
- How to raise awareness of your company to new potential customers
- How to convince those prospects that your company is the best one to solve their problems
- How to leverage relationships to close sales and increase revenue

Social Media and Revenue

Over the last several years, social media has grown from novel curiosity to proven revenue generator. In 2008 and 2009, Dell made over $6.5 million additional revenue from its Twitter accounts.[3] Zappos was a start-up whose marketing consisted almost entirely of social media (including hundreds of Zappos employee Twitter accounts) and was acquired by Amazon in 2009 for $928 million.[4] Numerous small- and medium-sized businesses made money on Facebook in 2011.[5]

The business-to-consumer marketer took notice. Marketing budgets began to move toward social media. But what about businesses that sell to other businesses (B2B)? Does social media work for them, too? And are they using it?

In 2011, Accenture completed a study demonstrating the following:

- Although five out of six business-to-business executives thought social media was very important, only 8% would say their company was "heavily leveraging" social media. They had started but weren't at full steam.

- Only 5% of B2B executives reported a strong formal link between their social media activities and their strategic customer initiatives—meaning social media had yet to be integrated with goal planning and tactics. Their social media activities were ad-hoc and not systematized.

- Nearly one-fifth of these executives doubted their company's ability to make the right social media investment decisions.[6]

Most businesses know social media is important and have begun some kind of social media marketing, but they are not using it to its full potential and aren't sure they know the best way to do so.

Increased revenue is almost always the ultimate goal, but many steps need to happen along the way to that goal. If you increase awareness of your company and its solutions, you can get more leads for sales. Better thought-leadership and prospect education can increase how many leads decide to buy (making the sales force's job easier) and how many customers you keep (making customer service's job easier).

Sometimes you can prove that social media efforts create new sales, especially if you have sophisticated tracking in place. Does your sales CRM (customer relationship management software) show if the lead came from LinkedIn, Facebook, or Google? If not, you'll have a tough time proving the true value of your Internet marketing. You sometimes hear from customers that they saw you on one website or another, but memory can be unreliable. We're busy these days, and we consume more advertisements than we even remember. We may not know exactly how we first heard of something or even why we bought it; other times, we're not capable of being honest with ourselves about why we make certain decisions. Good tracking removes some of these obstacles and can give us clear data about which marketing, advertising, and sales campaigns contribute to the final sale.

In situations where tracking is adequate, social marketers often report impressive results. But of course, it depends on how you're doing your social media marketing. Slipshod or inconsistent efforts are unreliable. The best thing to do is to find the companies that have been successful and follow their process. These lessons can come from other LinkedIn marketers, social media marketing with Facebook and Twitter (because of the similarities between them), and even other types of online marketing, including Google, AdWords, and email. In Chapter 2, I cover some of the best practices in social and online marketing that can be applied to

LinkedIn marketing. Later in the book, we look at tactics that have been proven successful, specifically on LinkedIn.

Even if you follow best practices, all social media marketing is relatively experimental, with LinkedIn marketing and sales even more so. Our understanding is immature and spread thin across many verticals. Metaphorically speaking, we're at a point in the frontier life where some scouts have barely made it back to safety and others have followed routes that led to riches. Your journey doing advertising, marketing, and sales on LinkedIn will be an adventure and an experiment, but you can ensure that failing tests are quickly recognized and stopped whereas successes are maximized and repeated. The successes will more than make up for the failures.

This is the time. By starting now in social media, you create an advantage for yourself. In the online world, the early adopters gain the lion's share of the spoils. This pattern has repeated itself over the last decade: New technological opportunities create new companies like Netflix and destroy or damage others like Blockbuster. If you're one of the business people who put off creating a website, put off doing Google ads, and put off search engine optimization while your competitors began to eat away at your market share, you know what I mean. Those in business who take a few calculated risks are the ones who win big. Companies that wait are forced to play catch-up in a field of greater competition, more obstacles, and higher prices. The biggest profits are there to be captured now. I realize that often the bigger the company is, the more risk-averse it may be, but I believe the systems and processes taught in this book will help you maximize opportunity while minimizing risk.

Although this book is about LinkedIn, the same lessons can be applied to Facebook, and this pattern won't change in the foreseeable future. Technology moves faster in the twenty-first century, so you don't have a year or two to think about whether you should leverage these social platforms. In fact, they may no longer be a good idea in a couple of years. What if smartphone platforms such as the iPhone and Android release apps that do all this without Facebook and LinkedIn, and people switched to them? Yahoo! has had its peak time and is now, according to sites such as Google Trends and Alexa, half as popular as Facebook.

A number of clients I've worked with find Google AdWords competition and prices to be rising. Some no longer spend money on AdWords, and others have cut back to only the most profitable keywords. Some businesses cannot use AdWords because people aren't aware of their products enough to search for them. A number of companies that use third-party pay-per-click optimization services are doing better than ever with AdWords, but these are companies that have enough money to spend both on agencies and their high-level tools.[7] Search engine optimization also has become more and more competitive. Companies working on their natural search presence constantly improve their content and increase their inbound links, raising their rankings or solidifying their authority. Every day, a company just starting in the natural search game faces more of a challenge.

The marketing mix decision is different for every company, and your mileage will vary with each marketing and advertising channel. If AdWords is a model, then these opportunities become more expensive for years until third-party companies properly calibrate ways to make them more efficient. While those costs are increasing, you should get involved in LinkedIn and figure out how it can benefit your business. LinkedIn will only become more competitive, so the biggest opportunity is now.

The History of LinkedIn

Here are a few statistics to illustrate the growth of LinkedIn:

- LinkedIn was founded in December 2002 and launched in May 2003—within one month, it had 4,500 members.
- By mid-2011, it had 33.9 million unique visitors, up 63% from 2010.[8]
- As of December 31, 2011, two professionals were newly signing up to join LinkedIn *per second*.
- As of February 9, 2012, LinkedIn operates the world's largest professional network on the Internet, with more than 150 million members in over 200 countries and territories. It is available in 16 languages.[9]
- There were more than 2 billion people searches on LinkedIn in 2010, and close to double that in 2011.

As you can see in Figure 1.2, which shows what people are searching for in Google, interest in LinkedIn has grown steadily, as has interest in Twitter, while interest in MySpace has plummeted.

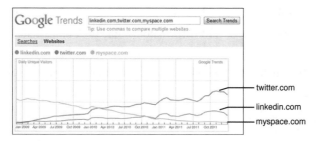

Figure 1.2 *As evidenced by Google search data, Twitter has grown to be the most popular of these three social networks, while MySpace's popularity has plummeted.*

LinkedIn is widely regarded as the most professional (the least whimsical, least personal, most formal) of the social networks. People don't normally put crazy photos on LinkedIn the way they do on Facebook. They are less likely to report what they're eating than they are on Twitter. LinkedIn is many people's online resume, and recruiters use it extensively to find viable employees. Many business people use LinkedIn Groups and Answers to network, find, and share facts, develop themselves as professionals, show off their expertise, and secure new business. Some people are thinking ahead about their business futures. As of December 31, 2011, students and recent college graduates were the fastest-growing demographic on LinkedIn. This makes sense because we know Generation Y is bigger than the Boomer Generation, and they continue to move into the workforce.

Why LinkedIn Is Relevant to Your Business

Many marketers believe LinkedIn is a profitable channel. A 2012 poll by MarketingSherpa reported that LinkedIn's effectiveness was supported by 65% of B2B marketers, Twitter's by 53%, and Facebook's by 47%.[10] LinkedIn has executives from all Fortune 500 companies as members. More than 2 million companies have a LinkedIn Company Page.

Who else likes to use LinkedIn? Some interesting answers come from Quantcast, a company that directly measures more than 25 million web audiences around the world. You can use it to check the audience of any website, as shown in Figure 1.3. The following is according to their data:

- Fifty-four percent of LinkedIn members earn more than $60K per year, and 36% earn more than $100K annually.

- LinkedIn has 29% more six-figure earners than the average website.

- The 35-to-49-year-old demographic uses LinkedIn, 19% more than the average website.

- Almost one-fourth of LinkedIn visitors come back at least 30 times per month.

- More than half (51%) of LinkedIn users visit at least once per month.[11]

Figure 1.3   *According to Quantcast, LinkedIn users are more affluent and more educated than the average website visitor.*

In June 2010, LeadFormix, a marketing automation company that offers lead generation and sales-enablement software to enterprises, published a study called "How Effective Is Social Media For B2B Lead Generation?" Their finding was that, of all the social networking sites, LinkedIn was the most effective for getting leads to B2B company websites.

In 2011, LeadFormix conducted a follow-up study focused just on LinkedIn for B2B marketing. They learned that website visitors from LinkedIn were remarkably good prospects. Many times it was these visitors' first trip to the company website. LinkedIn was raising awareness with new customers and generating leads. Of all the marketing opportunities on LinkedIn, people who came to the site from Groups and Advertising were most likely to fill out a lead form.[12]

If you want for new potential customers to come to your website and become a lead for your sales force, LinkedIn is a great place to find them. What's more, the data in this study suggests that LinkedIn Groups and Advertising are the *most* effective places on LinkedIn to find them, and having a company page and employee profiles gets potential customers to take your company seriously.

Why LinkedIn Is More Than a Modern Rolodex

If you're not old enough to know what a Rolodex is, it was a rotating file device used to store contact business info. It debuted in 1958 and was insanely popular with business people (back around the time when people were walking uphill both to and from school). If you think LinkedIn is just a modern version of that, you're dead wrong. Here's why:

- LinkedIn contacts stay up to date without your help, especially when people move from one company to another. I've had salespeople tell me that if all LinkedIn did for them was keep track of contacts who are switching companies, that feature alone would make it worth using.

- LinkedIn contains a heck of a lot more information about a person than a Rolodex ever could, often including recent tweets, blog posts, and colleagues who've recommended them. You can use this information to start interesting conversations and get a sales call off on the right footing.

- You can advertise, start groups and communities, and even market your company on LinkedIn—all obviously beyond the capabilities of a rotating file.

LinkedIn is more than a real-time Rolodex or resume; it gives you an entire marketing and advertising system. Plug it into a CRM such as Salesforce.com or ACT! and you've put your sales funnel on steroids.

How Your Advertising, Marketing, and Sales Teams Achieve Goals with LinkedIn

There are a variety of different goals for LinkedIn users, such as the following:

- Increasing your number of leads
- Increasing your lead quality
- Branding and positioning your company
- Capturing your target audience in a group for marketing or market research purposes

All of these are valid goals, and although you might start with just one or two, you may pursue all of them with LinkedIn over time. Regardless of your goal, you need to define how you'll measure your campaign's success, what quantified target you want to hit, and what strategies and tactics you'll use to get there.

For example, if you want to grow a LinkedIn Group for market research purposes, decide how many people you want in that Group. Have your LinkedIn advertising person do some research with the ad creation tool: How many people can you target on LinkedIn who might become your customers? Let's say there are 50,000. You might aim for getting 5,000 or 10,000 in your Group initially. Your strategy for membership growth may be advertising. This gives you quantified goals and a strategy with which to begin this marketing project. On the other hand, if you're going for a small group of extremely targeted folks—say, Fortune 100 CEOs—your Group may not be so large, but both quality (the right people) and quantity (because you won't get them all as customers) are important.

As you'll read later, most companies on LinkedIn use a combination of strategies and tactics to achieve their marketing goals, including contests, awards, polls, advertising, groups, content marketing, blogging, and integrating other social networking websites. And you'll want to base all of this on the Internet marketing best practices we discuss in Chapter 2.

If you're looking for leads, you'll enjoy the conversation in Part III about how LinkedIn Advertising can empower your lead-collection process. You may also have a marketing automation service in place such as Eloqua, which can help qualify and score your leads before they go to the sales force (having that in place actually means you can go for a larger volume of leads without worrying as much about how qualified they are). You may already have a process for salespeople to give marketing and advertising feedback about how qualified the leads are or aren't. They can give you specifics that might help you improve lead quality in your marketing and advertising. We'll cover this sort of team interaction and feedback in Chapter 14.

LinkedIn Marketing Success Stories

LinkedIn features a number of case studies on their website, illustrating a variety of strategies attempted and goals achieved. I've pulled out the more exceptional of those successes that are relevant to B2B sales and marketing. I thought it might be inspirational and motivational for you as you begin to digest the information in this book. I summarize and comment on these case studies in the following sections.

Cisco WebEx as Online Conferencing Leader

Cisco WebEx wanted to raise awareness and position themselves as the leader in online conferencing solutions. So, they created a set of awards and used LinkedIn ads to promote submissions. Their awards site generated 500+ entries and 11,500+ votes from 134,000 unique visitors. Half of their traffic was from word of mouth. Over 900 members joined the LinkedIn Group, and their Twitter account grew by 900. They announced the results at a live event that attracted 1,090 registered attendees. All of this led to 125 articles in the press and online news.

LinkedIn ads allowed Cisco to reach targeted business prospects affordably. Social media networks and shareability doubled their traffic, and the media stood up and paid attention. What do I mean about shareability? If you've tried to get press coverage for your company, you know that just putting out a press release won't cut it anymore. Anyone can put out a press release, and many do. You get lost in the noise and usually don't get major media coverage. But unique and innovative campaigns like this stand out and get the attention of journalists. What's more, anytime you do something new, people in social media are more likely to share it with their networks, thus increasing your exposure and traffic.

Qwest Business Understanding and Influencing IT Decision Makers

Qwest Business wanted to engage IT decision makers in specific geographies to build a community that they could use to do the following:

- Host technology solution conversations
- Influence decisions
- Increase sales

They created a LinkedIn Group, drove membership with LinkedIn Ads and Partner Messages, and then engaged new members with educationally interactive content. Their membership invitations were opened by 18% of the people they sent them to. They grew a 1,400-member community built from scratch and exceeded their year-end membership goal (1,000 members) by 40%. They also used polls (see Figure 1.4) and discussions to learn more about their audience to increase the effectiveness of their marketing and sales efforts.

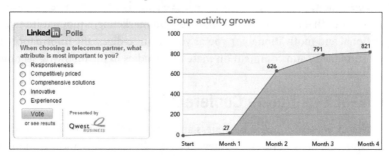

Figure 1.4   *Qwest used polls to gain valuable intelligence about their target audience after quickly growing their new LinkedIn Group.*

Many businesses have already learned the value of audience "ownership" with email lists and Facebook fan bases. How much more valuable is a group of prospects when it's highly qualified because you targeted the exact job titles, industries, or companies you serve?

Philips Market Research and Thought Leadership in Lighting and Healthcare

Philips wanted to be seen as an innovative leader in healthcare, lighting, and well-being. Their goal was to build credibility and drive discussion (see Figure 1.5) and awareness with key audiences for their two main B2B offerings: health and lighting. They created two LinkedIn Groups (Innovations in Healthcare and Innovations in Light) and grew them to 38,000+ and 27,000+ members, respectively. Over 60% of their members were manager level or above. They drove this membership through display ads, InMail, and word of mouth. Almost 10% of those who received an InMail went on to join the associated Group. What's more, their LinkedIn Groups became the go-to communities for their niches.

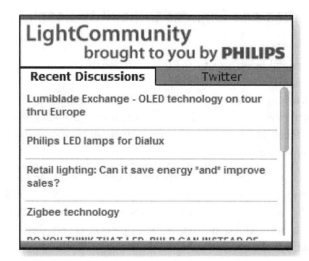

Figure 1.5   *A widget showing a sample of discussions in Philips' successful Innovations in Light LinkedIn Group.*

Exact Gets 40% of Invited Accountants to Recommend Their Financial Software

Exact is a company in the Netherlands that supplies software to entrepreneurs. Knowing that accountants are influential advisors in the financial process, and that 85% of the accountants in The Netherlands could be reached via LinkedIn, Exact used a Company Page, Recommendations, and Recommendation Ads to get 40% of their customers to recommend their SAAS product. It garnered 281 product recommendations and 5,924 new followers on their Company Page. Exact has 14 product solutions. It lists each one on its LinkedIn company page, and each one can receive recommendations from LinkedIn users.

You may have noticed that people shift where they spend time online much more frequently than they used to. A LinkedIn Group that didn't exist yesterday could be the hottest place in your niche three months later (as it was for Philips, discussed previously). If there's not a great place for one of your target audiences to discuss things, or if the excitement in a forum has faded or it's an older forum that doesn't have up-to-date social sharing capabilities, you can take advantage of that by filling the gap with your own Group, getting people to it, and trying to own that conversation niche with your Group.

Chevron Unifies and Engages Difficult-to-Reach Energy Leaders

Chevron wanted to bring together all those passionate about energy-related issues into one place. As you might imagine, in the energy industry, as in many verticals, there is controversy. It's an ongoing PR challenge to maintain a positive image for some companies. A social media solution that brings dignity and decorum to conversations that might otherwise be ugly is incredibly valuable from a PR and branding perspective.

So, Chevron created a LinkedIn Group (see Figure 1.6) and then used LinkedIn Ads and Partner Messages to target industry professionals, policy makers, academia, and the media. They reached exactly who they wanted to, exceeded their growth goals by 41%, and doubled membership via unexpected word-of-mouth recommendations. Although they worried about potentially contentious debates, they found the discussions on LinkedIn to be respectful and professional. About 90% of members visit the Group repeatedly, 87% read the discussions, and 92% read Group digest emails.

Figure 1.6   *This Group ad provides a live snapshot of current Group discussions. These ads can mention specific members in each ad viewer's network.*

Vistage Grows Its Business While Reducing Cost Per Lead

Vistage International provides ideas and strategies to business leaders, business owners, and chief executives. The company is looking to grow more members by reaching as many people as possible in highly targeted audiences. Before LinkedIn, they had trouble finding marketing and advertising options that yielded both quality and quantity results. Targeting their audience with LinkedIn Ads, they discovered a way to continuously reach more quality leads at lower costs. In one recent quarter, they increased lead volume by 114% month over month, while cost per lead decreased 26% (see Figure 1.7). The LinkedIn campaign generated 89% more leads than the same campaign on a leading ad network and at less than a third the cost per lead.

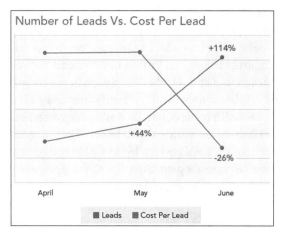

Figure 1.7   *Vistage International was pleasantly surprised to find that LinkedIn Ads performed better over time and dramatically outperformed any other ad network for their business leads.*

Here are the primary factors that affect profitability in B2B marketing and sales:

- **Lead Quality:** Are these the right people for your business?
- **Lead Quantity:** Are you getting enough potential customers to talk to? Can you increase this number without lowering quality?
- **Cost Per Lead:** Can you reduce the cost per lead without lowering lead quality? Usually this is achieved with good audience targeting and exciting or at least appropriate messaging.
- **Closing Ratio:** What percentage of leads turns into sales? If the lead quality is good and sales follow-up is prompt and skilled, this can be maximized.
- **Cost Per Sale:** The cost per lead and closing ratio determine your cost per sale. With your margins, how much can you afford to spend per sale on your sales, marketing, and advertising efforts? Is this cost per sale low enough?

That's the math of profitability. The ways to get more profits are to lower your cost per lead, increase the lead quality, and increase the closing ratio. When you can do two or three of these at the same time, you're a rock star. LinkedIn helped Vistage achieve that.

Joining LinkedIn Was Worth Nearly Half a Million Dollars

Bill Waterhouse is a Regional Director for Technical Innovation, a company that provides audiovisual products, services, digital signage, streaming media, and video conferencing. I spoke with him in 2011 in preparation to train at an event for the association his company belongs to: Professional Systems Network International. Bill has a sales background and was the first person in the company to use LinkedIn. It paid off almost immediately. Shortly after using his email contact database to grow LinkedIn connections, he was messaged on LinkedIn by someone he'd tried—and failed—to get business with before. They invited his response to a new RFP (request for proposal), which led to a $450,000 contract. Bill was only considered because he popped up on LinkedIn. One employee simply joining LinkedIn was a half-million-dollar payday for his company.

Endnotes

1. http://www.amazon.com/Quiet-Power-Introverts-World-Talking/dp/0307352145/

2. http://www.amazon.com/Flow-Psychology-Experience-Mihaly-Csikszentmihalyi/dp/0060920432

3. http://en.community.dell.com/dell-blogs/direct2dell/b/direct2dell/archive/2009/12/08/expanding-connections-with-customers-through-social-media.aspx

4. http://techcrunch.com/2009/07/22/amazon-buys-zappos/

5. http://mashable.com/2012/01/12/facebook-make-money/

6. http://www.accenture.com/us-en/Pages/insight-making-social-media-pay.aspx

7. http://insights.marinsoftware.com/analytics/fresh-insights-from-marins-2011-q4-report/

8. Womack, Brian. "LinkedIn Passes MySpace to Become No. 2 U.S. Social Network". Bloomberg. http://www.bloomberg.com/news/2011-07-08/linkedin-tops-myspace-to-become-second-largest-u-s-social-networking-site.html

9. http://press.linkedin.com/about. Any other stats not referenced in this section of the book are from this page.

10. MarketingSherpa 2012 Search Marketing Benchmark Survey – SEO Edition, August 18, 2011. http://www.meclabs.com/training/publications/benchmark-report/2012-search-marketing-seo-edition/overview?9641

11. http://www.quantcast.com/linkedin.com

12. http://www.leadformix.com/Why-Should-You-Use-Linkedin-For-B2B-Generation/

2

Best Practices: Online Marketing and LinkedIn

This chapter is about the best practices online market-ers have already developed and how to apply them to LinkedIn. While working for better social media results and teaching people to do the same, I've noticed a com-mon mistake: reinventing the wheel.

People sometimes start marketing with new platforms such as Facebook and LinkedIn without considering what best practices have created marketing successes on other platforms. For example, on Facebook, some companies assume they need fans even if email marketing is their most successful strategy to date. Perhaps they can simply use Facebook ads to get more email addresses and skip fans altogether. On LinkedIn, some advertisers forget—or never learned—that targeting the right people with mes-sages customized to fit them is what makes AdWords and Facebook advertising successful.

If you're already an online marketer, not using best practices from similar channels would be as foolish as never turning on the A/C after buying a new car, simply because the button looks different or is in a different place on the dashboard. If LinkedIn is the first online marketing initiative you are participating in, you're like a first-time driver. You need a driving instructor to tell you the rules of the road and what to avoid, as well as how to be safe and get where you're going.

LinkedIn marketing did not materialize in a vacuum. It entered a larger world of Internet marketing filled with other types of social media (see Figure 2.1). LinkedIn wasn't a viable Internet marketing channel until 2009, at which point Internet marketing had been developing for at least 10 years. More than a decade of research, wisdom, and best practices in online marketing can guide you to use LinkedIn successfully.

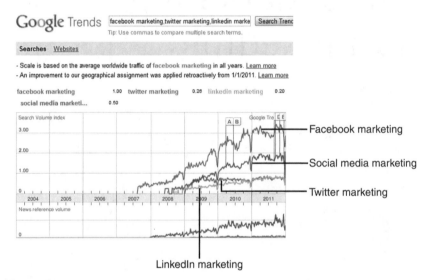

Figure 2.1   *Google's search trends. Facebook marketing leads the pack. Social media marketing, in general, took off in 2009 and is number two. Twitter marketing jumped up in 2009 but has stagnated since. LinkedIn marketing has slowly but steadily grown since 2009 and now rivals Twitter marketing.*

The History of Online Marketing and Its Best Practices

U.S. companies spent more than $300 million on Internet marketing in 1995.[1] The core Internet marketing channels of email, advertising, and search grew up during the first decade of the twenty-first century. Web analytics became more sophisticated and companies began to demand metrics and ROI-accountability (see Figure 2.2). Customer relationship management offerings such as Salesforce became the standard for online lead-generation and sales efforts. Inbound marketing (permission based or attraction marketing) became a viable and often preferable alternative to outbound techniques (such as telemarketing and direct mail).[2]

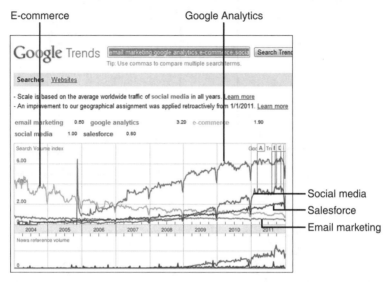

Figure 2.2   *Using the search terms people use in Google to compare general interest in elements of Internet marketing.*

In this group of searches, a list of some of the more commonly discussed elements in Internet Marketing, "Google Analytics" remains number one because almost every site can use it, it's free, and it's almost as powerful as paid analytics packages. Interest in "social media" has risen since mid 2009. Interest in e-commerce has consistently waned, even though it remains a fundamental part of online business. Salesforce, the most popular online service to help companies track and manage sales leads, has grown to number three (Salesforce is the most searched for CRM).[3] Email marketing has remained relatively consistent but has always been of much less interest than the rest.

Looking at a group of Internet marketing strategies, SEO (search engine optimization) has dominated the Internet marketing space for years (see Figure 2.3).

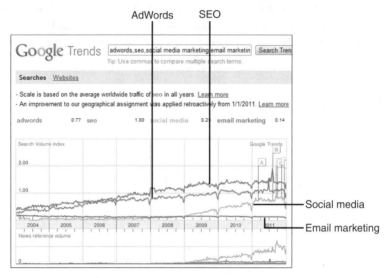

Figure 2.3   *Comparing the number of Google searches over the years for various Internet marketing strategies.*

The other side of the search marketing coin, paid search (Google AdWords and Yahoo/Bing/MSN), has been slightly less favored than SEO. In 2010 and 2011, social media marketing began to rival these two. Email marketing has slowly declined and doesn't attract near the interest of the first three.

LinkedIn marketing is one part of social media marketing, and its popularity has increased. When we compare interest in marketing on LinkedIn to several other major social media sites (see Figure 2.4), we see it beginning to outgrow Twitter marketing.

Social marketing   Facebook marketing

Figure 2.4   *Comparing searches for various types of social media marketing.*

LinkedIn marketing isn't as hot as Facebook marketing, but for business-to-business companies engaging in social media marketing, LinkedIn has become the mainstay. An April 2011 survey of U.S. marketers by eMarketer.com found that B2B marketers rated LinkedIn the most effective social platform (see Figure 2.5).

Social Media Platforms that Are Effective* According to US Marketers, by Primary Sales Channel, April 2011 % of respondents			
	B2B	**B2C**	**B2B/B2C**
LinkedIn	65%	23%	46%
Blog	63%	69%	63%
Twitter	53%	58%	59%
Facebook	47%	77%	80%
YouTube or other video-sharing	47%	51%	64%
Slideshare or other presentation-sharing	21%	12%	18%
Delicious or other social bookmarking	14%	29%	24%
Flickr or other photo-sharing	9%	21%	13%
Scribd or other document-sharing	9%	10%	9%
Note: *very or somewhat effective Source: MarketingSherpa, "2012 Search Marketing Benchmark Survey — SEO Edition," Aug 18, 2011			
131549			www.e**Marketer**.com

Figure 2.5   *For B2B marketers, LinkedIn leads the pack in perceived effectiveness, followed closely by blogging.*

Now that we've established the importance of LinkedIn for social media marketing and its context in the history of Internet marketing, what principles can we apply from Internet marketing to LinkedIn marketing? Surely it would be foolish to reinvent the wheel, and certainly Internet marketers have learned some principles that can be applied so you don't have to start from zero.

Fifteen Internet Marketing Principles That Apply to LinkedIn

Internet marketing varies for many kinds and sizes of companies and in many niches. Here are 15 principles from Internet marketing in general that also apply to LinkedIn marketing:

1. Think strategically and follow a process.

2. Know what your goal is and measure it.

3. Measure your progress with web analytics.

4. Optimize your tactics based on analytics.

5. Get to know your target audience.

6. Stimulate your target your audience with the right messages.

7. Test, test, test.

8. Fit everything into a coherent strategy.

9. Create value for your audience.

10. Make it easy for people to share what you create.

11. Create, build, and maintain relationships.

12. Be generous.

13. Grow an audience that is easy to contact repeatedly.

14. Set policies for Internet behavior.

15. Empower employees to contribute to the marketing and sales efforts.

Principle 1: Think Strategically and Follow a Process

Whatever results you're seeking from LinkedIn—more awareness, leads, PR coverage, or just interaction—you have to take your prospects through a process to get those results. Usually business people know the goal first and then discover the best target audience and how to get them to do what they want. Sometimes your target audience is fickle, and this affects what goals are realistic. The process and strategies to get them to take action may evolve with what you learn about that audience, but you must begin with a best guess. Knowing that you have to grow awareness with an audience and get their interest before selling them anything, you can have some patience and see when you're hitting essential milestones rather than expect sales to happen instantly. You may also know something about how long the sales cycle is in your business (how long it takes prospects to consider and then buy), and that informs how long you expect sales to take and what a realistic timeframe is for your goals.

A great standard process in the marketing industry is Attention-Interest-Desire-Action (AIDA), shown in Figure 2.6. AIDA was created in 1898 by advertising pioneer E. St. Elmo Lewis.[4]

Figure 2.6 *The AIDA advertising, marketing, and sales process.*

I don't think it's possible to achieve any worthy goal online without taking your audience through this process. You probably are already using it without realizing it. But knowing this process helps you identify where your problems are and what you need to improve to get better results. Here's how it works:

- You might grab a prospect's attention with an advertisement, a message to their inbox, a blog post that gets tweeted on Twitter, or any number of things. They can't buy from you if they don't know you exist.

- You may grab their interest right away or with another, later, contact. They have to be interested before they'll read your marketing or white papers or watch your videos. And they have to stay interested throughout that content consumption.

- Something in your ads, messages, or content will arouse their desire for what you are selling, and they may take action (buy), or a salesperson may need to persuade them. If you haven't connected the dots for them—that is, how your offering will benefit them, solve their problems, improve their business, and so on—they won't have any desire for it.

- Marketing, advertising, and sales activity keep prospects moving toward the action step. One of the skills of salespeople is to get consumers to take action. Advertising and marketing that creates urgency can also precipitate sales faster.

Make sure you know which parts of your sales, marketing, and advertising activities fit each step of AIDA, and ask yourself how you can do more in each stage, and where you need the most improvement.

Principle 2: Know What Your Goal Is and Measure It

As mentioned before, you probably know what your main goal is. You may have secondary goals, as well as milestones to the biggest goal. For example, you may want to increase sales as your main goal, but you also have a secondary goal to grow a branded annual event over the next five years. The secondary goal isn't as essential, but you still want to pursue it. While working on your main goal of growing sales, you know you need to look at milestones such as "a 30% increase in lead quantity" and "a 25% increase in closing ratio."

Each goal and milestone should be measurable and designated a key performance indicator (KPI). It's critical to have metrics in place and start tracking so you can create a history. This can be turned into all kinds of charts and analyses useful for determining what works and what doesn't, and comparing them over time.

You can't fix something or improve results if you can't measure it. Many businesses have seasonal trends (particularly around the holidays). Without knowing what's normal in your performance metrics over the course of a year, you can't know whether any performance dip is a failure or just a seasonal trend. If you're pushing forward, you're probably changing things in your marketing or advertising. When you make changes, a history of performance helps you know whether you made the right decision or should quickly reverse course.

Here are some goals and measurements for each of the main strategies this book covers:

Advertising

- **Awareness/Attention**—Number of impressions (how many times an ad was seen)
- **Traffic to a website or page on LinkedIn**—Number of clicks on ads
- **Interest in sales messages**—Click-through rate (percentage of ad viewings that resulted in a click)

Social Marketing

- **Captured audience size**—Number of people you can repeatedly contact, whether connections, group members, or company followers
- **Traffic to a website or blog**—Number of visitors and time on site
- **Engagement**—Number of likes or comments on posts
- **Viral effect**—Number of shares of posts

Sales

- **Pipeline volume**—Number of inbound leads, number of new prospects contacted, number of phone calls scheduled

- **Pipeline quality**—Percentage of leads designated good prospects after first digital contact, percentage of leads designated good prospects after first call

- **Closing rate**—Percentage of leads closed, percentage of quality leads (leads designated by sales as good prospects) closed

Applying Metrics to Your Sales Process

In almost every case, consumers go through the Attention-Interest-Desire-Action process in the top row of Figure 2.7 when considering and buying something.

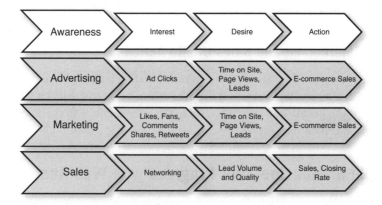

Figure 2.7   *How the AIDA sales and marketing process applies to LinkedIn.*

How Ads, Marketing, and Sales Create Awareness

Ads can raise awareness of your brand, but so can shares and likes from marketing content that's so good everyone wants to pass it on in social media. Sales can raise brand awareness with tactics such as networking and tradeshow booths.

How Ads, Marketing, and Sales Create Interest

An advertising specialist sees clicks and click-through rate as measures of interest. Marketing can look at how interactive their LinkedIn Group is as well as the likes, comments, and the passing along of content on the blog, Twitter, or Facebook. Salespeople gauge interest in how people respond initially in conversations. They can create interest by being physically attractive.

How Ads, Marketing, and Sales Create Desire

An advertising specialist can look at web analytics to see how much time the people who come to the website from LinkedIn ads spend there: Is it the same, less, or more than people who came in from Google or Facebook ads? What about how many pages the LinkedIn ad visitors view compared to people from other sources? What percentage of them contact the company to become leads?

Marketing can perform the same analysis by looking at the behavior of web visitors based on whether they come from the blog or LinkedIn Groups. Which blog posts, white papers, or other content drive the highest volume and highest quality of potential buyers?

Salespeople are concerned with the quantity and quality of these leads. If advertising and marketing go overboard, they can bring in lots of low-quality leads, which frustrates salespeople because they spend too much time dealing with too many people who'll never buy.

How Ads, Marketing, and Sales Create Action

Advertising and marketing can be involved in creating online sales for e-commerce, where the transaction happens without a salesperson. Otherwise, their part is to get the lead and pass it on to the salespeople, who specialize in closing and getting the sale.

Principle 3: Measure Your Progress with Web Analytics

This is the natural next step after setting goals and deciding on metrics. You need to verify whether the analytics on your website can track the data you require. Can you see where your traffic came from? Can you tell what ad sources, marketing campaigns, or blog posts brought in the leads? Can you identify lower quality traffic sources by seeing that people from one source or another spent too little time on the website?

And for sales, do you have a lead and sales management service such as Salesforce set up? Other providers include SAP, Oracle FusionApps, NetSuite, and Intuit's QuickBase. These offerings help you track which marketing and advertising sources create the highest volume and best quality leads, not to mention helping sales managers plan and increase the productivity and efficiency of sales reps. Salesforce claims that by using its software, the average customer obtains a 29% increase in sales, a 34% increase in sales productivity, and a 42% increase in forecast accuracy.[5]

Principle 4: Optimize Your Tactics Based on Analytics

None of the key performance indicators or analytics will do you any good if you don't regularly review the numbers, evaluate the viability of your various tactics, and change course accordingly.

Decision-making in online marketing and sales can be difficult. To make the process manageable and to ensure your decisions are good ones, you need sufficient data to be sure that what you're seeing is an accurate average. Many advertisers and marketers shut down tests too early. Statisticians try to measure how much "confidence" they have that their data is a true picture of reality. For example, if you have seen 3% of people fill out your lead form in the past, and you're testing a new form or new advertising audience, you need at least 33 people to demonstrate a 5% rate. That might cost you $100, just for that one test. If you're testing five new ads or audiences, that's $500.

Sometimes marketers make decisions based on temporary spikes or dips in data, and their results worsen. Snap decisions can come from anxiety or from accounting or executive pressure to spend less money on tests. To avoid this, ask from the start: What will it take to achieve statistical confidence? Factor in the cost of each test and then decide how many tests you can do at once.

Principle 5: Get to Know Your Target Audience

Ideally, we are always getting to know our best customer better. Mature businesses may begin social marketing with a good understanding of who buys what they sell, but start-ups may not have a clear picture. Even mature businesses may understand their customers only in terms of more traditional marketing channels—you might know their geography, job title, or demographic, but have no idea what kind of blog post will excite them the most.

Here are some of the things you'll want to know or learn about your target customer:

- What are their age, gender, and location?
- What are their job title and level of seniority?
- What LinkedIn Groups are they in?
- What are their biggest obstacles and problems?
- Do they think more creatively or more logically?
- How button-downed or wild-and-crazy are they?
- What magazines and blogs do they read?
- What's their typical workday like?

- What trends are they facing within their industry or in their role at the company?
- What are they most afraid of?
- What are they most excited about?

Outstanding advertising and marketing are composed of two things: communicating to the best of our understanding with our audience, and experimenting with new approaches to which we're not sure how they'll respond. Experimenting is indispensible because it confirms or disproves our theories about our audience. Numerous clients learn surprising and useful things about who their audience is and what they would or wouldn't respond to. Open-mindedness plus these digital insights help your company become more effective.

Principle 6: Stimulate Your Target Audience with the Right Messages

I've learned from my consulting work that some B2B companies aren't getting near the reaction from their target audience that they could. You can see room for growth when people don't interact with your corporate B2B Facebook page, don't comment on your corporate blog, don't share your content in social media, and don't come to your website from Facebook, LinkedIn, Twitter, and the like. The average B2B marketing approach just might not be stimulating enough to get big social results.

One of the biggest liabilities in marketing is being stuck in how you think about your products and services. Companies that get outsized results understand their target customers. Once you understand them, you can figure out how to tell them about your products and services in a way they'll care about.

Being curious and generous makes sense to us in other parts of life, but we often forget it at work. For example, are you a better parent when thinking about yourself as the ideal parent, or when you're thinking about your children's needs? Are you more fun as a date when talking about yourself or when listening to your counterpart? Are you a more effective salesperson when reading the brochure to a customer or when discovering their needs?

Advertising, marketing, and sales are about building bridges from your company to your target customer. The bridge starts with you, but you can't build it if you don't know where it ends—in the psyche of the customer. Focus on them and speak to their specific situation. This is a theme throughout the rest of the book, in particular in Chapters 5, 10, and 13.

Principle 7: Test, Test, Test

Successful online marketing is driven by curiosity. Day to day, it involves creativity, experimentation, and reviewing measurements of your results. The main reason for failure is lack of experimentation. If you make it normal to more frequently try more ad ideas, more marketing messages, different blog posts, and new white papers, and if you search for prospects in new places and try new messages for contacting people, you will discover the approaches that generate extraordinary results much sooner. If you don't have ideas, you probably aren't trying to learn more about your audience. And if you don't have ideas, you can't get better results.

What I've seen in testing thousands of advertising and marketing message ideas is that roughly only 5%–7% of what I try will perform excellently. If I only try a couple of ideas, I have a much lower chance of getting results. If I try 10–20 ideas, I'm much more likely to find that one thing my audience really responds to. And what they do and don't respond to teaches me something about them that I can use when developing my next set of ideas. With every round of testing, I understand them better and get better results. But you have to try bad ideas before you find the good ones. Rejoice in discovering that a test didn't work. That means you're closer to finding what does work.

Principle 8: Fit Everything into a Coherent Strategy

What happens if your print advertising doesn't fit your online marketing messages? Maybe it works, but not as well as when they're coordinated. In sports, which team wins? The one where everyone freelances, or the one where everyone is on the same page? This book contains several chapters focused specifically on how advertising, marketing, and salespeople can coordinate and help each other with LinkedIn marketing efforts.

But you should also make sure your offline marketing and advertising, your PR, and your customer service approaches fit your online and social media efforts. Here are a few ways they can work together for better results:

- If customer service repeatedly finds customers have had the wrong expectations, maybe marketing and sales are overpromising.
- If PR has to deal with a crisis, how can online ads and marketing messages help out? You can target journalists and media companies with advertising that supports PR messaging.
- When you're launching a new product or service, how can all these teams work together to get the message out to more people, with more repetition and clarity, thus driving more leads and sales?

If you're like most businesses using LinkedIn, you're also using some or all of the following: blogs, Twitter, Facebook, YouTube, Google SEO (search engine optimization, which is increasing your website's search rankings), Google AdWords, and others. You need a strategy for how to best mix and match efforts on multiple Internet marketing channels. How does your LinkedIn marketing and advertising fit in? What audiences are you able to go after on LinkedIn that you can't elsewhere? Which of your blog posts does your LinkedIn audience like best? Does some of your content do better on Twitter and some on LinkedIn? Is it better to post whitepapers on LinkedIn and blog posts on Twitter? That's a lot to learn over time about your audience, your content strategies, and your social marketing. As you learn, evolve your overall strategy.

Principle 9: Create Value for Your Audience

Why should anyone care about your ads, marketing, or sales messages? Why should they pay attention to you? How are you different from any other company?

The best way to get attention is to start a positive relationship and begin a sales conversation to provide content (blog posts, white papers, videos) that solves a problem for your target customer. That doesn't mean giving away the farm; the problem might be as simple as how to evaluate the competitive field in your niche (for example, "Ten Mistakes Made by Buyers of Used Ultrasounds").

The opposite and worst way to create content is to talk about things at your company that only your company or executives care about, such as the following:

- A LinkedIn post or blog post about how so-and-so was promoted.
- Bragging on your LinkedIn company page that "We're the biggest and best" without spelling out the benefits to your customers (make sure you're in compliance with LinkedIn's User Agreement!)[6]
- A bunch of photos of your employees going bowling on Friday night.

Why are these bad ideas? Because who really cares? Maybe only you! How do those things help your customers achieve their goals? They're not headlines that make customers care. If any of them are for investors, create a special section, targeted ad, or LinkedIn Group for investors and make sure that this type of content only reaches them.

On social networks such as LinkedIn, people like to see and interact with pieces of content. They're conversation pieces. Pinterest.com, a site where all you do is quickly and easily share photos with people, has been making big waves lately. It drives as much traffic to websites as Twitter and more than Google Plus, LinkedIn, and YouTube combined, yet it's just under two years old.

Pinterest's audience and its photo content make it most applicable to B2C e-commerce and perhaps not great for B2B. However, you can distribute any infographics you create on Pinterest as well.

The lesson is clear: Without interesting content, you come across as too boring or too direct with your sales messages. But with them, you can set in motion a virtuous cycle of social activity, search engine authority, and brand awareness (see Figure 2.8). The website traffic from this virtuous content cycle feeds an inbound marketing system (see Figure 2.9) that creates more leads and business for your company.

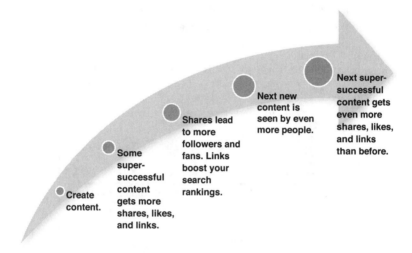

Figure 2.8   *Creating content frequently leads to occasional word-of-mouth successes that increase awareness of your brand and the social activity around it.*

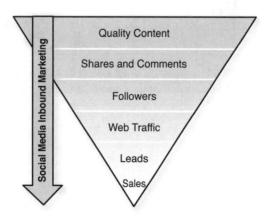

Figure 2.9   *Great content leads to social interaction, search engine authority, a growing audience, web traffic, leads, and sales.*

Principle 10: Make It Easy for People to Share What You Create

When you create valuable content, you have to host it somewhere—on your website, blog, YouTube channel, or Pinterest. Then you can share the link with your audiences on social networks and advertise it. Once people get there to experience it, is there an easy way for them to share it via Facebook, Twitter, LinkedIn, or email? Have you set up social sharing buttons like those in Figure 2.10? If not, you've just prevented yourself from experiencing the benefits of viral marketing. Not every piece of content will be shared 10,000 times, but some will. Make it easy for people to facilitate that the way Mashable does. You may want to try the free ShareThis.com service to set yours up (see Figure 2.11).

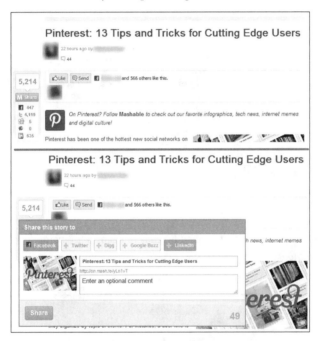

Figure 2.10 *Mashable has a custom sharing widget that shows how many people have shared overall and on each of the major social networks, and allows you to share on whichever ones you want.*

Figure 2.11   *ShareThis.com offers a free and easy way to create sharing buttons and get the code for your website or blog.*

The result of creating great content and making it sharable is, in the best cases, viral word-of-mouth activity. About 10% of your content will dramatically outperform the rest in terms of interaction and shares. The more you create, the more of these viral experiences you'll have. You can learn from your company's content successes and failures. You can also use a tool such as InfiniGraph.com to see what kinds of content are getting the most interaction in any niche.

Principle 11: Create, Build, and Maintain Relationships

Some people have networked naturally their whole lives. Others were forced into it by circumstance (a new job, PTA, civic or other groups) and came to see its business value over time. Some people have less experience or aptitude for networking, including some online marketers, who are introverted by nature.

I can speak from experience that after growing up a shy computer nerd, I had some great social experiences with groups such as Toastmasters. Being so overly social felt unnatural to me, but it helped. I also tried standup comedy, which is really the boot camp of public speaking. If you can survive that, everything else seems easier. In keeping with my introverted side, I performed the first tweeting-only stand-up comedy set one Friday night in 2008. That and my other Twitter activities planted the seeds for strong offline relationships that blossomed at Internet marketing conferences. These friendships led to business opportunities and revenue for the agency that employed me.

Regardless of your personality type, this combination of online and offline activity is powerful. You find and meet people online that you'd never encounter elsewhere; then, you use offline interaction, whether face-to-face or on the phone, to solidify and deepen these new relationships.

Many of the same rules of successful offline networking apply online as well. Being nice helps. Saying positive things about people publicly makes them like you more (praise in public, criticize in private). All of this can create cheerleaders and advocates who share your content with their networks. They extend your reach, business referrals, and new leads. Regardless, the best way to start and build relationships is with generosity (discussed next).

Principle 12: Be Generous

Humans are built to reciprocate. Most of us feel indebted when someone does something for us, so we try to even the score; otherwise, we feel guilty. When you give people useful information, a free consultation, a valuable blog post or white paper, or an entertaining video, you make a deposit into their emotional bank and they usually repay you in some way.

You might tell them how to repay you—with a like or share, or by entering their email address. Or you might continually build goodwill with a prospect until you can ask them for the sale. In my experience, generosity is a strategy that yields a positive ROI. Any company with social, generous, and positive employees has a competitive advantage over companies who insulate their employees, or whose employees appear to be negative or focused only inwardly on the company.

Principle 13: Grow an Audience That Is Easy to Contact Repeatedly

There's a hard cost associated with getting a message out with advertising. Every single time someone clicks, you pay. But when you create connections, groups, or followers who see your messages repeatedly, there's no incremental cost to contact them. A captured audience is an asset that you can mine for gold again and again, whether that gold is direct sales or social media shares that lead to further word-of-mouth exposure and a constantly growing audience. With that audience as an asset, you can get your PR or sales messages out whenever you need to.

A word of warning: You have to stay useful and generous, or you'll kill the golden goose. People can get bored, turned off, ignore you, or leave. Selfish marketing reduces the size and value of your audience. Although you might initially use advertising to help you grow an audience, later you can lead that community and nurture relationships. When they recommend you to others, the value of your audience grows.

Principle 14: Set Policies for Internet Behavior

The more employees you have with LinkedIn activity, Twitter accounts, or blog posts, the more potential marketing and audience they can give you without adding to your marketing budget. But quantity without quality in social media can be dangerous. In 2008, Zappos had hundreds of employees representing them on Twitter, and this only helped them. Other brands, such as Nestles, have suffered big PR gaffes when less-than-friendly social media representatives reacted emotionally and said the wrong thing. Each company must decide for itself whether every employee should be able to post, how they should do it, how involved they should be in marketing and PR, and how formalized such practices should be.

The safest route may seem to be putting one well-qualified and experienced social media person in charge of all communications, and to have them vetted by marketing, PR, and other teams. But that can slow things down to the point of ineffectiveness and inability to respond to customer issues. Social media needs to be agile.

You definitely need a social media policy for employees, and should probably designate which employees can speak for or about the company in social media, while making it clear to the rest of the employees that they are *not* to speak for the company online. SocialMediaGovernance.com has a database that lists 188 real corporate social media policies you might use as examples.[7]

Keep in mind that, when choosing resources, what make someone a good person to trust as a social media or blog poster is not simply age. I've seen a situation where a 20-something was put in charge of social media just because it seemed like a young, hip thing to do, and yet that employee had no experience with marketing or PR. Business experience and maturity count in social media personalities.

Here are some of the things I believe qualify an employee to post in social media:

- **Discretion**—Knowing what information about the company is private and proprietary.
- **Respect**—Thinking highly of the company, its employees and executives, and its customers. Is this a glass-half-full type of person who can address reality but is on your company's side?
- **Expertise**—Experience with and knowledge of what makes social media effective, good writing skills, as well as a good understanding of the company, its offerings, and its customers, and how it wants to be perceived.
- **Poise**—The wisdom to pause when emotional, not to post whatever comes to mind and not to react negatively or unprofessionally to customers when they are unhappy. The ability to turn negatives into positives.

- **Agility**—Some people are very quick with words and responses. Speed, when combined with the preceding qualities, is impressive and gets social media results.

Note that only one of these criteria is about knowledge. The others are about maturity and character. Some employees, although extremely valuable to your company, don't represent the company well. And some employees don't want to be out front. But don't overlook employees who are not in PR, marketing, customer service, or sales who might enjoy and be great at representing their department online.

Principle 15: Empower Employees to Contribute to the Marketing and Sales Efforts

Once you've created a social media policy and identified employees who might contribute, take some time to think about the following:

- How sales, PR, marketing, customer service, the executive team, and perhaps even departments such as product development should participate in LinkedIn Groups and Answers.
- Who in those departments has time (and the qualities mentioned earlier) to do this?
- How will they collaborate? Who is in charge of what? How do you leverage each others' networks and audiences to achieve goals but without annoying or overwhelming those audiences?
- Do you have an internal chatting platform (one better than email) that this "Social Media Team" can use to coordinate efforts? You might use a private LinkedIn or Facebook Group, chat in Google Mail, or an intranet messaging group.

The advantage of empowering more employees is that you leverage their personality and connections to increase your company's overall audience reach and word-of-mouth potential. Each employee is like an outpost in the frontier as you expand your reach. Each employee's unique personality attracts a different audience, thus increasing your chances of reaching more new customers.

Summary

These 15 principles, in my opinion, embody a great deal of the wisdom the Internet marketing profession has developed over the last 10–15 years. Most of the problems I've seen and helped fix through consulting were due to the neglect of one of these best practices. Because so many companies miss one or more of them, the more you're able to adopt and habitualize (or even better, integrate into your everyday processes), the more of a competitive advantage your company will have. I'm not sure if any of them are optional, but if I had to choose a few to emphasize that would ensure your success (and which most people neglect at their peril), they'd be test (7), create value (9), build relationships (11), and grow an audience (13).

Endnotes

1. http://www.arcamax.com/mediacenter/blog/post/1118736

2. http://www.seomoz.org/blog/inbound-marketing-is-taking-off

3. The few Google Trends comparisons shown in this book were built on the foundation of a number of searches. To see a comparison of CRMs, use this link: http://www.google.com/trends/?q=salesforce,+zoho,+act!,+marketo,+netsuite&ctab=0&geo=all&date=all&sort=0

4. http://en.wikipedia.org/wiki/AIDA_(marketing)

5. "Voice of the Customer Survey Results," Issue 5, *Salesforce.* http://www.salesforce.com/ap/assets/pdf/crmnews/Issue5_VoiceoftheCustomerSurveyResults.pdf

6. http://www.linkedin.com/static?key=user_agreement

7. http://socialmediagovernance.com/policies.php#axzz1izJiwLuP

3

Impressive Employees: LinkedIn Profile Enhancement, Findability, and Thought Leadership

These days, with social media, your employees are more visible than they used to be. Their Facebook profile may be private, but their LinkedIn profile is public. What if the first thing potential customers see about your company is your employees?

Employees coloring people's perception of companies isn't new—for decades, people have attended conferences and networking events and met employees of companies with which they're not familiar. They speak with the employee and make good or bad judgments. Is this person impressive? Do they appear competent? Do they have exceptional experience or achievements? Now we need to ask that question of every employee's LinkedIn profile because your prospects may see one of these profiles before they've ever met one of your employees in person.

The LinkedIn profiles of your employees reflect on your company. They affect how interested clients are in learning more about your company. They affect how professional, effective, and interesting clients think your company is. There are a lot of competent but boring companies out there. How do you stand out? The impression employees make on LinkedIn can help.

Socially Networked Employees Are Influential and Create Valuable Audiences

A strong impression from an employee can change someone's mind about your company in a good way. Let's say your company has image problems, such as Exxon or BP had after their oil spills. If you meet someone who works for the company and they're likeable and can explain in a reasonable and humble manner what the company has done to clean up the oil, you may change your mind about the brand. The next time someone else says something bad about the company, you might even tell the story of the employee you met and liked.

Employees can impress and affect more people if they're socially networked. When employees help people online, are kind and courteous, and share or blog useful information, people like them more and may even feel obligated to them. By extension, customers are more likely to like or be open to that positive employee's company. If your employee is remarkable (for example, if he is a thought leader), prospects might even talk about him in a social media environment. People might quote an employee. Media people might want to interview them. Event planners might want them to speak at their conferences.

Employees develop audiences you can market to and lead. If your employees are active in social media (growing connections, blogging, and participating in Groups), they may have thousands of LinkedIn connections, Twitter followers, Facebook friends, and fans. Every employee you have that grows a small following is helping you create a larger and more diverse audience for your company's marketing messages.

Some go so far as to call this your potential "brand army." That means that any one of your employees can help your company. Be careful with this because LinkedIn profiles belong to the employee—you may not be legally empowered to dictate that they post all your company's marketing messages. It's essentially a volunteer army. You can make participation an option, and some employees will be more gung-ho than others. These gung-ho employees might help get you more PR than your company has experienced in the past.

I asked Melissa Madian, senior director of solutions consulting and field enablement at Eloqua if LinkedIn was putting more of their sales employees in the public sphere. She replied, "LinkedIn is a fabulous way to facilitate a positive first impression. If you leave a message for someone you've never spoken with before, they will likely Google you. Your LinkedIn profile may be the first thing that comes up. A completed LinkedIn profile significantly increases your visibility and professional branding with prospects. It shows you're a credible person working for a credible brand." Alex Shootman, SVP of sales at Eloqua, added, "We are requiring our field employees to be in the public sphere; it is the way you do modern prospecting. And it is impossible to be in the public sphere without authentically using LinkedIn."

As we discussed in Chapter 2, you need to have policies in place to deal with the business versus personal aspects of social media. It's not fair to expect employees to spam their friends with your business messages. They may need separate business profiles on social networks for their marketing and sales activity. Alternatively, you can craft messages that sound natural, or even better, you can tell employees what's going on and let them put the message in their own words. Make sure your company has a plan for personal versus business profiles and that it is clearly spelled out in employment contracts.

The average Facebook user has 130 friends.[1] If you have 100 employees, that's as much as 13,000 people your employees know directly. The average LinkedIn user in my network has 358 connections. According to LinkedIn, I have 757,600 friends of friends I could reach out to through introductions, and these are potential business contacts, likely much more relevant for B2B marketing and sales. I personally have 2,119 connections at the time of this writing (see Figure 3.1). Those are my first-level direct connections. When you hire a salesperson and she brings the value of her LinkedIn network to your company, that's like the traditional black book of customers and prospects, or more recently, the Blackberry full of emails. You can use this network to get messages out and sell your offerings.

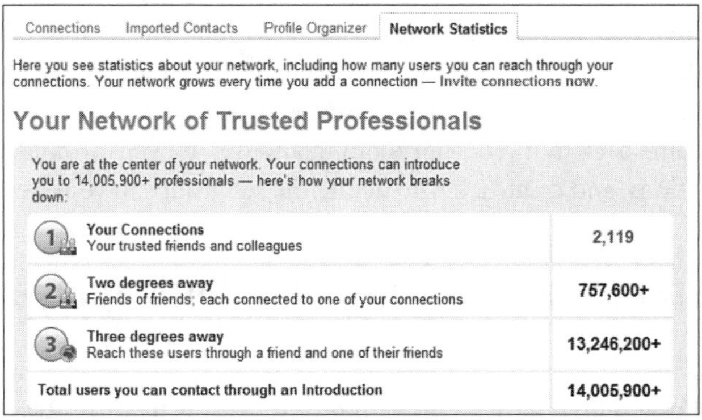

Connections	Imported Contacts	Profile Organizer	**Network Statistics**	

Here you see statistics about your network, including how many users you can reach through your connections. Your network grows every time you add a connection — Invite connections now.

Your Network of Trusted Professionals

You are at the center of your network. Your connections can introduce you to 14,005,900+ professionals — here's how your network breaks down:

1	**Your Connections** Your trusted friends and colleagues	2,119
2	**Two degrees away** Friends of friends; each connected to one of your connections	757,600+
3	**Three degrees away** Reach these users through a friend and one of their friends	13,246,200+
	Total users you can contact through an Introduction	14,005,900+

Figure 3.1 *The statistics on my LinkedIn network as of January 2012. Note how many more people, two degrees away, to whom I could connect with introductions.*

LinkedIn also tells me about the primary locations and industries in my network (see Figure 3.2). Some of this is affected by the sheer size of each city. I'm not surprised to see NYC at the top because there are so many professionals working in a large city. But a tech programmer living in California might have many more San Francisco connections than I do. My industries make a lot of sense, too. I'm in Internet marketing, although I have begun to develop more PR contacts in the last year.

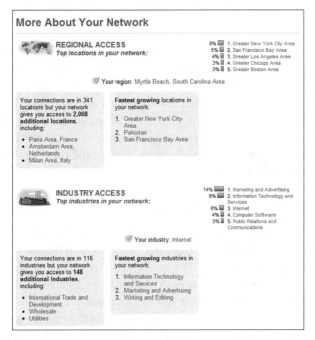

Figure 3.2   *LinkedIn summarizes the primary locations and industries of my contacts.*

And if you're a visually oriented person like me, you might want to take a look at LinkedIn Maps, which creates a color-coded map of all your connections. The first time might take it a little while for LinkedIn to process the map, but it will be faster when you come back to it. You can zoom in and out, move it around, look at specific connections, and create a key to define the subgroups in your network by color.

How to Create Impressive LinkedIn Employee Profiles

Every employee should have a LinkedIn profile. This is their professional face in the social media world. In this section, I discuss what makes profiles impressive, what your options are for customizing them, and examples of people who are already doing a great job.

LinkedIn Profiles That Impress

Impressive LinkedIn profiles have five characteristics:

- They're complete (everything is filled in, according to LinkedIn's definition).
- They have a strong, compelling headline.
- They include recommendations from coworkers, managers, employees, and customers.
- They appropriately incorporate the employee's other social media activity, such as presentations, blog posts, and books.
- They use apps that pull in content from other websites.

As suggested, every employee profile is an opportunity for your company, so you don't want to miss out. A complete and interesting profile that leads people to content that's useful and promotes your company can bring you new business.

An incomplete or unimpressive profile may be interpreted several different ways by prospects. If you're lucky, they'll think you're too busy to bother with LinkedIn because you're working so hard on your clients. At worst, they'll think you're too boring to have anything to say, or don't care enough to represent yourself well. A risk of doing anything poorly is having prospects assume you do everything at same low quality level.

Just as you care how your employees look, dress, and speak when clients are around, so should you care how they present themselves publicly online. Getting employees to do a good job with this shouldn't take too much time; your marketing people can and should help them improve their profiles. This is a win-win for employees because, however long they continue to work for you, they'll look good and so will your company.

Don't skimp on this out of fear that they'll look so good they'll move onto another company. Employees switch jobs more than they used to, and you can't expect to have them forever. According to the U.S. Department of Labor, the average employee stays with a company for 4.4 years. And for those ages 25—34 it's only 3.1 years.[2] I realize that employees moving on might be a disturbing idea to some managers and executives, but it's a reality—and the best companies and managers not only understand this, they make sure good employees have every reason to stay.

Make Sure Profiles Are Complete

LinkedIn says that complete profiles are 40 times more likely to receive opportunities than incomplete profiles.[3] That means completing your profile is worth doing. LinkedIn has a specific definition for a "complete" profile, which is one that includes the following:

- Your current position
- Two past positions
- Your education
- Your profile summary
- A profile photo
- Your specialties
- At least three recommendations

I won't cover all these items in this book because some of them are no-brainer "duh!" obvious (like which schools you attended). What I will do is cover the areas where you can really make your profile stand out. And the one piece of advice that applies to all of them is to give everything you can a description that looks good to people and, if it can contain keywords people might search for (discussed later in this chapter), even better. Just don't use extra keywords in a way people wouldn't write normally. This might get your profile more views, but it'll look so spammy that it can actually hurt your and your company's image.

How long does it take to completely fill out a profile? You should be able to do it within 60 minutes. If you take a bit longer to make it excellent, so much the better. Recommendation requests from your connections are covered later in this chapter. Positions and education are fairly obvious, although you'll modify them later in this chapter when we talk about findability and keywords. Let's first talk about how to do a good job with the other parts of your complete profile.

A Powerful Profile Summary

The profile summary is like a bio or a resume cover letter, but instead of addressing it to a potential employer, you might be addressing the type of customer you serve and how you serve them. Answering the following questions can help you create a powerful summary:

- How are you different from other people who do what you do? Everyone has competition, both in their industry and position. Talk about how you do your particular job in a unique and better way.
- What are your values and your history? Think about the things that you care about in your work and how that helps your customers and coworkers.
- For whom and what are you grateful? If you have had great customers, coworkers, or mentors—especially if any of these are well known— mention them and how they've impacted the way you work.

- What's your story? Show some personality.

- Who are you and who are you not? Take a stand without offending.

- Do you have a guarantee to those who work with you? Set a bar for the level of work you do.

- What benefits do you provide? Express how you help customers and coworkers. Quantify this with numbers as much as possible.

- Also, what have you achieved? You can add summaries to past jobs, but if any stands out, you might want to put it in the profile summary.

Think twice before using a lot of jargon and acronyms in your profile summary. This is like any other written marketing or sales piece; it should be easy to understand and fulfilling to read. It should make people like you or want to know more about you. It shouldn't bore them or put them to sleep. That said, if you are a highly technical expert and your goal is to impress other experts, by all means, make your profile summary as incomprehensible as possible, but also throw in something wise or insightful to add depth, and consider how you might humanize yourself.

 Note

If you haven't read Strunk and White's *The Elements of Style*, you should read it before writing this section. It's the best known guide in the world on how to write clearly and powerfully. It's a very short book and is available online for free at http://www.bartleby.com/141/. The most important parts to read are Chapters 11–14.

A Professional and Flattering Profile Photo

LinkedIn is a professional network. Your photo is not the time to get goofy. Although it can differentiate you, using a goofy photo is discouraged. Even the professional humorists and corporate comedians I know use a serious-but-positive headshot for LinkedIn. This is the picture you'd want going out in a corporate newsletter or in your bio if you speak at professional conferences. Your picture needs to answer the following questions:

- Should I pay this person money?

- Can I trust this person?

- Is he or she going to take my problems seriously?

A good headshot isn't always easy to come by—not everyone has one. Your company might choose to sponsor a photography day where everyone gets a headshot done in the same style. Although it's true that companies don't typically pay for your haircuts or clothing, it's normal, easy, and affordable for most employees to provide those themselves. Quality photography that represents your company in a consistent and professional way, making each person look their best, is different. One qualifier: If the photographer asks everyone to put their chin on their fist, or insists on laser backdrops, fire him immediately and don't pay him.

In my case, I used a photo taken of me speaking at an event (see Figure 3.3). The microphone is visible in the picture. I do this on purpose to visually communicate that I'm a speaker. I've found that saying I'm an author and speaker increases my authority in the minds of potential customers as well as increases my likelihood of getting speaking gigs.

Figure 3.3   *My headshot, using the microphone to emphasize that I'm a speaker.*

Specialties

Specialties are your areas of expertise. You can probably think of at least one or two off the top of your head, and then search LinkedIn for people with your job title in similar companies. You'll probably see specialties that apply to you but that you hadn't thought of. I would make sure you have at least five to ten listed. This is a prime area for keywords, as we discuss shortly.

Create a Compelling Headline

The most obvious headline is the same as your job title: "Vice President of Sales at XYZ Company." If that's the way your company does things, that's great. And sometimes, you need to create an unassailably professional image that's simple, clear, and direct.

But you have other opportunities here. You can include search keywords, and you can make yourself stand out with unique word choices. For unique word choices that create an extraordinary degree of interest, how about "VP of Meeting Your Goals at XYZ Company" or "VP of Glad You Bought from Us at XYZ Company"? I don't want to be redundant in emphasizing that uniqueness doesn't fly at every company, but if you give your employees the freedom to try things like that, and if marketing helps craft interesting headlines, you might find you get more responses from prospects. Even a simple, "Hey, what's with your weird job title there?" can start a conversation with a potential customer. Sometimes, getting that first contact and conversation is the most difficult thing in sales.

You can also use that headline space to throw in the company slogan or summary, if your company isn't well known (see Figure 3.4). Every time someone sees your profile, they'll see the headline and learn something about your company.

Figure 3.4 *An example of a LinkedIn profile headline that adds important information about the company.*

You may prefer to use the headline to express your primary service's biggest benefit and who you provide it to (see Figure 3.5). The term "benefit" in marketing means what a product or service does for people. Why do they want it? What do they get out of it? Put yourself in their shoes and think about what you do for them and why they should care. Write several versions of this benefit and let other people help you choose the most compelling one.

Figure 3.5 *The profile of a LinkedIn member who uses the headline to express her service's main benefit and who she helps achieve that benefit.*

If you use jargon, make sure your audience is going to understand it. In the current example, "Web Visibility" might be unfamiliar to some of Tinu's prospects. Another way she could have phrased her headline is, "I Make Sure Future Customers See Your Website—For Successful Entrepreneurs". However, she may want to invest in the branding of the phrase "Web Visibility". It's a tradeoff. You'll have to decide whether findability or branding is more important to you.

Recommendations: Give to Receive

Of course, we know *you* think you're great. You have the chance to tell us why in the rest of your profile. But what do other people think of you? Do your coworkers respect you? Do your superiors value you? What about your employees?

Customers? Clients? Peers? People who don't know you are much more likely to believe you're great if other people say you're great. And recommendations from within your own company are essential, but not sufficient on their own. We can all visualize a meeting where everyone decides to recommend each other. Therefore, you should include people outside your company recommending you. It would also be nice to see recommendations for your work in all the positions you've held (although this understandably might be harder to do for positions you held 20 years ago). People want to believe in your greatness, so get the recommendations that validate it.

A complete profile has at least three recommendations, but strong ones have ten or more. It takes time and networking to grow them. But if you already have strong relationships and a good history in your niche, you might be able to get these recommendations rather quickly. After you request them, you'll be able to see any incoming recommendations and choose whether or not to display them.

In my experience, giving someone a recommendation first will dramatically increase their likelihood of honoring your recommendation request. Go through your contacts and make a list of the people you'd like recommendations from. You might not feel it's appropriate to recommend all of them yourself, for one reason or another, but for those that you do, contact them first with a note like this:

> "Hey, how have you been? *(Include something positive and more personal here if you can.)* I've been getting more active on LinkedIn and would like to recommend your work at your company. Is there anything specific you'd like me to focus on in my recommendation?"

Notice I didn't suggest you ask exactly how to word your request, because that would lead to inauthenticity. It needs to be your voice. You're being generous and hoping you can get a recommendation in return.

You're also asking for their input on how to recommend them. That's not at all because you want the recommendation to be fake. It's for two reasons. The first is that I've received some recommendations from well-meaning people that were unusable because they focused on a service or situation that was positive but that I didn't want to promote anymore. If I could have given them some parameters, the recommendation wouldn't have been wasted. The second reason is because of an experience I had once: I was asked for a recommendation and after I asked what to focus on, they told me something about what they were trying to do that surprised me. As I thought about it, I could see what they meant. But it was bigger and different than what I thought they were doing. It was an angle that made for a more impressive and more accurate recommendation. The fact is, we may not really understand what the other person values or is trying to accomplish; likewise, they may not understand where you are coming from. Communicate about it.

You can get mediocre recommendations without going this extra step, but mediocre recommendations don't make a profile really shine. What's more, you want people to be happy with the recommendations you give them; it can make a business relationship suddenly uncomfortable when you receive a recommendation you can't display on your profile. And LinkedIn doesn't make do-overs easy.

Incorporating Facebook and Twitter

If you're active on other social networks, and what you share there adds another dimension to the picture of your professional activity, you might want to include those feeds in LinkedIn. You might be tempted to automatically publish everything from them to LinkedIn, because it's easier, but it's better to send only some updates to LinkedIn.

For Twitter, select the Edit My Profile option on LinkedIn and choose to publish only tweets that contain the hashtag #in or #li, which are shortened versions of "LinkedIn" (see Figure 3.6). It takes a bit more presence of mind to remember to add a hashtag while tweeting, but it is necessary if your Twitter profile is somewhat personal and you don't want everything going to LinkedIn. This simple approach allows you to think about which tweets your LinkedIn network should and shouldn't see.

Figure 3.6 *Managing your Twitter settings for LinkedIn.*

Incorporating Facebook into your LinkedIn profile is difficult because Facebook doesn't provide an easy way to stream your Facebook content outside its walls. This is a strategic and cultural decision on Facebook's part. And there's no easy way to stream LinkedIn activity to Facebook. But who really wants to read that anyway?

I don't think this lack of interactivity is the end of the world; each social network has different norms, and people behave differently on them. It doesn't work very well, for example, when people stream Twitter into Facebook, because those posts don't take advantage of many of Facebook's features. As a result, they look boring, don't get much interaction, and hurt your visibility. It's generally better to custom-tailor your approach to each social network. So, do your LinkedIn activity on LinkedIn and your Facebooking on Facebook, and leave it at that.

Adding Apps to Your Profile

LinkedIn allows you to add apps to your profile that enable you to display richer content, to share and collaborate, and to get insights from your connections. Several apps are available, including Projects and Teamspaces (for project collaboration), the Polls application, an app for syncing your WordPress blog with LinkedIn, an app for embedding Google or Slideshare presentations, and many more.

I would be disappointed in LinkedIn's apps if I thought extending my profile was that important, because there are only a few of them. The positives: The SlideShare plug-in looks great for people who upload a lot of presentations to their SlideShare account. I would experiment with integrating your Wordpress blog if you have one, partly for direct exposure and also for the SEO benefit of the links from your profile to your blog posts.

Growing Initial Connections

Adding connections is easy, and LinkedIn insists on helping you by asking you for your email login information (see Figure 3.7). There's nothing to fear here; they won't read your email and they won't save your password. They will go through your contacts, find those people on LinkedIn, and allow you to request they connect, all in one fell swoop.

You'll also be asked if you want to email the people who aren't on LinkedIn to join and become your connection. It's so little to ask and such a popular professional network that most people will do it. Besides, so many professionals are on LinkedIn now, you are actually considered odd if you don't want to use it.

LinkedIn can easily hook up to online mail such as Hotmail and Gmail to make this happen, but if you don't have one of those, you can export your contacts from Outlook, Apple Mail, or whatever program you use for a CSV file. Upload the file to have LinkedIn find your contacts on their network. This takes less than 30 minutes, and within days you might have hundreds of LinkedIn friends.

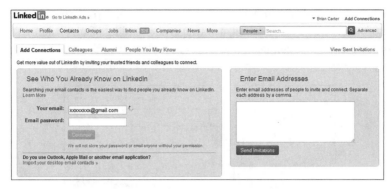

Figure 3.7   *LinkedIn helps you request your email contacts become your LinkedIn connections, quickly and easily.*

Afterward, as you use LinkedIn, it may suggest people to you who you know but didn't have email addresses for, and you can request them. And as you go through your business life, every time you meet someone, you can find them on LinkedIn and request them as connections. Over time, you'll grow a substantial network.

Making Sure Employee Profiles Are Visible and Findable

As we've discussed, the more of a rock star any one employee is, the more attention they'll grab and the more potential business they can pull into your company. Also, if they have a job title that's hot and newsworthy, they may be found by bloggers and journalists looking for experts to interview. But regardless of an employee's potential to bring your company attention, without the right keywords in the right places, they'll be much less visible. This section helps you show employees how to become more findable, increase their value to the company, and grow their careers.

How People Get Found Online

You can search Google or LinkedIn for a specific area of expertise or for your own name. This is done via a search box, whether it's through Google's main search box or LinkedIn's search (see Figure 3.8). LinkedIn's search box always starts as a People search, but can be switched to Companies, Answers, or Groups. We discuss how to use Answers and Groups in Chapter 5. This section is about making profiles more visible doing a People search.

In Chapter 13 we talk about Advanced People Search, and your saved searches, some of which are keyword-based, can trigger the sending of email alerts. That means that using the right keywords in your employee profiles could make people with saved searches aware of your employees and your company!

Figure 3.8   *The Search box in the upper-right corner of the LinkedIn interface defaults to People but can be used to search other parts of LinkedIn as well.*

Researching the Search Terms

Go to Google's keyword tool—it has a free version for people who don't spend money on their ads (https://adwords.google.com/select/KeywordToolExternal). You just have to fill out a CAPTCHA challenge to use it.

This tool helps you find what people are searching for in Google. You can type in a job title or area of expertise and see which ways people look for it most. This isn't necessarily exactly how people search for it in LinkedIn, but LinkedIn doesn't have a keyword tool, so we have to assume this is close enough. You can also use the Google Keyword Tool to enter a website address and get keywords related to that web page.

For example, let's say you're an account executive at ReadyTalk, a company that provides web conferencing solutions. It doesn't make sense to use your job title, because potential partners and customers aren't looking for account executives. They're looking for conferencing solutions, so let's look at keywords for that. Of the keywords I got back from Google (see Figure 3.9), the most relevant searches with the biggest number are "web conferencing solution" and "web conferencing service."

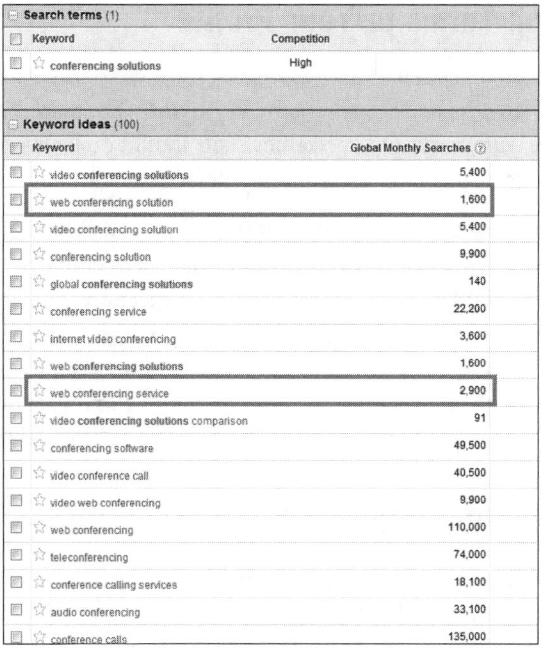

Search terms (1)

Keyword	Competition
conferencing solutions	High

Keyword ideas (100)

Keyword	Global Monthly Searches
video conferencing solutions	5,400
web conferencing solution	1,600
video conferencing solution	5,400
conferencing solution	9,900
global conferencing solutions	140
conferencing service	22,200
internet video conferencing	3,600
web conferencing solutions	1,600
web conferencing service	2,900
video conferencing solutions comparison	91
conferencing software	49,500
video conference call	40,500
video web conferencing	9,900
web conferencing	110,000
teleconferencing	74,000
conference calling services	18,100
audio conferencing	33,100
conference calls	135,000

Figure 3.9 *Suggested keywords from Google's Keyword Tool, with their relative popularity as searches.*

If you had web analytics data about which of these keywords got more or better leads and analytics about which one led to more sales, the information would influence your decision. It's not always the most popular keyword. Because we don't have that info in this example, let's go with the more popular one: web conferencing service. Given that keyword, you could change your profile headline from "Account Executive at ReadyTalk.com" to "Account Executive for the Web Conferencing Service, ReadyTalk.com" or "Web Conferencing Service Account Executive at ReadyTalk.com." What if people look for web conferencing experts and you try that in the Keyword Tool, too, but it comes back with zero results? Then you don't use it in your profile.

You can choose more than one keyword. You might want one for your job title, one to describe your company, and a few for areas of expertise. Use some of your company website's URLs to look for keywords. Spend some time thinking about where you can use them in your headline and summary.

If you want to win online, you need to get to know what the most popular search phrases are in your niche, and use them everywhere, not just on LinkedIn, but in blog posts, on Twitter, in press releases, and in YouTube video titles.

Adding Search Terms to Your Profile

When you have your chosen keywords, search for these phrases in LinkedIn and review the first few profiles. See where the key phrases are placed; the best places are the headline, summary, and specialties. You should do likewise, and don't forget to include keywords in job titles and job descriptions.

If you're reading this chapter because you're in charge of these aspects of marketing for your company, draft a few paragraphs that every employee can add to their profile summary. You know how most press releases end with a blurb about the company? You can create one of these that uses one or more keywords and suggest employees place it at the end of their profile summary and job description. As mentioned elsewhere, it might not be legal to require employees do this, but you can suggest it and explain that it will help both the company and the employee.

Keyword Spam: Don't Overdo It

There are LinkedIn experts who suggest you use the same search keyword everywhere you can in your profile. If you go overboard, it may help you rank higher in LinkedIn search results, but it will look so redundant and spammy that it might create a bad impression.

This is the line that bloggers have had to walk for years. You have to learn to include keywords in a natural way that enhances search rankings without looking spammy and hurting your image.

Please do not put your keyword in your LinkedIn name. It's possible to throw some extra words in as a middle name or in the last name section, and LinkedIn won't reject it, but again it looks spammy.

Did Your Keywords Work?

You can check your homepage from day to day to see how many people have viewed your profile and how much you're showing up in search results. If the results and views go down after making keyword changes to your profile, you probably went the wrong direction. If they go up, it was a good change.

Keep in mind, though, that during holidays and weekends, when people are less likely to use LinkedIn, you may see a drop in searches and views that is unrelated to your keywords.

Shaping LinkedIn Profiles for Employees

Each employee has a unique brand. What does that mean? A company's brand is how we perceive it. The company has some control over its brand by choosing its colors, logos, and slogans. It creates commercials to shape that brand. Hopefully, the company doesn't do anything that leads to negative press or makes people dislike the brand. Each employee can have a brand, too, as much as you want them to. How they dress, speak, and work can be unique and have meaning to them and their customers.

Think about how unique the announcements are from Southwest's flight attendants (check out the rapping flight attendant at http://www.youtube.com/watch?v=G9lZV_828OA; "before we leave, our advice is, put away, your 'lectronic devices"). Their daring announcements bring a smile to their customers. Flying can be such a numbing, depersonalizing experience. You can feel like just a number in the crowd, someone who must surrender rights and conform to regulations, choosing your food from a limited set of options, lowering your expectations, and suffering until it's over. Suddenly the flight attendant starts rapping or telling jokes, and she has broken the spell of the mundane. You feel a burst of hope. Maybe this flight is different, this airline is different, and you feel like a unique person. Maybe the attendants will actually meet your needs. You can create the same experience for your prospects and customers by taking the time to express a unique personality even in boring places.

The more employees develop their abilities, the more of a resume or body of work they develop. Have your employees written blog posts that were well read or shared? Have they been quoted or interviewed by the media? As their skill set develops, so does the list of achievements. Every employee might have or develop a specific skill set, and that creates unique perspectives and philosophies. Each employee, by virtue of his uniqueness, attracts a different set of people you might market to, and that increases your potential customer base.

Each employee has a set of specific values. A technical salesperson might value helping you achieve your strategic objectives. A customer service person might talk about valuing people's time. Your company's image informs the words you use to phrase everything. If you have a buttoned-down image, your customer service people might talk about how they value customers' time. But if your brand is more playful, you might say how much you love making sure you're not driving them crazy...unlike your competitors.

Marketing Employees

Human Resources might have input on LinkedIn profiles from a resume standpoint, but sometimes this department has too much of a conformist approach. If your corporate culture is button-down (think IBM), maybe you want that. But if you want something more attractive to outsiders, these profiles are going to need some creative copywriting. If you're a marketer, you can help.

How do you help the various types of employees market themselves? Check each employee's profile first, so you can say something positive about it when you speak to them. Tell employees the company recognizes the importance of how it and its employees look in social media, and has dedicated itself to upgrading its social media image. Also, tell them how it can help them get better results at work and enhance their careers in the long term. Ask whether they mind if you help them spruce up their LinkedIn profiles. Then schedule 15 minutes with them to discuss the profile. This time investment pays off for your entire company, if you can raise the bar for the quality of how each employee looks online. At the very least, do this for the executive team, VPs, and directors.

Before the appointment, make sure you've taken a look at people in similar roles at companies that do a stellar job of social media marketing. If the employee wants to do some research like this, too, so much the better. At that appointment, ask them about their values, their process, what customers like about them, what they enjoy most about their job, and why they think they're successful. Take some notes.

Next, when you're alone, start an email to the employee about what you wrote down. If you're the marketing person and the person with the most experience writing sales copy, you might want to edit their ideas into full sentences in the most compelling and attractive form you can devise. Make sure you include whatever keywords you've found that fit the job title and the company, and even the suggested keyword/sales-optimized piece about the company. Again, watch your company policies because if the employees haven't agreed to let you influence their LinkedIn profile, this may seem intrusive.

Employees Promoting Themselves

How should each type of employee promote him or herself? Why is this helpful? Your most socially proactive employees will keep forming new connections and interacting online without any prodding. They'll interact on Twitter, they'll interact in LinkedIn Groups, and they'll ask questions and answer them in LinkedIn Answers. Even more germane to the title of this chapter, their blog posts can show on their LinkedIn profiles. Other people won't do much online no matter how you try to persuade them. Expect that you'll have some who are more gung-ho than others.

A theory from Jakob Nielsen called "90-9-1," and shown in Figure 3.10, states the following:

- **Contributors** are 1% of the online population. Only 1% of people online create content from scratch.

- **Participators** are 9% of the online population. They edit wikis, comment on blog posts, and like, comment, or share socially.

- **Lurkers** represent 90% of the online people. They simply consume information and don't interact at all.[4]

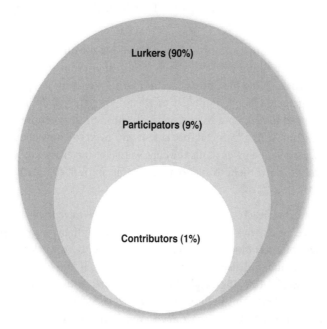

Figure 3.10 *A diagram illustrating the three types of people online, by behavior.*

Sometimes just a few employees provide the bulk of the social media interaction, exposure, and opportunities for your company. Don't restrain the enthusiastic 10% of creators and participators at your company too much because they can bring your company attention and praise. They are a social media asset from a Human Resources standpoint. You don't want to be the one company in your space at a disadvantage in social media because your competitors figured out how to leverage their enthusiasts and you didn't.

Also, even lurkers care what happens on this score; more than half of college students say that if they encountered a company that banned access to social media, they would either not accept a job offer or would find a way to circumvent corporate policy.[5] Many in Generation Y see Internet access as more important than having a car.[6]

Make sure you have social media policies in place for how employees are to represent themselves and the company, and ensure they are responsible and reasonable people who aren't likely to make your company look bad. Make sure they know the policies. Tell them about companies such as Nestle, where in March of 2010, the Facebook page administrator posted while angry and made the entire brand look bad. Two years later, this incident still shows up very high in Google results for the search "nestle facebook," which 3,600 people use each month to find their Facebook page. This mistake will be a ding on their brand image for years. The rule should be to never comment when you're emotional. Step away from the computer, go outside, and do something else. Then look at the situation again in three hours.

What's more, share your corporate strategies and goals with the active 10% and spend some time speaking with them each month about how their activity helps achieve those goals. What blog posts can they write? What infographics can you brainstorm together? (This is a preview of what marketers will do in Chapter 5.) Who do you need to reach out to and network with to achieve those goals? What are they doing and seeing in social media that you need to know about? This group of enthusiasts should be given signs they are valued at the executive level, and their managers should allow them to spend a reasonable amount of time helping the company in this way.

Some of the most active 1% of Internet users might also have their own personal blog. Therefore, be clear about whether or not you want them to even mention their employer on their blog. If they have another blog that's work related, this can be more problematic, but also more of an opportunity. If you look at AdAge's list of the most powerful 150 blogs, eight of the top 20 are written by just one person, or were for many years. This includes well-known social media and marketing names such as Chris Brogan, ShoeMoney (Jeremy Shoemaker), Anne Holland (Which Test Won), CopyBlogger (Brian Clark), Seth Godin, Brian Solis, and Andy Beale.

Never look down your nose at solo bloggers; they can be a powerful part of your marketing strategy. Even if they aren't currently one of the top bloggers in the world, their activity, notoriety (microfame), the power and networks of the people with whom they connect, their speaking opportunities, and the SEO value of their links might help your business significantly. It's reasonable to expect that an employee who writes well can write as frequently as once a week for their own blog without negatively impacting their work output at the company.

The ROI to you from this activity is difficult to predict, but the reasons it can be profitable are many. If they are good, they may be invited to write for influential blogs or online magazines within your business niche; how valuable would it be to have someone at your company with that kind of influence? Bloggers also can get free conference passes in exchange for writing about an event; for a small company, this can significantly decrease your employee education and event marketing costs.

The Corporate Blog

Corporate blogs are notoriously boring and sparse, although there are certainly exceptions. The lack of creativity may be because a company has reluctantly agreed it should have a blog but hasn't fully committed to it, or because its view of professionalism eliminates divergent views, controversy, and creativity.

What makes a good blog are good writers, good content, and passion. If you want employees to write blog posts, the two biggest problems are their not having enough time to write and just not being a good writers. The fact is, some people will never be great writers. Don't make them write. If you do, you'll get bad blog posts that no one cares about and that won't make your company look good. Other employees have writing potential and just need a little guidance. They need to use good grammar and spelling, because spell-checkers aren't perfect, and spelling mistakes scare off sales. No matter how smart you are, if you can't spell, people will think you're stupid. And, if you can't create a quality blog, people might wonder whether you have high standards for your core business.

Make sure your writers read *The Elements of Style* and follow the blogging tips in these next sections. Even if they don't read all the grammar points in *The Elements of Style*, they should at least check out the stylistic ideas. For example, they need to know the value of short sentences and clear phrasing. If your blog writers aren't open to learning this, they won't write good blogs, and they'll make your company look bad, or at best, mediocre. Push them to be better.

Blog Post Titles

First, start with the title. The blog post's title is the most important part because the title might be all that someone sees on Twitter, Facebook, or LinkedIn. It determines whether readers will click the post and influences whether they will share it.

Search Google's BlogSearch for title ideas, and check out the hottest blog posts according to Technorati in various categories (http://technorati.com/business/). I'd caution you that in highly technical industries, you're more likely to find boring blog posts. You do want to be aware of what's being written by your competitors, but you should also look in consumer categories and model your posts after them, because they tend to be more creative in their approach and get better results because of it. Think article titles on the cover of magazines at the grocery checkout. Look at the Mashable articles that get the most Facebook shares and Tweets. Check

InfiniGraph for your brand or bigger brands in your category and find the most interacted with and shared content.

For examples of high quality B2B blogs, take a look at the following:

- B2Bbloggers.com
- SocialMediaB2B.com
- LiesDamnLiesStatistics.com
- ContentMarketingInstitute.com/blog

The easiest way to write a good title is to put a number in it, some aspect of your business, and something exceptional:

- The 9 Biggest Mistakes People Make When...
- 25 Amazing...
- 5 Reasons You Should...

Adding elements of usefulness, news, warning, vanity, greed, surprise, contrary views, and the cool factor help make the post topic interesting.

Blog Post Layout

One aspect of blog post creation that can take you a long way, even with mediocre content, is the layout. Start with an outline, and then begin writing. Turn the outline points into headlines using H2 headers (not just bolded subheadings, but make them actual H2s, which are HTML headers), both for SEO purposes and to break up the flow of text. People should be able to skim through the headlines alone and get the gist of the article. Don't write any long paragraphs (over five or six lines) and be sure that your paragraphs aren't all the same size. Occasionally have a one-sentence paragraph. You're trying to create something interesting for the eye.

Make sure the width of the body text isn't greater than about six inches. People get tired of reading horizontal lines that are long.

Insert one to three nice images (in every blog post), ideally with the first image visible before the reader has to scroll down the screen. People like pictures and they hate blog posts that are all text. It helps if any of these pictures are infographics (visually pleasing diagrams that make data simple and easy to understand), historical timelines, or charts. For business-to-business (B2B) purposes, often there's something in the data you can put into an easily understood chart that proves the effectiveness of what you offer. But if your target audience isn't geeky, stay away from charts. Sometimes the best images are just happy people, or happy customers. Make sure the image not only fits what you're trying to convey, but also the audience.

Viral Blog Posts

People share because they want to look smart or look good. They won't look good if they share a boring post that's hard to read, so they won't share it. If you combine all the elements suggested previously, you're more likely to get clicks to your posts and see people sharing them with others.

Some blog posts succeed far more than others, and you won't know why. After you have 20–50 posts, you might see a pattern to the topics that do well versus the ones that don't. The low-performing topics will probably surprise someone. You may have to convince the writer that no one cares about their pet topic. Hopefully that person is not an executive.

Profile Maintenance

Once you've set up your profile and optimized it, it's easy to forget about it. Most people will need to update it annually, at a minimum, but quarterly is even better. If you're very active and frequently have new achievements, you might need to update it monthly. Whatever frequency you think best, put it on your calendar so you remember. You may be surprised—even if you have little that needs to be altered, after a bit of time passes, you may change your mind about the best headline or some aspect of your summary. As they say, writing is rewriting, and the best writing takes several passes. As you look over your profile, multiple times, you'll find ways to improve it you didn't see before.

Summary

Both employers and employees can benefit from employees developing impressive LinkedIn profiles.

For employers, this chapter tells you how to get more social media mileage out of your employees. LinkedIn profiles are public, so they might as well look good. Think of employees as potential volunteers in your "brand army." All of them can directly or indirectly help your company with PR and marketing.

For the employee, this is an opportunity to help your company and grow as a professional. LinkedIn profiles that contain the right keywords in the right places get more views. LinkedIn profiles that are complete and well written and that highlight original content written by the employee reflect well on both you and your company.

Endnotes

1. "The Average Facebook User," Bianca Bosker, *Huffington Post*, Nov 19, 2011. http://www.huffingtonpost.com/2011/11/19/the-average-facebook-user_n_1102902.html

2. "Employee Tenure Summary," Bureau of Labor Statistics, U.S. Department of Labor, Sept 14, 2010. http://www.bls.gov/news.release/tenure.nr0.htm

3. Profile Completeness, LinkedIn Help. http://www.linkedin.com/static?key=pop%2Fpop_more_profile_completeness

4. Participation Inequality: Encouraging More Users To Contribute, Alertbox, Jakob Nielsen, Oct 9, 2006. http://www.useit.com/alertbox/participation_inequality.html, and What is the 1% Rule, Charles Arthur, The Guardian, July 19, 2006. http://www.guardian.co.uk/technology/2006/jul/20/guardianweeklytechnologysection2

5. "Cisco Gen-Y Study: Mobile Devices Value More Than Higher Salaries," Rachel King, Nov 2, 2011. http://www.zdnet.com/blog/btl/cisco-gen-y-study-mobile-devices-valued-more-than-higher-salaries/62246

6. "Study: For Some Millenials, Internet Is as Important as Air, Water, and Food," Kevin Allen, *PR Daily*, Nov 7, 2011. http://www.prdaily.com/Main/Articles/Study_For_some_millennials_Internet_is_as_importan_9964.aspx

4

Amazing Brands: Company Pages That Grow Business

Company pages are LinkedIn profiles for companies. A company page serves as a home away from home for your company. It's an outpost or mini-site inside of LinkedIn. It's also an opportunity. You can use a company page to sell your products and services, attract employees, gather followers, and do PR and marketing.

LinkedIn characterizes a company page this way:

- *A central hub for your brand*
- *Your engagement tool*
- *A way to grow your business virally—through word of mouth*
- *A rich source of analytics[1]*

You have a lot of options for providing a compelling and professional view of your company with a LinkedIn company page. Search for Eloqua's company page and take a look at it (see Figure 4.1). You can see its latest blog post, an overview of the company, specific employees, how many followers the company page has, how many connections are in the company (actually, I know two people who work there, and this is a reminder for me to connect with them—see, it's working!), a tab for careers and products, and a link to see more statistics about the employees.

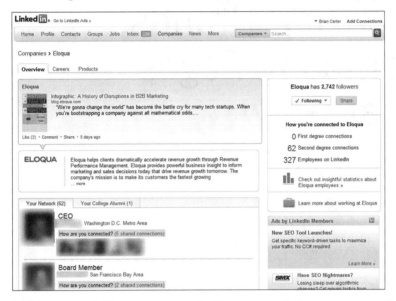

Figure 4.1   *The LinkedIn company page for Eloqua, a marketing automation software provider.*

The Statistics page shows employee composition by job function (see Figure 4.2), years of experience, and education. It also shows company workforce growth (this is measured by LinkedIn profiles and thus influenced by the number of people who join LinkedIn) as well as compares that growth to similar companies, shows job title changes, and shows incoming and departing employees.

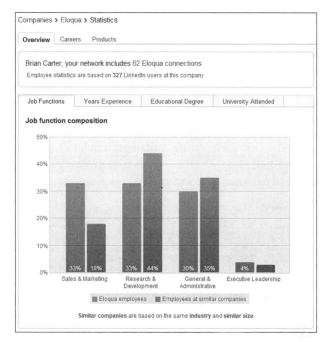

Figure 4.2   *Some of the statistics people can view on a company page.*

The Careers tab can also be impressive to people who might be a future employee (see Figure 4.3). Note the custom banner and sales pitch to potential employees.

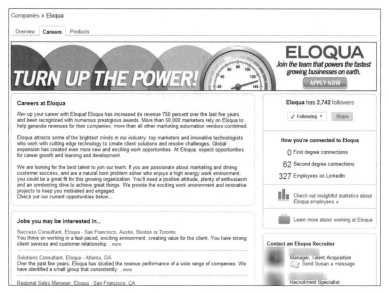

Figure 4.3   *The Careers tab on Eloqua's company page.*

After the summary about why people should work at Eloqua, there's a live and ever-changing list of open jobs, and off to the right is an easy way to contact one of their recruiters. The company's advertising people can run ads targeted to the kind of employees they want to attract and have their ads direct to this page. You can also talk to LinkedIn directly if you want a premium Careers page with even more options.

Similarly, the Products tab can display products and services. Note how Eloqua has included a slideshow, with each picture containing a link to a landing tab on their website (see Figure 4.4).

Figure 4.4 *The Products tab on a company page.*

Also, note how the Products tab displays people who have recommended their products on LinkedIn. As you can see in Figure 4.4, LinkedIn selects, if they exist, people from the visitor's own network (labeled "2nd") and, secondarily, connections of their connections (labeled "3rd"). In this example, one of the two people works for Eloqua, and, fortunately, the other two do not. Remember, it's always more credible to have people outside your company recommending you, so you'll want to create a marketing effort to request company recommendations.

Company Page Setup Tips

Some aspects of setting up a company page are self-explanatory, but others are not. Here are some less-obvious tips for setting up your company page.

Company Name

When you first create your company page (go to http://www.linkedin.com/company/add/show), you'll be asked to enter the company name and your email address at the company. Once you've done this, employees will need to go to their profiles and make sure they've selected the company from the drop-down (see Figure 4.5), rather than just typing in the name of the company. The drop-down appears as you type in your company name. Choosing the drop-down option standardizes the company name and associates all employees with your company page so that it accurately reflects the size and composition of your company.

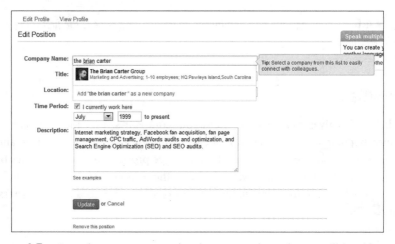

Figure 4.5 *Once the company page has been created, employees will be able to select it from a drop-down menu for their own profiles.*

Admins

You get to choose who can administer your company profile (see Figure 4.6): either all employees with an email address at the corporate domain or designated users only. My recommendation is to use specific employees. Your company profile is like a website; you don't want everybody and anybody to be able to change things willy-nilly. Also, as with a Facebook page, right before terminating an employee, you should remove their admin. Don't wait until after, or your social accounts can be hijacked.

Figure 4.6   *Choosing who can administer your company page is the first thing you'll see in edit mode.*

Specialties

LinkedIn also gives you a place to input your company's specialties. You can include popular keywords that describe your company's products, services, and niche areas. As we did in Chapter 3 for employee profiles, use Google's Keyword Tool to find the most popular ways to phrase these specialties. You can include up to 20 specialties, but the total length of all entries cannot exceed 256 characters (see Figure 4.7).

Company Blog RSS Feed

Here you'll need to get the URL for your company blog's RSS feed (see Figure 4.7). RSS stands for Really Simple Syndication, and it's the standard format websites use to link to blog content across the Web. Once you've entered the RSS URL, LinkedIn can automatically pull in the most recent blog posts for people to view on your company page. These continue to stay up to date through the magic of RSS. If you want to learn more about RSS, check out Wikipedia, or Common Craft's short video "Video: RSS in Plain English."[2] (The link is in the endnotes, but it's probably easier to Google it or search YouTube for it!)

Figure 4.7 *The Specialties and RSS Feed areas of the company page in edit mode.*

News Module

You can turn on the automated News module, which shows news about your company from across the Internet. If your company is not making news, it's best to select "Don't show news about my company." Otherwise, this module may display irrelevant and distracting items.

Promoting Your Products and Services

How do you set up products and services on the company page? As you can see in Figure 4.8, my company page has only services and no products. In addition, it has a banner that forwards to my keynote speaking website and also a video down in the lower-right corner.

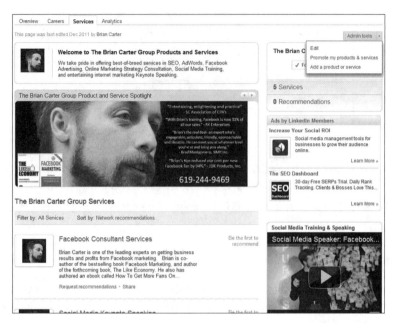

Figure 4.8 *The Services tab of a company page.*

Under the Admin Tools button, you can add a product or service. Apply all the lessons concerning keywords we discussed for employees in Chapter 3 to filling out the Products and Services tabs.

Company Status Updates

People who've followed your company can see corporate posts on the company page overview or directly on their homepage. They can also comment on, like, or share your company posts.

Company Page Analytics

Only administrators can see the Company Page Analytics tab. You can use it to understand your follower composition—who they are, what they do, and what products, services, or jobs interest them. Probably the most important thing to ask yourself is if this audience composition fits your customers and potential customers, or if you need to target some outreach to change the composition.

Getting Connections to Follow Your Company

Most likely, the first connections you get will be your employees and closest peers, colleagues, and customers. If you're starting from zero, you might take the route most every new social media profile does: Get your family and friends to follow it! That's common, but not enough. The next step is to share it with your LinkedIn connections and Twitter followers, and it's best if every employee does this as well (see Figure 4.9).

Figure 4.9 *When you click Share on your company page, you are given the option to post about the page to your connections, your Twitter account, to LinkedIn Groups, and to specific individuals. You can even enter email addresses.*

Then you might create a specific email to your corporate email list announcing the company page, what great content it has, and why people should go follow it. Make sure you tell them in the email to click to the page and follow your company.

You can make it easy for people who go to your main website to find and connect to you on LinkedIn, the same way that many sites now show Facebook and Twitter icons with links. Eloqua's homepage has an expandable bar at the bottom that contains links to its profiles on six social sites, including LinkedIn (see Figure 4.10).

Figure 4.10   *Eloqua's homepage with its Get Social tab expanded and links to its homes on six social networks.*

If you click Promote My Company from the Admin Tool button, you'll be taken to LinkedIn Ads to create an advertisement (see Figure 4.11). The ad can be targeted to whomever you want, and people who click it can be sent to whatever section of the company page you choose.

Figure 4.11   *Promoting your company page with a LinkedIn ad.*

Also consider using AdWords and Facebook ads to drive people to your LinkedIn company page, but first you'll have to make some decisions about your strategies and goals. You likely have a limited ad budget and want to distribute that between ad platforms and goals. As discussed in the advertising chapters (Chapters 7 through 10), you may get more bang for your buck by sending people to your webpages than to your LinkedIn company page. It's critical to have a LinkedIn company page; therefore, make sure its content represents your brand positively and that it has enough followers and recommendations to not diminish the brand image.

Creating Multiple Views and Targeting Segmented Audiences

One overlooked feature is the ability to create multiple "views" of the company page that are tailored to specific audiences. Want to show different things to people in different geographical regions, or with different job titles, or of different levels of seniority? All you need to do is click the button to create multiple audiences and then create the different content for each audience.

Go to your company page and select Edit from the drop-down under the blue Admin Tools button. First, create a default version and then click Create New Audience to create more versions of your company page. For example, I created a version of my company page targeted to Human Resource managers (see Figure 4.12) because they are sometimes the decision makers for events.

Figure 4.12 *Creating a new view of the company page for an HR audience. Note how the headline calls out to Human Resource managers by profession.*

Summary

Company pages need to be created and should look good. They provide great opportunities for HR and some opportunities for marketing, if you're willing and able to grow a following. They also can play a role as a quality Google search result for your company to protect against SEO reputation issues. (If you control the top ten results for your brand, any negative sites about your company will remain on the less viewed second page.) However, there are much more powerful marketing opportunities than company pages available on LinkedIn, which we'll discuss in the next chapter.

Endnotes

1. "Company Pages—LinkedIn Marketing Solutions," LinkedIn.com, March 2011. http://marketing.linkedin.com/sites/default/files/ attachment/LinkedinCompanyPageGuide_Mar2011_1.pdf

2. Video: *RSS in Plain English*, Common Craft. http://www.youtube.com/ watch?v=0klgLsSxGsU

Generating Leads with Content Marketing and LinkedIn Answers, Events, & Groups

As a social marketer, how will your success will be judged? Every company is different, and you'll have your own set of goals and priorities, but here are some of the things you may be held accountable for:

- *How well did you support the sales team?*

- *How many leads did your efforts generate for the sales team?*

- *What have you done to differentiate your company's brand from your competitors?*

This chapter shows marketers how to excel in all three of these areas using LinkedIn Answers, Events, and Groups to showcase your company's thought-leading expertise and your custom-created, value-adding, persuasive content:

- **LinkedIn Answers** is a place where you can ask or answer questions. You and your coworkers can use this to have productive, niche-oriented Q&A. You and other employees can generate leads and find prospects for the sales team by demonstrating expertise, being visible, and creating relationships in LinkedIn Answers.

- **LinkedIn Events** is a place where you can promote real-world events or online webinars, both of which can generate leads or take prospects deeper toward a sale. If you already run events, this can help you get more attendees. If you don't, the functionality here might lead you to start holding events.

- **LinkedIn Groups** is a great place to reach captive, already-organized segments of prospective customers. You can engage in discussions other people start, or you can start your own. What's more, you can and should create your own Group to attract prospects to a place you moderate and control. Both can generate more leads.

To be an excellent marketer in each of these three areas of LinkedIn, you need quality content and you need to act like a thought leader. Therefore, before we go into detail about Answers, Events, and Groups, let's look at how content marketing and thought leadership work.

Content Marketing and Thought Leadership

Content is a word for any created work. Examples include blog posts, white papers, videos, books, PDFs, songs, and infographics. Content marketing uses these forms of media to engage your prospects, demonstrate your expertise, get website traffic, and drive prospects to become a lead or complete the sale. Content marketing has to be exciting enough to grab people's attention. When the content is useful and objective, it doesn't feel like a sales piece, so they're more open, the piece is more influential, and it gets shared more through social websites like LinkedIn, Facebook, and Twitter. Your content piece might be a whitepaper such as "The Five Biggest Mistakes to Avoid When Choosing an Electronic Health Record" or an infographic that shows how much activity there is per minute on each social media site.

How important is content marketing? Very important. The average B2B marketer spent 26% of his budget on content marketing in 2011, and 60% of B2B marketers plan to spend more in 2012. The most effective content marketers have the buy-in of their higher-ups.[1]

Thought leadership means being a leader in an area of expertise. Thought leaders lead by asking questions, shaping public discourse, creating content, and speaking publicly. Often, thought leaders are bloggers or authors. They have or they develop a large audience (large relative to the size of their niche) and they create content that helps people learn, understand, move forward, and do their jobs better. Their content is widely seen and shared. How do you know if they're a leader? If they have followers, they're leading. In social media, this can be Twitter followers, Facebook fans and subscribers, LinkedIn connections, and LinkedIn Group members. Some companies have stand-out employees who are thought leaders, and these leaders increase the company's visibility in their niche. I performed that function for my former agency, Fuel Interactive. Chris Barger did so for General Motors. Steve Jobs did it for Apple. Sometimes CEOs are niche thought leaders, sometimes they aren't. There's no one right way to do it. You might even say that Stephen Colbert and Jon Stewart are thought leaders in politics, because despite their comedic approach, many people get their news and views through their TV shows.

Content marketing and thought leadership aren't new. Companies send investors their "investing prospectus," which gives the facts along with sales points about why people should buy their stock. We could go all the way back to Socrates as an early thought leader. Or more recently, people such as Zig Ziglar, John Maxwell, Malcolm Gladwell, and Seth Godin have led the sales, leadership, and marketing fields with their writing and speaking.

You can use the power of content marketing and thought leadership for your company even if you don't have a famous or micro-famous personality in your company. You can create white papers, infographics, blog posts, and videos with a reasonable amount of time and effort. The easiest of these to create are blog posts, but blog posts usually don't drive as many sales leads as white papers. According to MarketingProfs and the B2B Content Marketing Institute, blogs, videos, and white papers were the content marketing tactics used by the most companies in 2011. The percentage of B2B marketers using these three increased from 2010. Print magazines and print newsletters were the fourth and fifth most used content types, although use of these decreased from 2010 to 2011. E-books were sixth, and they almost doubled in usage from 2010 to 2011.[2]

Those are the *most* used, but which type of content marketing is best? A separate study asked B2B marketers which types of marketing they thought drove the *highest quality* leads and found that educational webinars were number one, followed by periodic content such as e-newsletters, product trials, and white papers and e-books. The degree of separation was remarkable; 50% more marketers said webinars drove high quality leads compared to white papers and e-books.[3]

There are some shocking stats about content marketing in an infographic on Mashable called "Marketers Who Share Content Drive Traffic, Gain Customers."[4] Whether they call it by its name or not, 90% of B2B marketers use content marketing. Marketers' top goals for content marketing are brand awareness, customer acquisition, lead generation, and customer retention. Even more interesting, 62% of companies outsource their content marketing. If you don't have a budget or line-item for doing so, it might be time to start asking for one.

Infographics have become more and more popular (see Figure 5.1). They have all the characteristics of the content that goes viral most often:

- **Visual**—Infographics look impressive right away, so people think that sharing or forwarding one will make them look good, too.

- **Understandable**—The point of infographics is to quickly create comprehension and meaning from data that would otherwise need pages of explanation, which is pages of text people would be would be less likely to read.

- **Useful**—Often the insights of an infographic change your tactics or your perspective on your business for the better.

A stellar infographic may become a mainstay of how people in your niche understand something. If your corporate name is on it, your company gets big exposure and positions itself as a leader in the niche.

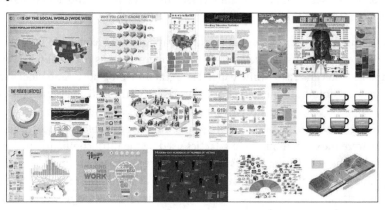

Figure 5.1   *A selection of infographics. Each infographic is usually bigger than one printed page, so this image demonstrates their extent and layout.*

Leveraging LinkedIn Answers for Inbound Leads

LinkedIn Answers has numerous benefits for the LinkedIn marketer. You can use it to do the following:

- Generate contacts
- Find new suppliers
- Discover new content for blog posts

- Get feedback on marketing and content ideas
- Identify industry influencers
- Find guest bloggers
- Learn how prospects write and think (as opposed to your jargon)
- Find keyword ideas for SEO and LinkedIn

Asking Questions

When you ask a question, LinkedIn requires you to select some of your own connections to answer it. This also allows you to limit the answering to just these contacts, but you really want anyone on LinkedIn to see and respond. Therefore, leave it open.

You could restrict your answers to experts you know, if you believe that will generate higher quality results. Another reason you might restrict your answers to your first-degree connections is if you're already connected to all the prospects you want to ask. Still, this limits the potential prospects who might see your question in three months or six months, so I never do that.

Once you start getting answers, stay on top of those responses. Some people try to game the LinkedIn Answers system by answering as many questions as they can, while leaving very short, not very helpful answers. You can hide these answers and report people if you want. I would be cautious about reporting people, unless you find the same people leaving poor answers on all your questions. I noticed one such spammer after asking just three or four questions, and one of the quality answerers even complained to me about this person. I believe part of keeping your questions high quality is filtering through these answers and helping LinkedIn be aware of people who are trying to game the system.

Why Ask Questions?

You might ask prospects and customers a question that helps you calibrate your sales or product development—anything that you know is part of your target customer's needs, or your existing customers' goals, is fair game for a question in LinkedIn Answers (see Figure 5.2).

When you have specific people in mind you'd like to shine on a particular topic, you set them up to succeed. You might ask some of your own company's experts a question that will allow them to shine (but remember, your company name will appear in the answers, so have them wait until some other good answers are posted).

Figure 5.2 *Asking a question in LinkedIn Answers.*

Look at the existing questions already posed for your industry, and see how many answers each gets to determine which topics are sparking the hottest conversations. Then use those topics as fodder for your business blog.

Using LinkedIn Answers to Understand Your Prospects

There's a lot to know about any company's prospects. There's probably more for you to learn about yours. Here's a list of some of the things you might want to know about your company's prospects, and if you don't know them all, create a LinkedIn Question about them:

- Their biggest problem.
- Their biggest frustrations while solving the problem.
- How they feel about you and your competing providers.
- What makes a good or bad provider.
- What's the best result or outcome they've ever had using the kind of thing you provide?
- If they've never purchased the kind of thing you offer, what is holding them back?
- What are their favorite magazines, websites, and blogs? (You can use the answer to this to target them with Facebook ads.)

Using LinkedIn Answers to Find Industry Influencers

Just as you and your coworkers will be searching for questions on LinkedIn to answer, other marketers and experts will be as well. There are niche media people and highly communicative customers participating, too. Scan through 30 to 50 answers in your niche, and watch for people who show up three or more times, especially if they are chosen as the best answer. Find out who these people are and make a connection with them. Even if they aren't prospective customers, is there some way you could partner with them? Will they blog about you? Interview you? Tweet your content in the future? As always, begin with generosity; blog about them, interview them, tweet their content (so long as it's good). Strike up a relationship. See the six steps to relationship building in Chapter 13 for more about this process.

Using LinkedIn Answers to Find Guest Bloggers

Shift your search toward the topics you'd like to find bloggers to write about. Let's say you're in the business of selling software such as Dragon Naturally Speaking, and you'd like to find some interesting things to go on your blog. You can do anything along the lines of language, culture, and translation; maybe you could find some flamboyant translators who'd want to do a video of a funny dance while saying common words from their language. Too crazy? Try an interview series where you ask three experts each three questions on topics that are important, controversial, or fun.

Using LinkedIn Answers to Eliminate Jargon

Jargon includes those words, phrases, and acronyms that people at your company use freely. But your prospects and customers may not know what they mean. Often, when people don't understand, they don't ask because they don't want to look stupid. You can't assume that people who aren't asking questions are understanding you. Using jargon introduces the risk of being misunderstood or increases communication time because you have to explain what the jargon means to each person.

LinkedIn Answers is one place where you can find alternatives to jargon. As you read answers in your niche, you may notice people phrasing the same things differently.

Remember the discussion of the profile that used the term *web visibility*? When we want to explain how findable a person or website is online, what should we call that? Search visibility? Findability? Visibility? And what about people for whom it isn't second nature to think of the value of being visible? Visible to whom, and where? We know people are searching Google and LinkedIn all the time, and you have to be visible in the search results to be found. But not everyone knows that. The term *web visibility* may not flip the mental switches that you think it does.

I gave training once to an association of audiovisual professionals whose biggest problem was (and still is) that their niche doesn't have one good name. These are the highly technical A/V guys who fulfill million-dollar contracts for the Department of Defense, TV control rooms, digital signage in public places, and even worship experiences. There's no agreed-upon name for this niche, and there's a plethora of jargon. Even digital signage is a phrase of dispute; it includes those LED boards you see on the side of the road telling you the price of a gallon of milk and the cool screens that guide visitors around malls, casinos, and airports. Unfortunately, we didn't solve the entire industry's naming problem that day, but I'd suggest they call themselves the Corporate Audiovisual industry. Audiovisual is the only thing that ties it together, and only main problem with the A/V label is differentiating from the freelance guys who have lesser capabilities.

Your industry probably has jargon, too, and you won't see all of it until you start looking or try to explain what you do to your neighbor at a backyard BBQ. Keep an eye out for it, know how to rephrase it, and learn from how other people how to explain it.

Answering Questions

As I discussed in Chapter 2, helping others ultimately helps you. The person you help will feel an obligation to you on some level. If you help them while demonstrating your expertise, you walk away with a sales lead. One warning: If you give too much to the wrong people, you attract people who would never become customers. Always keep your eye on the prize: your target customer.

Answering questions can make you look like an expert and may encourage the asker to reciprocate. It could lead them to investigate your profile and your company, and even to contact you. Or you could connect with them after answering their question, tell them you answered it, and say, "Let me know if I can help further."

How to Find Questions to Answer

First, go to http://www.linkedin.com/answers (see Figure 5.3) and check out new questions from your network and the categories of questions on the right that you can "browse."

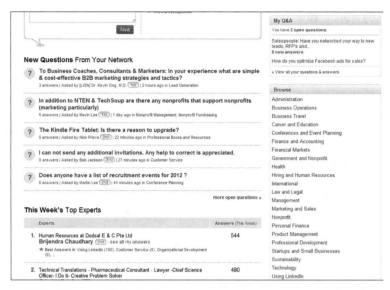

Figure 5.3   *The main LinkedIn Answers page, with recent questions from your network and the categories of questions on the right.*

Next, check out the advanced search options by clicking Advanced next to the search box in the upper right of your screen. Alternatively, you can go to http://www.linkedin.com/searchAnswers. There you'll see the options shown in Figure 5.4.

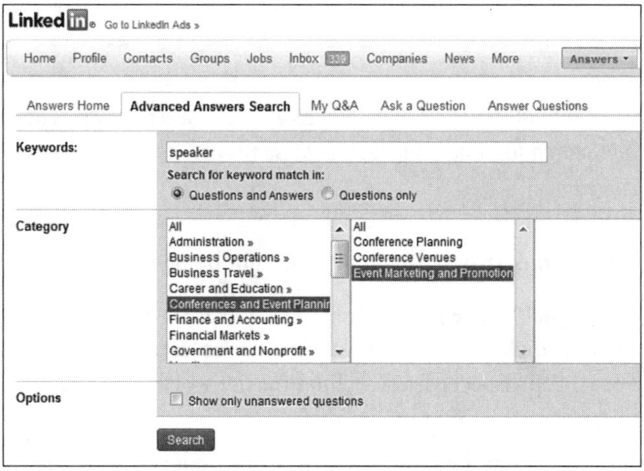

Figure 5.4   *The Advanced Search section for LinkedIn Answers.*

Using Keywords to Find Questions to Answer

The next thing to do is to take your company website's major search keywords and see if there are related questions you should answer. You should seriously consider answering any questions related to your major keywords. If you can, get the main search keywords from your company's SEO person or consultant. If your company hasn't done any of this, go to the AdWords Keyword Tool (https://adwords.google.com/select/KeywordToolExternal), put in your website, and see what keywords come up (see Figure 5.5).

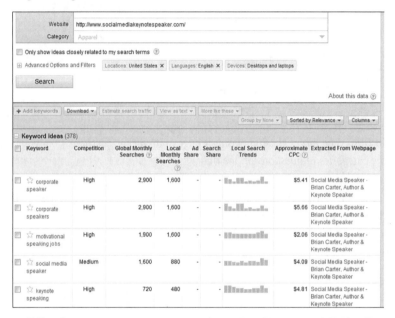

Figure 5.5   *If you put in your company website, Google's Keyword Tool will suggest phrases people search for, and you can use these phrases to search for questions to answer on LinkedIn.*

If these keywords look wrong to you, there might be one of two problems:

- The first is that you're just finding out how customers think of your offerings. It might not be your normal way of talking about it. Maybe none of your prospects are searching for the words you're thinking of. They may be using different words.

- Your website might be poorly search-optimized, so you're seeing how Google sees it, and you need SEO help.

What else might you answer questions about? Think about your customers; what do you help them with? There are all kinds of other topics you can look for. Here are some examples:

- If I want to help my target market as a keynote speaker, I should talk to event planners. What are they concerned about? What other types of professionals are involved in my niche? What questions are they asking on LinkedIn?

- An audiovisual design company can search for questions related to control rooms and worship centers.

- An engineering company can search for answers related to its type of engineering, such as civil engineering.

All of these ideas can be run through the keyword tool for more phrase ideas and then through the LinkedIn Answers search, to find the questions you might answer. For example, I searched for "Pinterest," found a question to answer (Figure 5.6), and referred to my own Pinterest profile.

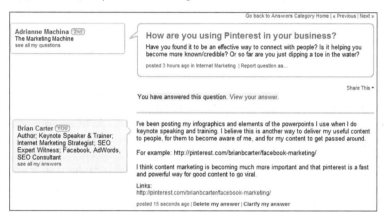

Figure 5.6 *My answer here uses my own case study and links to a post I wrote about it.*

Let me get crazy here for a second: Consider whether your job title should change if you're going to be more active in social media. Maybe VP of Customer Success sounds better to prospects than VP of Marketing. Marketing is a selfish activity, known for creating "spin". Many people will assume you're biased, so you'll have to fight against that. Will they believe you? Will they think you care more about selling than what's best for them? Follow the tips in the next section to make sure your answer is more credible and welcome.

What Makes a Good Answer?

A good answer is one that will meet your goals on LinkedIn. You want to look like a thought leader: positive, informed, practical, and smart. You want to build relationships and get website traffic and leads. The idea is to get responses or be selected as the best answer. Because your answer will sit on LinkedIn publicly and be found by searchers for years to come, you want it to represent you and your company well.

Here are some ideas and guidelines for writing LinkedIn Answers:

- You can include a link to a relevant blog post on your website, but only after fully answering the question. If you don't answer the question on LinkedIn, you'll appear as if you are just promoting your blog.

- If you can take a contrary stance that's backed up by experience or research, and you can do so in a respectful way, do it. Leaders don't just follow the herd, so a thought leader often has original ideas that challenge people.

- If there are already answers to the question, take a look at them first and think about how you can make your answer stand out. If you're not trying to have the best, most helpful answer, why show up as just another "me, too"? Quote research from well-known and credible sources (you can find these by Googling for a couple of minutes), tell a true story, or quote someone.

- Just as with a blog post, don't use too many solid lines of text in a row. Make your paragraphs varying sizes. A paragraph can be just one sentence, if it's a powerful line.

As you review the questions and answers you've found, consider who is asking and answering the questions. Is the questioner your competitor? Be sure to answer with courtesy. If the questioner is someone who might hire you, definitely answer if you have good ideas because they will get a LinkedIn message and an email with your answer.

Your help has even more meaning if you have a subject-matter expert at your company. (See how the answer in Figure 5.6 includes a blog post.) Let them be a thought leader, or at least an expert answering a question accurately. Certainly, you can answer questions as a marketer. Some of the salespeople who are most enthusiastic about LinkedIn may also want to answer. However, you must consider how each person's job title will look next to the answer.

Using Answers to Generate Leads

Steven Shimek, a PR firm employee, brought in business worth $250K with LinkedIn Answers. He simply answered questions, developed relationships, and within three months had brought in 20 business development leads. For more on how to take contacts from LinkedIn Answers toward a sale, read Chapter 13.

Participating, Creating, Growing, and Managing LinkedIn Groups

LinkedIn members have created more than one million Groups.[5] Because there are 150 million users, that tells you that Groups are an important part of the site. Advertising to Groups versus other targeting options has shown that Group members are the most active LinkedIn users.

There are alumni, corporate, conference, networking, nonprofit, and professional Groups. Each Group has specific topics of conversation. Some Groups are on general topics, are completely open, and are easy to join. Some are just online versions of membership organizations. For example, some LinkedIn Groups were created by associations; they're private, and your request to join won't be approved if you're not a dues-paying member of that association.

Why are Groups so important for B2B marketing? You control the space, and you grow your own Group of customers and prospects. That LeadFormix study I mentioned in Chapter 1 found that, among LinkedIn visitors to websites, those who come from Groups and Ads are the most likely to fill out a lead form.[6] In other words, if you're posting updates to your LinkedIn profile itself, you might want to switch that time and activity to participating in and creating Groups. The people in Groups are more likely to see your post there than on your profile, and they're more qualified website visitors.

Groups is one of the main menu items at the top of every LinkedIn page. If you hover over that menu, you'll see "Groups You May Like," which will take you to a page of suggested Groups (http://www.linkedin.com/groupsDirectory?recommend ations) based on your LinkedIn profile and friends.

If you've participated in an online forum or commented on blogs actively, LinkedIn Groups are very similar, except the topics are professional (see Figure 5.7). What's a little bit different is that LinkedIn Groups can be totally private, so what you say in posts and comments may not be indexed by Google and visible to the entire world; most online forums are public. Still, you're participating professionally, so it's important to think about how you, your posts, and your comments will be perceived by others.

Figure 5.7 *Some discussions summarized on the front page of the "B2B Marketing" LinkedIn Group.*

How to Find and Join Groups

There are a few ways to find the most important Groups in your niche. One way is to look at the LinkedIn profile of people in your industry who are heavy LinkedIn users, or even your competitors at other companies, and see what Groups they belong to. Start with the Groups most germane to what your company does. For example, Figure 5.8 shows the Groups of someone who's a salesperson at the Huntsville branch of an audiovisual integration company.

Figure 5.8   *You can find Groups to join by looking at the Groups your peers and competitors have joined. You do not have to be a first-degree connection with someone to see their Groups.*

Another way to find Groups is to go to the Groups Directory at http://www.linkedin.com/groupsDirectory. You can search Groups by keywords, categories, and language (see Figure 5.9).

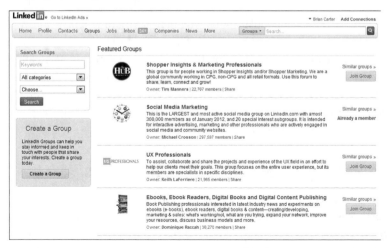

Figure 5.9   *The LinkedIn Groups Directory and its search feature.*

How to Post in Groups

Active Group members create their own posts. Often these posts are links to your company's blog content, but they can also be questions or polls. Questions are one of the most common types of posts. You can ask general questions or perhaps something in the news related to your niche. You can create your own five-question poll in any Group you're a member of.

When you do post your own content in a Group you don't manage, be courteous. Add something personal like, "We just wrote this and are really excited about it! Hope you find it useful!" Even better, explain why exactly you think it's relevant and useful. If you ask a question, you may stimulate people to comment on it. This also shows you're open-minded and plan to be present in the Group, not just show up every week or two to push your posts down people's throats. Never post out of frustration. If no one responds to your post, either no one saw it, or it didn't hit a nerve. There are other places to distribute your content, such as Twitter. And not every blog post resonates with people. Ironically, some of the blog posts I'm most proud of and spent the most time on received the least response. You never know what's going to work until you see the results—or lack thereof.

Make sure your post is relevant to the Group. This sounds like a no-brainer, but I can tell you as a Group admin, there are lots of people who must just post all their latest blog posts to all their Groups. If the admins have to repeatedly delete your posts rather than approve them, they'll remember you, and even when you do post on topic, they might not approve it. Not all Groups are managed that tightly (with the admin deciding whether each post should be approved or deleted), but the best Groups are, because this keeps the post quality high and Group members more engaged.

If you post on the most popular topics, you may get more visibility- but your post can disappear faster too. Find a balance of high-, medium-, and low-traffic Groups. If you've noticed when you comment, the check box to send you an email for later comments is automatically checked. There's a good chance everyone who commented before you will see your comment. Of course, don't comment on everything just because of this. If you have little to say, people will see through it, and they'll view you as a spammer.

How to Generate Leads from LinkedIn Groups

People may watch your activity in LinkedIn Groups for a long time before it occurs to them to use you for business. This is true in all of social media, and to some degree in all business. It usually takes multiple exposures to make an impression. Even an extremely successful viral infographic may only be the seed that, upon further exposures, leads a person to realize, "Oh I remember that company; they're the ones that...."

When you're posting and commenting in social media, you're making a long-term impression on people who don't even know they're potential customers. Eventually, though, their problem will be big enough and you will be the most obvious solution.

Over time, you need to continue to be visible, be positive, and appear to know what you're talking about without ever being too pushy. There's a reason why telemarketing isn't a great marketing solution anymore. People are busy, and they know what they want (or at least they have pride in thinking they know what they want). They resent being interrupted. But if over time they come to believe your company is competent, professional, reliable, approachable, and able to solve a problem for them, they will seek you out. These leads will be easier to turn into customers than any cold call ever could be. That's inbound marketing (and I discuss that more in depth in Chapter 13).

The subtle way to get leads by commenting in Groups is to find discussions you can contribute to, add something meaningful or useful to, or add something funny to the conversation. Make this about 80% of your comment. Then, mention briefly in an "oh-by-the-way" fashion how your company solves the problem or some related content you've created. If you don't have related content for that topic, use it internally to come up with ideas for new content.

Your mission is always to make a meaningful connection with your target customer. Always have your target customers and their needs in mind when you write Group posts and comments. Stand out among the Group participants by being more of an expert or voicing customer needs and challenges more accurately. Stand up for their rights. Let them know you understand them, and that creates a subtle connection. Speak about goals they care about and how they can achieve them, even if it's not always through your company—remember, generosity!

Share information, tips, and news. Every time you post something worth reading or sharing, people see you again. You remain visible. You're thought of as a valuable resource.

Commenting is important. If you've ever posted and received no response, you know it doesn't feel good. Someone who's listening, reading what you've posted, and saying something about it creates a good connection. Even if you only form a positive relationship with the most frequent posters in Groups, that's valuable. If they become your allies, they're more likely to like, support, and share your posts, which makes you look good to prospects who are reading.

Be positive. Say nice things about other comments and commenters. The worst thing you can do in social media marketing—and it's so easy to do—is to sound like a negative person. A negative person is someone who can't help you, who you won't enjoy working with, and who makes things more difficult. People know a critical person is likely to criticize them, and most people are sensitive to criticism even if they never tell you. A positive and complimentary person is a joy to work with, so there's no obstacle to them contacting you and no stain on your company's image. Endeavor to put forward your most positive face. However, try not to gush or be fake. Sometimes being too familiar is off-putting as well.

One rule that's worked for me over the years is to praise people in public and criticize in private. And I think two or three times before I decide to criticize. Usually, I decide that the low chances of people using valid criticism positively aren't worth the risk of losing an ally or creating an enemy.

Build relationships with other Group members, get to know them, and let them know what you can do and how you help people. Don't try to connect with everyone willy-nilly. Connect when you have a real mutual interest or genuine praise to share. If you've seen someone comment several times, and you think they could be a good partner, contact, or customer, request them as a connection and mention how much you've liked their contributions to the Group. One warning: Make sure you never sound patronizing. Some people's praise seems to have the subtext that they are the King Arbiter of Good. And beware that a small subset of people who are actually offended by praise, as if anyone could doubt their goodness! These are incredibly insecure narcissists, but they're out there.

The Value of Networking Beyond Your Industry

The most obvious people to network with are your customers and people who have the same job function as you. I did that a lot initially in social media myself. But later I found additional opportunities, partnerships, and even wisdom by networking with people in related or complementary fields. I've been in Internet marketing for some time, and that led me to learn PR to some degree. The more PR professionals I met, the more I learned about public relations. My PR contacts became a professional advantage, in part because I've learned things I can apply for myself or my clients. Also, we can pass business opportunities back and forth because we're not exactly competitors.

Ask yourself: What types of companies also help your clients but don't compete with you directly? Who are they and how can you find and network with them? For example, an architect can network with engineers, interior designers, and construction companies. A wedding photographer can network with florists and catering companies.

As you look at related job functions and niches, you can find other LinkedIn Groups to participate in. In my case, if I want to continue to develop those contacts, learn from them, and market to them, I can join their Groups. A quick scan of several of my PR contacts reveals some great Groups I could join, including "Solo PR Professionals." Others appear to be associations for PR pros that I don't belong to, so they probably won't let me in. Once in, I can read what they're concerned about and comment if I might be able to help. I won't horn in and say, "Look at me!" I'll start by listening, and then engage where appropriate. Over time this can lead to opportunities and partnerships.

Why Create Your Own Group

There are many benefits to creating your own Group. LinkedIn Groups allow you to do the following:

- Lead discussions
- Grow contacts and prospects
- Grow an email list
- Be at the center of the conversation
- Get more visibility for your company
- Be a thought leader by having a place to distribute your content and controlling who posts and what is posted
- Choose to feature your favorite posts as "manager's choice"

Most importantly, it can be a place to attract business prospects. Much like someone who runs a conference, once you have attendees, you have control over opportunities. You can choose to moderate everything that gets posted, but if you do, you need to moderate as much as daily. If you can't check that often and feel that's preventing true discussion from happening, you might let more postings happen.

You can send an "announcement" (see Figure 5.10) once a week to Group members; this sends an email to each one of them. Some of the Group members may have opted out of these, but this is rare. What this means is that your LinkedIn Group is also an email list. So, let me put it this way: Would you like to have a free email list of niche professionals that grows passively over time and that you can email weekly?

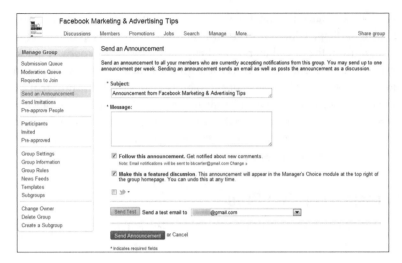

Figure 5.10   *If you run your own LinkedIn Group, you can send an email (yes, to a real email, not just a LinkedIn mail) announcement to members once a week.*

The passive growth part is cool. I have a "Facebook Marketing & Advertising Tips" Group on LinkedIn, and I've only tweeted or Facebooked about it a few times. When I created it, less than 100 people joined soon after. But over a year later, 800 more people have somehow found the Group and joined it. Most likely, they searched LinkedIn for Groups, found mine, and joined. Anyone can create a Group like this for free.

How to Promote Your Group

Initially, invite your connections to the Group by clicking Share Group and then Invite Others in the submenu. You can use that same Share Group menu to post a link to your Group to Twitter and Facebook. You can create Facebook or LinkedIn ads to promote the Group, as well. But if you're not in a rush, you can just let it grow over time.

And if you didn't read the case studies at the end of Chapter 1, note how Chevron, Cisco, and Philips used premium LinkedIn ads to promote their Group. If your company has big money and big goals, that's the way to go.

Leveraging LinkedIn Events to Promote Your Company

LinkedIn Events is a great place to promote events your company puts on, whether they're real-world meetings or virtual webinars.

Social Proof: Which of My Friends Will Be There?

The LinkedIn Events page (see Figure 5.11) has a number of valuable features. It provides a place to get more info about the event, helps you start networking with people who will attend, enables you to see if you already know some of the attendees and the main companies that are bringing the most attendees, and enables you to post questions or comments about the event.

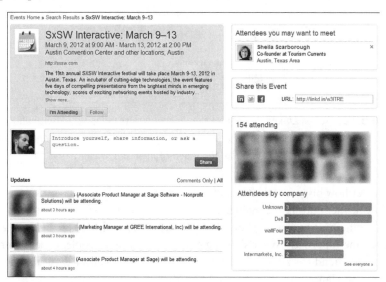

Figure 5.11 *An active LinkedIn Event page.*

Creating LinkedIn Event Pages That Attract Attendees

When you're ready to start promoting your event, create a LinkedIn Event page. In my opinion, a good logo differentiates your event, makes it stand out, and makes it seem more professional. It reflects positively on what kind of professionalism and diligence people can expect from the event itself. Look at the example in Figure 5.12. Do the events with the logos look more interesting than the ones with just the standard calendar icon? The logo is only 60×60 pixels, which is small, so it has to be well designed to convey your brand, be clearly read, and impress. In other words, the logo designed for your conference may or may not look good at this size. You might have to customize it or get the company designer to take a look at it.

Figure 5.12   *When LinkedIn suggests events, you can see who you know who's attending, and you are affected by whether there's an event logo. Create and use an impressive and clear event logo. I like the touch of including the city and date.*

No matter how big your event is and how many years it has been going on, you might consider putting the main benefits of the event in your title. Although there's something to be said about the "you must know who we are because we're so awesome" approach, you risk being overlooked by new people. Unless everyone who could attend has attended in the past, not everyone knows about it. Make it clear at first glance how the event will help them.

If you already have a slogan for the event, use it, especially if it contains benefits. If you haven't thought of one, take 20 minutes to brainstorm one and run it past some coworkers. For example, the SES New York 2012 event could read: "SES New York 2012 | Get Better Digital Marketing Results." Alternatively, they could brag about their longevity for credibility purposes: "SES New York 2012 | 10 Years Of Marketing Training" (I don't know if it's actually 10 years; they don't even brag about their longevity on their website!)

In the Events description, use all your copywriting skills. Make sure you include any and all details that can persuade and help people decide to attend. Put the most important parts at the beginning, because when people view a LinkedIn Event, the display initially shows only the first five lines. To view more, they'll have to click

Show More (see Figure 5.13). If the first part wasn't that interesting, they might not click for more information. Also, in the description, use a call to action: Tell people what to do. Don't forget to tell them to register.

If it's a webinar, you'll use something like GoToMeeting or WebEx. Depending on how the service you use works, you'll be able to capture emails from the event; it's always valuable to have an email list of new prospects. You can set up some questions people have to answer when they register, which can give you more information about whether a person is a good prospect. Assuming you got opt-in permission, you can follow up with them directly, or put them into your lead-nurturing system. If there are other things you'd like them to do after the webinar, such as join your LinkedIn Group, make sure to mention the Group several times during the webinar, and include the link to the Group in a post-event email.

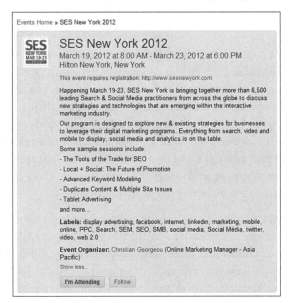

Figure 5.13 *Viewing the full details of a LinkedIn Event. Note how the event planner entered specific details, including the titles of seminars as well as labels that will help LinkedIn suggest the Event to the right people.*

Facebook also has an Events function, so you might want to create and manage an Event page there as well. If you or your team has friends or fans on Facebook who might want to attend, they're more likely to hear about it this way. Don't worry too much about confusion between multiple Events pages—you likely have some more formal way for them to actually register (such as filling out the webinar form or via a conference registration system), so it doesn't matter too much whether they've indicated on Facebook or LinkedIn that they'll attend.

The only reservation I would express about LinkedIn Events is that when you direct people there, they still may have to go somewhere else to actually register. Creating a LinkedIn Event is a good idea, and it may attract some attention. When you have a choice, such as with advertising, I recommend sending people to your Event registration page first and then let them know about the LinkedIn Events page subsequent to their registration.

Promoting Events

Creating the Event is just the first step. Now you need to get people to attend! And there are some things you should be doing during the Event, in part to make post-event promotion possible.

Pre-Promotion

Your event has a cool website, right? One with a list of speakers, the location information, and so on? If not, and if you do events infrequently, the best option is a page on your main website (linked to from your homepage) because Google will index that new page and include it in search results faster than a new website. Use the Google Keyword Tool to find event-related keywords and use those in your event webpage. It can take the Googlebot program a couple weeks to come back to your site and find new links, so create posts on your social media profiles with a link back to the new page, and Google will find it faster. Once it's in Google, people doing a Google search may discover your event.

The problem with creating a new website just for the event only is that, until you link to it from a more authoritative site, such as your corporate site, Google won't have indexed it or ranked it. It takes many months and good links to get rankings, so the big question is, do you have months before your event? But of course, if you have a strong marketing and advertising plan that doesn't require people find your event through Google, you don't have to worry about it—create that super-cool event website.

Send the link to your event out on Twitter, LinkedIn feeds and Groups, LinkedIn ads, your LinkedIn company page, Facebook, Facebook ads, and email. I would start at least 30–60 days out so that people can look at their calendars. Many live events are advertised three months ahead of time. Some people make their conference decisions for the year ahead, based on events that happen every year.

If you can give away material with the event, that helps. At a live event, you can give away tchotchkes such as pens and flash drives with the company or conference name on them. After a webinar, you can give attendees a PDF of the PowerPoint slide show or a video of the presentation for review later.

Sometimes combining the event with a giveaway of a book or one of your products can increase attendance. If it's a free webinar, the first battle is to get sign-ups. The next battle is to get them to show up. If you've never done a webinar, you need to know that sometimes only 20%–30% of people who've signed up for a free webinar actually attend. Another subset of people will not attend but will watch a video replay if you email it to them.

Ask the speakers and presenters to promote the event, too, using their Twitter, Facebook, LinkedIn, and email audiences. If it helps, supply them with some brief information to use in those communiqués. Even if you're a B2B company, notoriety about your organization isn't bad. It can lead to connections and information with strategic value that you would never have received otherwise.

Consider using LinkedIn ads to promote your event. You can target all the LinkedIn Groups you normally participate in and send those who click the ad to either the LinkedIn Event page or your event webpage.

What to Do During Your Event to Get Ready for Post-Promotion

Can you create a video stream to show portions of a live event to people who couldn't make it? Consider offering them access to this at a lower rate. That way, you can get revenue from people who can't afford the entire traveling expense. At the event, get a lot of photos: Get photos of people speaking, get group photos of smiling attendees, and get photos of the speakers with their arms around some attendees. You'll use these after the event to continue to market.

This works for live and virtual scenarios. If possible, have comments, questions, and answers happen on Twitter with a hashtag and link back to the event. If the content and interaction is powerful, it can draw in spontaneous attendees during the event.

For webinars, record the audio and video. Most webinar services, such as GoToMeeting, WebEx, and ReadyTalk will do this. You can also run a backup with camtasia in case something happens to your first recording.

Getting Your Company Even More Exposure After the Event

Don't forget to promote *after* the event. A lot of event planners breathe a sigh of relief—"Thank goodness it's over!"—and move on to something else. But remember, the whole point of the event is marketing, and events create content. You can market content. You can use content to say, "Look how awesome this event was! Look how valuable the information is! Aren't you sorry you missed out? Aren't you coming to the next event?" You can also, assuming you have the permission of the speakers, use portions of their presentations to hammer home the quality of the information your company is associated with. If the speakers were from your company, so much the better, because that expertise means you're the right company to work with.

Post photos to your Flickr account, do a slide show, click Share, and get the embedded code to put this slide show into a blog post on the corporate blog. For webinars, you can go back to the recording and take screenshots of interesting slides, and then use those images in the same way you'd use live event photos.

Send out the Flickr photo stream link via Twitter, LinkedIn profiles, on your LinkedIn company page, in your corporate Group, and anywhere that that's appropriate. Don't post it in a Group you don't moderate if you have any doubts about whether it will seem too promotional and irrelevant. Think back to all the guidelines about posting in Groups. Be useful and relevant. If the post-event promo content is more like "Look, we had an event" than "Look what valuable things were taught here," it is best not to post that content in Groups other people run. You have a bit more leeway in a Group you created and manage. Even so, if too many of your posts are promotional, people will participate less.

If you don't have a corporate Pinterest account, create one. Ideally, you will associate it with the Facebook account of someone who has a lot of Facebook friends who are in the industry you serve—because that's how you get connections on Pinterest. That's one current limitation of Pinterest for B2B purposes—Facebook wants companies to have pages, not personal profiles, but Pinterest finds contacts for you based on your friends. You can't use a business page or its fans to find people on Pinterest. Post the best photos on your Pinterest account, adding a link to something (in the following order: the most relevant web page to the content, the event web page, and then the homepage) on your corporate site. Post them in a board that has a name with keywords in it that fit your company, your event, or both.

Tweet or post on LinkedIn any particularly great individual photos. Pinterest can hook up with Twitter and Facebook accounts to do this automatically. I'd suggest connecting your corporate Twitter account to Pinterest, unless you have strong thought leaders with their own Twitter and Pinterest accounts.

You can do the same things with video from the event; just use YouTube. For extra mileage, use keywords from the Google AdWords Keyword Tool in your YouTube video title. This may bring in people from Google searches. For example, let's say you have a video from a corporate insurance seminar on the topic of Cyber Attacks and Privacy Claims. Be careful not to name the video something people aren't searching for.

Take a quick look with the AdWords Keyword Tool at what people are actually searching for (see Figure 5.14). First look at the types of different phrases, and then look at which ones get the most searches. The results suggest you might consider using the keywords "professional liability insurance" or "commercial business insurance." Sometimes your actual topic is too specific, and you need to tie it to a keyword people are actually looking for. But put it at the end of the video title so you don't confuse people—for example, "Cyber Attacks & Privacy Claims— Commercial Business Insurance."

Another quick way to grab keywords is to look at the suggested keywords that automatically drop-down while you type into Google or YouTube's search box. The downside of this quicker method is that it eliminates what AdWords calls "related keywords" (related phrases using totally different words) and only gives you phrases that begin with the exact words you type.

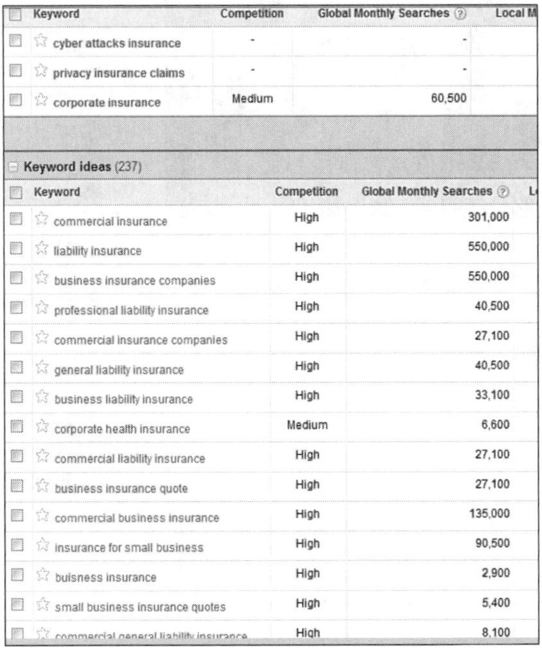

Keyword	Competition	Global Monthly Searches ⑦	Local M
☆ cyber attacks insurance	-	-	
☆ privacy insurance claims	-	-	
☆ corporate insurance	Medium	60,500	

Keyword ideas (237)			
Keyword	Competition	Global Monthly Searches ⑦	L
☆ commercial insurance	High	301,000	
☆ liability insurance	High	550,000	
☆ business insurance companies	High	550,000	
☆ professional liability insurance	High	40,500	
☆ commercial insurance companies	High	27,100	
☆ general liability insurance	High	40,500	
☆ business liability insurance	High	33,100	
☆ corporate health insurance	Medium	6,600	
☆ commercial liability insurance	High	27,100	
☆ business insurance quote	High	27,100	
☆ commercial business insurance	High	135,000	
☆ insurance for small business	High	90,500	
☆ buisness insurance	High	2,900	
☆ small business insurance quotes	High	5,400	
☆ commercial general liability insurance	High	8,100	

Figure 5.14 *A search in the AdWords Keyword Tool for keywords one might use in a YouTube video title.*

If it's an online event, you won't have attendee photos but you can get screen-shots of specific slides or of the speaker and moderator in a split screen. Record the webinar and then excerpt a particularly interesting two-minute segment (the easiest way for PC users is with the freely downloadable Microsoft MovieMaker 2.6,[7] and for Apple users, it's iMovie). Upload that short video to your corporate YouTube account, putting keywords into the title and tags.

To get people to find your video and increase its presence in Google, embed the video in a blog post. Go to the YouTube video, click Share, click Embed, and then you'll get the HTML code you need for the blog post (see Figure 5.15). It's the code that starts with <iframe. Then post the links to the video and to the blog post on all your social networks and in your Groups. For bonus points, post the video on your Facebook account and then create a sponsored story ad to show the video to whomever you want to target.

Figure 5.15   *To get the code to embed your YouTube video into a blog post, click Share and then Embed. You might want to turn off "Show Suggested Videos" because your competitors' videos might come up after yours is done playing.*

Summary

This chapter includes some important strategies and tactics for marketers. In fact, chances are, most of the effective work marketing people do on LinkedIn is covered in this chapter. Content marketing and thought leadership could increase your company's competitiveness dramatically. LinkedIn Answers and Groups present deep and novel networking and marketing opportunities. LinkedIn Events may raise awareness and add value for event attendees. There's a lot of work to do to get all that done. We'll discuss the balancing and scheduling of all that work in the next chapter.

Endnotes

1. "Free Friday: Downloadable B2B Content Marketing Report 2012," Veronica Maria Jarski, *Marketing Profs*, January 13, 2012. http://www.mpdailyfix.com/free-friday-downloadable-b2b-content-marketing-report-2012/

2. "Free Friday: Downloadable B2B Content Marketing Report 2012," Veronica Maria Jarski, *Marketing Profs*, January 13, 2012. http://www.mpdailyfix.com/free-friday-downloadable-b2b-content-marketing-report-2012/

3. "How to Demonstrate and Deliver Lead-Nurturing ROI," Jim Lenskold, *MarketingProfs*, August 3, 2010. http://www.marketingprofs.com/articles/2010/3807/how-to-demonstrate-and-deliver-lead-nurturing-roi

4. "Marketers Who Share Content Drive Traffic, Gain Customers," Joann Pan, *Mashable*, February 8, 2012. http://mashable.com/2012/02/08/new-content-marketing-tactics/

5. "About Us," LinkedIn.com. http://press.linkedin.com/about

6. http://www.leadformix.com/Why-Should-You-Use-Linkedin-For-B2B-Generation/

7. http://www.microsoft.com/download/en/details.aspx?id=34

Get It All Done: Your Weekly LinkedIn Marketing Routine

You might be saying, at this point, "Oh my gosh, how am I ever going to get all this stuff done, Brian?" Everything I've outlined so far is doable, and I'm going to break it all down for you so you can get everything done, achieve results, and feel like a productive rock star who loves the guy who wrote that LinkedIn book.

The key is to get the setup done and then follow a manageable schedule. Always keep your goal in mind, and track what works and what doesn't. Figure out which 20% of things get the most results. Then invest 80% of your time into them.

One-Time Setup Activities

The first set of things you need to look at are the one-time activities. These might take a while to complete, but once set up they'll become your true long-term weekly routine. Setup activities include the following:

- Mapping your activities, sales process, and existing marketing materials to the AIDA (Attention -> Interest -> Desire -> Action) process.
- Deciding on campaign goals and key performance metrics.
- Helping the advertising folks with images and messages they can use.
- Ensuring that tracking on the website is adequate. Do you know how to use your analytics to get the data and reports you need?
- Reviewing employee profiles. Helping employees make them more findable and presentable.
- Deciding how extensively you want to use a company page and what you'll feature there.
- Organizing what you know about your audience, customers, and prospects. What questions do you still have about them? Brainstorm and research for answers.
- Inventorying the content marketing pieces you already have. Adding to them any content that can be improved for marketing purposes. Determining what resources and people can help you create new content.
- Taking stock of what events your company normally has each year. If the company can do online webinars, what would it take, what would it cost, and can you pull it off?
- Thinking about cost per lead and cost per sale, and how your activities affect those metrics.
- Making sure social media policies are clear for everyone who will be interacting online.
- Meeting with executives or your superiors about all the things in this list prior to going full-steam with marketing.

Ongoing Marketing Activities

You may only be able to do two or three things a week, so don't think you have to make progress with everything every week. As time goes on, you'll discover what strategies work best; for example, are events as productive for you as LinkedIn Group activity? Spend the most time on the few that work the best. If you're not sure what works best, go back to the optimization and testing best practice principles (numbers four and seven) in Chapter 2.

Employee Profile Updates

After you help polish the employee profiles, until there are new hires, there's not much to do with them. However, the employee profiles do need to be up to date. Create reminders (perhaps by creating appointments and notifications for yourself in your calendar) to check on profiles and prod employees to update them quarterly. Also, have employees update you and any PR folks so you can keep informed about the great new things going in their profiles, in case something warrants a special blog post or press release.

Event Marketing

If you've mapped out two live events for the year and a webinar every other month, you have eight events to coordinate and promote for the year. Map out each aspect of event planning, preparation, and execution, and put them in your calendar. There are many other aspects of event planning, but the amount varies so much with the size and number of events, it's difficult to give specific guidance here. Chances are, you're better at event planning than I am!

Internal Social Media Marketing Group

We mentioned your volunteer brand army and bloggers in Chapter 5. In that spirit, establish a group of coworker-experts who help with LinkedIn Answers, blogging, and webinar events. If they get enthused about this, you can increase your social media marketing momentum. Have a meeting with them monthly on the topic of social media marketing for the company. Keep them apprised of new trends. Keep them motivated. Let them know if the results of their contributions are remarkable. Make sure some part of your company's executive team is vocally supportive of this group.

Blogging

Get your volunteer bloggers to agree to a once-a-month schedule. Then, just remind them, edit their posts, and you'll have the thought leadership and content marketing balls rolling. The only other support role you might play is to guide future topics, such as the following:

- Check the AdWords Keyword Tool for search traffic on various topics.
- Use web analytics to see what content gets the most traffic.
- Check any Twitter, Facebook, LinkedIn, or other sharing buttons you have set up to see what posts got the most social traction.

Let your bloggers know what topics are most in demand and which get the biggest response. Gently guide experts toward what people really want to read.

Groups

Stay in your LinkedIn Groups. If people post everyday in a Group you created, you need to be there everyday. Moderate the Groups you've created for quality; don't let promotional or low-quality content in the door. Post about your latest content. Find other good content and post it as well.

The Group is a place to deliver value. You can deliver value by letting the members know about pieces other people have written. If you're worried about traffic going to other sites, take an excerpt, put it on your blog, and link to the actual content from there with a new window. That way, they'll go to your site, and when they're done with the content, your site is still open in the browser.

Analytics, Leads, and CRM

You should be looking at your social dashboards (your web analytics, CRM, LinkedIn company page's analytics, and any others you're using). You want to see what impact your marketing has on the website and on leads. You might only look at your analytics once a week. If so, make it earlier in the week so that if you need to change something, fix tracking, or redo content, you have more time to address the issue before the week is over.

If you see zero leads, you are either a very high-priced, low-volume company, or your analytics aren't set up correctly or your marketing isn't working.

Is the sales department complaining about low-quality leads? Use your web analytics to see where most of your leads are coming from. Are the search keywords wrong? Try new ones. Are the ads not targeting the right people? Test more targeting criteria. Is the new white paper campaign not working? Figure out why and apply it to your next content marketing idea. Is the blog pulling in the wrong people? Figure out how to attract the right people.

Scheduling It!

I think I'm a pretty good example of someone who keeps a lot of plates spinning while juggling chainsaws and protecting a box of baby kittens...so to speak. Here's what I do to make sure everything gets done on time and that I have enough time for everything. It's really simple: I schedule everything in my calendar. I mean everything—not just my meetings with other people, but exactly what I'm going to do each minute of each workday.

After a while, you'll find out if you need more or less time for a particular activity. You'll also be able to avoid, wherever possible, too many meetings, because you know the value of your non-meeting time. You'll see when you're spending too much time in email or social networks and your to-do list schedule is slipping. You'll be less likely to slip on to-do items. When things come up, as they will, and your schedule slips, move the item you couldn't accomplished to a later time. For that reason, it's always best to have some wiggle room (30–60 minutes) in each day. Sometimes you'll discover extra time in a day, if a meeting runs short. (It does actually happen on occasion.)

It's tough to give specific LinkedIn marketing scheduling guidelines that will fit everyone. You might spend most of your time in LinkedIn, or you might balance duties such as AdWords, SEO, email marketing, print materials, website copy changes, Facebook, Twitter, and so on.

What Percentage of Your Time Should Each Part of LinkedIn Get?

What are the minimum and maximum times *per week* you should spend on the LinkedIn marketing tactics described in the first part of the book? As you can see, blogging and other content marketing are included in the list, but not other social networking, such as Twitter or Facebook, because some companies won't do much or anything with them. Here's the breakdown:

- **Promotion**—Posting new company content to LinkedIn Groups, the company page, your profile, and sending content to employees to see if they want to post on their LinkedIn profiles. Minimum 30 minutes, maximum 2 hours.

- **Answers**—Looking for new questions to answer in LinkedIn Answers. Minimum 15 minutes, maximum 2 hours.

- **Groups**—Moderating LinkedIn Groups and replying to posts where appropriate. Minimum 30 minutes, maximum 5 hours.

- **Other content marketing**—Facilitating the production of other new content such as white papers and infographics. Minimum 1 hour, maximum 8 hours.

- **Networking**

  - Searching LinkedIn for more journalists, media, and industry peers to network with. Minimum 30 minutes, maximum 2 hours.

  - Accepting connection requests and connecting to others. Minimum 1 hour, maximum 3 hours.

- Reviewing your LinkedIn Group members and participators for people to reach out to and network with. Minimum 15 minutes, maximum 1 hour.

- **Events**—Setting up and promoting upcoming LinkedIn Events. Minimum 1 hour, maximum 8 hours (may overlap with blogging and other social networking activities listed here).

- **Analytics**—Reviewing website analytics (what visitors from LinkedIn are or are not doing on the website), LinkedIn company page analytics, and employee LinkedIn profile visibility. Minimum 1 hour, maximum 3 hours.

- **Blog**—Moderating blog comments, writing blog posts, coordinating coworker blog posts, and editing coworker blog posts. Minimum 1 hour, maximum 10 hours.

If you do somewhere between the minimum and maximum on these tasks, LinkedIn could involve about 20 hours of marketing a week for you. The minimum is about 7 hours per week. The maximum is 44 hours per week. Figure 6.1 shows the average proportion of your time spent on these LinkedIn marketing activities.

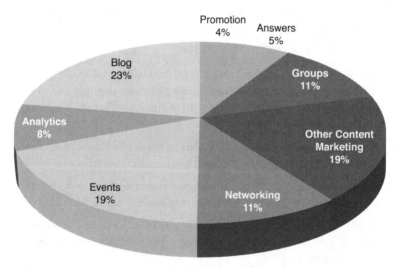

Figure 6.1   *A suggested balance of how to spend your marketing time on LinkedIn activities.*

This mix is just a suggestion based on how important I think these activities are to most companies—and how time-consuming each is. Naturally, your time spent on LinkedIn marketing is going to be decreased when you have other important marketing activities to do, and increased if you find that your LinkedIn marketing is unusually effective for your company. If you're creative and the ROI is there, you might find ways to spend more than the maximum I've suggested for some of the listed tasks. If your company doesn't do any event marketing, that time can be used elsewhere. By all means, tailor this suggestion to fit your goals and results.

Suggested Weekly LinkedIn Marketing Schedule

Table 6.1 shows a suggested schedule for when to perform the various LinkedIn marketing tasks during your week.

Table 6.1 Weekly Schedule for LinkedIn Marketing Tasks

	Monday	Tuesday	Wednesday	Thursday	Friday
Morning	Review website analytics, LinkedIn company page analytics	Upload new blog posts; moderate blog comments and Group posts	Search for new contacts to network with; reach out to Group members	Moderate blog comments and Group posts; accept LinkedIn connections; respond to InMail	Write new blog posts; edit coworker blog posts
Afternoon	Accept LinkedIn connections; respond to InMail	Promote new content by posting and tweeting	Look for and create questions in LinkedIn Answers; host a webinar	Promote new content by posting and tweeting	Work with others on new white papers, infographics, and so on

Of course, you can move the activities around to best fit your routine! My suggestions in the following list have reasons, though, as explained next:

- **Analytics**—Monday morning is a good time to find out analytics in case you need to report them during the week.

- **Uploading blog posts, tweeting, and posting links on LinkedIn**—Many people are focused internally on their companies on Monday and don't have time to see new content until Tuesday. I read years ago that the best time to get email opens (in the U.S.) was Tuesdays and Thursdays at 1:30 p.m. EST, and my experience trying various times has borne that out. This timing avoids lunchtime for the two coastal time zones, which are more populous than the middle of the country. That's also a good time to post and tell your social networks about new blog posts or other content. However, some data indicates that 4 p.m. EST is the best time to get retweets.[1] Other data indicates that more shares happen on Thursdays between 8 a.m. and 12 p.m. EST, and that page views are highest before 1 p.m. To play it safe, upload your blog posts Tuesday or Thursday morning, and tweet and post links to your social networks in the morning and again later that afternoon. And of course, watch your analytics and see what days and times works best for your customers.

- **Writing blog posts**—The work week winds down on Friday, so it can be a great low-stress day for sitting back and writing that new blog post, as well as for having a fun meeting to brainstorm the next big content marketing piece.

Summary

This chapter gives you a more practical idea of how to get all these great LinkedIn marketing ideas done. Of course, it's impossible to anticipate every marketer's individual situation, responsibilities, and priorities, so these are just suggestions. I highly recommend you do what you can to create and nurture your volunteer brand army because that will improve your results and lighten your load.

Endnotes

1. http://www.problogger.net/archives/2010/12/06/whens-the-best-time-to-publish-blog-posts/

7

Best Practices: Online Advertising and LinkedIn Advertising

Advertising has long been an essential communication tool for business. It's a way to raise awareness for your brand or get consumers to take action. Businesses pay those who have audiences (publishers, networks, TV stations, radio channels, and websites) for the privilege of getting their message out.

Online advertising is a huge and important part of the marketing world. Total money spent on Internet ads is expected to surpass print advertising for the first time ever in 2012. Internet advertising is also expected to be about half that of television advertising in 2012, and may equal TV advertising by 2016.[1]

Businesses advertise because it's effective for a number of goals, including profitable sales. Advertising gets you new customers and helps you fight off the competition. In some ways, online advertising is more effective than offline advertising. Let me explain why that's the case by telling you a bit of my story.

My personal web marketing journey did not begin with advertising, but with a content-oriented site I created and for which I wrote hundreds of articles. I saw the power of optimizing websites to create profits and revenue as early as 1999. Optimizing my website for search engine rankings made my previously unknown alternative medicine website one of the 10,000 most popular sites in the world by 2004.

I learned how to do Google advertising in 2004. I was able to increase the advertising profitability of my first client, an alternative medicine e-commerce store, by 41% within a month. Another early success was helping a woman market her custom-made Polish pottery. She sold each piece for about $69. I optimized her Google AdWords account and she was able to get each sale for just $3. That's a 2,200% ROI, which is exceptional. Many businesss owners are happy to just get a 400%–500% ROI with advertising. Years later, employees I trained at the agency Fuel Interactive achieved between 300% and 1,100% ROI from Google AdWords for their clients.

Because my start in advertising was highly trackable and profitable, I was a staunch believer in that as the standard—and a skeptic about branding and high-budget TV ads whose results couldn't be tracked. But Internet advertising initially resembled TV and radio advertising, and social media advertising has similarities, too. For some context, let's flash back to 1994, the beginning of Internet advertising, and see how the Internet advertising industry matured. Then we'll fast-forward to what LinkedIn ads mean for businesses in 2012 and 2013.

Internet ads debuted in 1994 on Time Warner's Pathfinder portal[2] and *HotWired*,[3] the first ever commercial web magazine. These ads were display ads (image-based ads), and they continued to run over the years on sites such as TechWeb, WebConnect, ESPN, and CBS.[4] DoubleClick, in 1995, was the first ad network to use cookies (unique code placed on the web visitor's computer) to track user behavior online. Cookies gave them the power to serve each user more customized ads, thus moving toward giving each web user a more personal and relevant experience. That more relevant experience made website users happier (or less annoyed by irrelevant ads), and so the ads were clicked on more often, which in turn increased the value of Internet ads to advertisers.

Early ads were measured only by impressions—that is, how many times the pages with those ads on them were loaded by users.[5] The Interactive Advertising Bureau standardized the display ad sizes (see Figure 7.1), making it easier for media buyers at large companies to get designers to create ads that could be used on many sites.

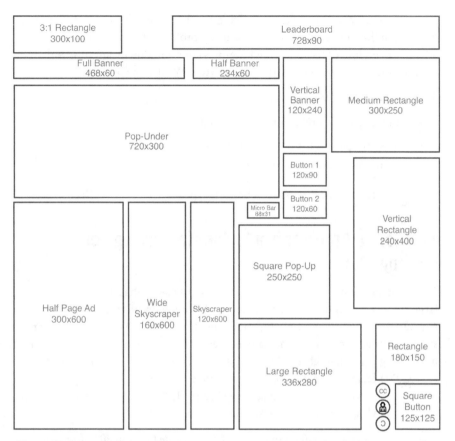

Figure 7.1   *Some standard display ad sizes.*

Websites charged for ads based on the number of times the ads were shown. The measurement was CPM (cost per thousand views—the M is Latin). Advertisers were used to thinking simply in terms of how much exposure they received— how many newspaper subscribers, how many radio listeners, and how many TV viewers—and historically these numbers have all been estimated, not exactly quantified. Many businesses traditionally set a fixed budget for ad spend and didn't see advertising profitability as essential to their marketing activities. Although Claude C. Hopkins attempted to measure that as far back as the 1910s,[6] it was uncommon.

Discussion about measuring the profitability of each ad began in 1994. Some companies used web analytics to measure ROI, but they were the exception. Google Ads and its conversion-tracking technology made tracking Internet advertising ROI much easier. Companies began to expect the ability to measure their online advertising profitability around 2005.

You can see how recent this is, and what a big shift it represents. That's important because, in their excitement about measuring profitability, some marketers and advertisers no longer see any value in impressions and don't want to spend money on anything they can't track with web analytics. We'll come back to that.

There several goals for advertising:

- Branding, exposure, and traffic-focused ads
- Direct-marketing profitability-focused ads
- A combination of the two

The following sections discuss each of these types.

Advertising Approach #1: Media Buying for Branding Purposes

There's an entire industry of "media planners" whose job has been to manage a large corporate advertising spend, placing ads for big brands across the Web. They may also be responsible for buying radio and TV ad spots. They sometimes are simply putting into action a media plan created by someone else. Their focus is on negotiating prices and generating a huge number of impressions. Their metrics (like CPM) focus on the number of people they can reach. They ask questions like: "What is the cost for a thousand ad views?" and "Is the placement going to reach the company's general target market?"

Figure 7.2 shows a current comparison of the average CPM in 2012 for various advertising locations.

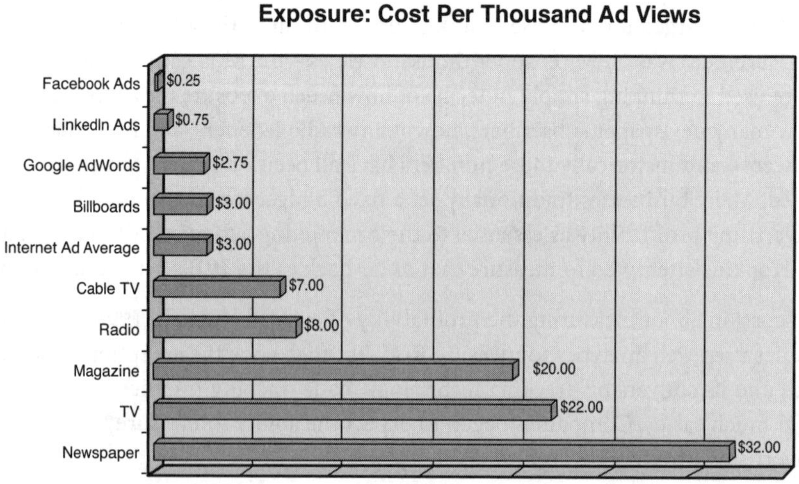

Exposure: Cost Per Thousand Ad Views

Facebook Ads	$0.25
LinkedIn Ads	$0.75
Google AdWords	$2.75
Billboards	$3.00
Internet Ad Average	$3.00
Cable TV	$7.00
Radio	$8.00
Magazine	$20.00
TV	$22.00
Newspaper	$32.00

Figure 7.2 *For various advertising channels, the cost per thousand ad views.*

As you can see, the top three most affordable ways to get exposure for your brand are all types of online advertising. Offline advertising is about ten times more expensive. What's even more amazing is which online ads are the most affordable, because not all Internet advertising makes it easy to target your ads to your specific customers. The regular "media buy" places you on well-known sites such as Yahoo! and Forbes. You have a very general sense of the typical reader of this site, but all kinds of people, in reality, read these sites. Therefore, maybe only 25%–50% of your ads are shown to the people you want to see them. The top three most affordable advertising options in this chart all allow you to target your ads more specifically than this.

It's amazing to me that the most affordable online ads are also the most efficient. Usually, things with higher value are more expensive. When they're not, there's an opportunity. This also means the websites that sell to media buyers are overvaluing their inventory. Media buyers won't benefit from the cheaper CPMs until they learn the optimization and marketing skills that Facebook, LinkedIn, and Google ads all require. Another obstacle keeping media buyers from these cheaper CPMs is that it's difficult to scale them to the massive degree of exposure they need without yet another time investment, training, and a learning curve.

LinkedIn advertising can bring in highly qualified leads for your sales force to work with. But it also, dollar for dollar, generates a higher amount of exposure to B2B decision makers than AdWords can.

Advertising Approach #2: Direct Marketing and Profitability

These days, the many marketers say, "Why would I pay for just exposure? I need to know—and my CFO needs to know—whether there's ROI there." And they're right. Why shouldn't all advertising be profitable, if we know that some of it can be? Why can't we at least track what's going on? It's great that we've been able to change the advertising culture into one that has a focus on tracking and profitability. Advertising, wherever possible, should be held accountable for results. Advertising personnel now ask questions like the following:

- Is this bringing in sales and leads?
- Is the cost per sale or lead low enough?
- Are these leads high quality enough that the sales department can turn them into revenue?

These are responsible questions that the executive team wants answered and that we can usually discover through the conversion tracking of the advertising method (AdWords conversion tracking), with our own website analytics (Google Analytics,

Omniture, and the like), or with a third-party setup (SalesForce plug-ins, Prosper 202, and so on).

Advertising Approach #3: A Combination of the First Two Approaches

Back in 2005, I was disturbed that so few people were counting the costs and looking at the profitability of their advertising. Now, we've come a long way toward expecting profitability. But I believe people have gone too far; they no longer value exposure (branding) at all, and that's not right either.

In fact, I don't even think many decision makers realize they're devaluing their branding. If you ask them if they value branding and exposure, they'll say yes. But if you show them a report where some of their advertising is profitable (but low in volume), and some gets them zero revenue (although it provides major exposure), many will be so distracted by the negative profitability of the second set, they'll tell you to stop doing those ads. People have gotten so hooked on having gobs of data from their analytics for every tiny action that when they don't see a direct correlation to profit, they get scared.

My wife and I, who have medical backgrounds, saw a similar thing in caring for patients: Sometimes people wouldn't believe an accurate diagnosis made by a health professional (with decades of experience) on the basis of physical examination and inquiry, but when we would show them one piece of paper with a score from a laboratory on it, they had no doubts as to its accuracy. In reality, some health conditions have no agreed-upon lab measurement, and lab results are not accurate 100% of the time. But our culture trusts science and numbers in the face of uncertainty.

In business, branding is important. It's valuable for people to know your company exists. Customers can't choose you, or even search for you or your company's offerings if they aren't aware of them. Sometimes advertising raises awareness and gets a lead or sale all in one shot; and those ads look great on a report! But sometimes your company slowly filters into a customer's consciousness through multiple advertising exposures. "Oh, I think I've heard of them before!" they'll say. They aren't aware they saw or glanced over that ad five times before they clicked it. And over time, if your business's competitors are raising more awareness than yours is, the growth of yours may level off.

In my opinion, advertising needs to both raise awareness (brand your company) *and* get bottom-line results. I put my money where my mouth is. For my own consulting and speaking business, I run ads that are meant to get me business, but I also run ads that increase awareness of me and my company. I spend money on branding because I believe in the value of top-of-mind awareness.

And here's another counterintuitive insight from a guy (me) with a decade in this profession: If you spend enough time with web analytics, you become disillusioned about their accuracy. Web analytics promise you the answers to all your questions, but sometimes you come away from your analytics program with *more* questions. The difficulty of tracking a real customer through multiple interactions with ads, marketing efforts on many social platforms, and sales exposures has convinced me that analytics cannot see it all; it's not omniscient. It can't measure everything. Relying only on what you can measure is dangerous, unless you can measure everything. We can't, so we have to have a healthy respect for the value of those things that are hard to measure.

Another way to see the value of branding is to start paying attention to how you learn about products, and watch your own decision-making process. It takes a while to get in the habit of being conscious of this. But it's worth it. I guarantee you'll begin to see situations later on where branding has led you to give a company money.

The power of LinkedIn ads (much like Facebook ads) is that a lower overall click-through rate means that for every click you pay for, you get dramatically more awareness than you would from Google AdWords. This is one reason I recommend a multichannel advertising approach for B2B. Some ads generate more leads per click, and others generate more awareness. Both are necessary to your success.

When it comes to LinkedIn, you want to set up your web analytics and CRM systems to make your advertising as accountable and profitable as possible—but always remember the value of the impressions, too. Even if, no matter what I did with them, LinkedIn ads never brought me a single lead or sale, I would still spend the money to make key business people aware of my company.

IMPROVED LINKEDIN TARGETING

LinkedIn's advertising initially was not as powerful because it gave you fewer targeting criteria. In February 2011, LinkedIn rolled out the ability to target people by their company names, job titles, and Group membership. If you formed your opinions of LinkedIn ads before that improvement, you might not realize how powerful they actually are.

Social Media Advertising

Advertising via social media is just one piece of the Internet advertising pie. Total social ad network revenues in 2011 were about $5.5 billion out of $32 billion spent on all Internet advertising. LinkedIn's piece of the social ad pie was just $140 million, but this is forecasted to double by 2013.[7]

A May 2011 survey of agencies and marketers found that 41% had already deployed LinkedIn ad campaigns, and 21% planned to do so in the next 12 months. That demonstrates that it's on people's to-do lists, but keep in mind that in the same survey, 93% had already tried Facebook ads and 78% had advertised on Twitter.

LinkedIn advertising is not as popular as other social advertising networks, but as we've examined in other parts of this book, LinkedIn is a professional network. It's niche and focused. It also provides some very special advantages and options you can't get with Facebook or Twitter advertising. And to be fair, one reason LinkedIn's ad revenues are smaller is that many LinkedIn ad campaigns target a smaller group of people, so they get fewer clicks. There's simply not as much click traffic going through LinkedIn ads as there is in Google or Facebook ads, because LinkedIn advertisers are laser-targeting their ads.

Online Advertising Best Practices

Before you start doing LinkedIn advertising, you want to understand what makes an online ad effective. My experience advertising on Google, Yahoo!, Microsoft (Bing), Facebook, and LinkedIn has shown me some commonalities as to what makes ads succeed or fail. The rest of this chapter looks at those online advertising best practices, and later chapters look more specifically at LinkedIn advertising.

I love the NBA, and one thing I've noticed during my excessive spectatorship is that there are a bunch of good players who survive on talent alone, but the *great* players (the hall of famers, and even those who aren't so athletically gifted but manage to carve out long and rewarding careers as role players) all spend a lot of time on "the fundamentals." They look at the skills and moves of other great players who've come before them, learn the basics of the game, and then practice them relentlessly until they're second nature. A player can learn defensive habits that give his team a chance to win. A prodigious scorer might only need to learn one more move to become "unguardable," which opens up opportunities for other players because the other team may have to use two players to defend against him. This explains why Kobe Bryant, at age 31, already an NBA champion, would go learn footwork and moves from Hall of Famer Hakeem Olajuwan.[8] There are best practices, proven over the years, that will help any of us at any level.

In online advertising, as in basketball, certain habits and tactics have helped other advertisers be effective in the past. Your willingness to learn and follow these will increase your results.

Testing

I don't think I can say it enough: If you don't view advertising as a laboratory for testing ideas and finding out what works, you will likely be disappointed in your results. Sometimes you get lucky; your very first advertising campaign may get great results. But if it doesn't, then what? Test!

Successful online advertisers are always trying to think of new ad copy, headlines, and images. And in social media advertising, targeting requires almost as much testing as these creative elements do.

People unfamiliar with Internet advertising often think they just need one big idea, and they're done. In fact, even when we know clearly which consumers we want seeing our ads and how best to target them in the advertising interface, we still don't know what message will impact them the most. Which words, or which offer, or discount, or graphic will get the biggest response? Which one will get them to click and which will get them to buy, or put their name into a lead form? And, yes, there are some ads that get lots of clicks but no leads or sales.

Your first idea isn't always your best. Start thinking of your ideas as theories. If you think back to your first science class when you learned about the scientific method, you probably remember the word *hypothesis*. A hypothesis is a theory. It's what you suspect. I don't care how much natural confidence you have, what your job title is, how many years you've been doing it, or whether you're wearing Sure deodorant. Your theory may not be true. You have to test it to find out.

If you doubt me, go to the website WhichTestWon.com. They have more than 150 case studies of testing two somewhat different web pages against each other to see which one got more responses from consumers. I guarantee you will get more than half of them wrong when you try to guess which page won.

And we experienced advertisers don't develop any prophetic capabilities after ten years. We don't grow a sixth-sense magical insight about how people will respond. There's no question we may develop some ego about our wisdom, but that's even more reason to keep testing our ideas.

The upshot is that when you create an ad campaign, you need to show multiple images, headlines, and advertising copy to the same audience and then let the numbers tell you which one grabbed their attention and made them click.

And the testing doesn't end there; there is always more than one way to target your audience. On Google, there are multiple keywords. On Facebook, there's demographic targeting, interest targeting, topic targeting, and more. On LinkedIn, we can target job title, groups, seniority, and so on. We can slice the segments who will see an ad campaign by a combination of criteria; for example, you could target manager-level event planners (seniority plus job title), or event planners in the

Meeting Talk LinkedIn group (job title plus group). Which one gets us the more responsive and qualified ad viewers? We have to test these targeting segments. And if we test all those versions of our ads against those targets, that's a lot more tests, isn't it? Yep, testing is a fact of life if you want to be successful at online advertising.

But the good news is that sometimes you find amazing ads, and you get excited about them, and they get you better results than you expected. As long as you're disciplined with testing and creative about what you test, you'll do well.

Copywriting

There is much history that goes into our current Internet marketing practices. And some of what people have learned before has not been applied to new technologies like LinkedIn ads. These old ideas can be great things to test anew, and it's never a bad thing to have more ideas to test. One area of marketing wisdom is copywriting.

If you go to Amazon and search for "copywriting," you'll find a lot of books on the subject. This book is *copy*, as in written material. *Copywriting* is actually a technical word in marketing for writing persuasively. It's a huge field that people have been working in and writing about for decades, although few people are aware of that. Amazon says there are 854 books relevant to copywriting. I looked through the first four pages, and yes, there are at least 100 books in which you can read about how to write more effective, persuasive copy. Once you accept that some words are more convincing than others, you'll want to learn what those words or phrases are. "I want that magical power of the pen to make everyone do what I want!" If copywriting were easy, there wouldn't be hundreds of books about it.

The bottom line is, you need to know what wording gets the best results. Should you say "Click here to get the white paper" or "Click now to download this white paper"? What if one of these two very similar phrases yielded 20% more leads? I would bet you (based on that experience I'm so proud of) there's at least a 10% difference.

I remember being astounded in 2004 by how two AdWords ads, different only in that I changed the word "purchase" to "buy," differed in ROI by 18%. In a much more recent test promoting specific musicians on Facebook ads, I found that some musicians did better when I simply used their name as the headline, and other musicians got better results when the headline was "Like (so and so)?"

You must test your copywriting ideas. I've read at least ten of those aforementioned copywriting books. But don't get too excited about them. Many are from other eras. They use phrases from the 1930s or even the 1980s that now sound cliché. Consumers may not respond to them. You may be able to use some of these books' formulas and ideas, but you'll have to continue to use the testing framework to see which words, phrases, and offers your consumers respond best to today.

What's more, the consumer you're targeting may be more or less formal, or there may be cultural references you want to integrate. You should combine your knowledge of the consumer with your knowledge of what your company offers in your writing. And by testing and watching what people respond to more or respond to less, you learn more about those consumers' psychology.

You may wonder why I'm so apt to give pep talks about testing. The primary reason is that, even though I have seen its value over and over again, I still have to push myself to do it. The main enemy of diligence in advertising testing is laziness. It might only take you a few more minutes to create a couple more versions of an ad that will increase your results dramatically. The ROI on your time is worth it— but it's so easy to cut corners and just hope for the best. Don't do that.

Message/Target Fit

In the real world, we always vary what we say depending on who we're talking to. You might explain LinkedIn differently to your mother than to your work colleague. When you talk to your boss, you might leave certain information out or add persuasive elements to get your way. With some people, we're more matter of fact. You've probably spent years learning the best way to speak to your spouse. The most influential people are able to figure out what each person likes, dislikes, fears, and loves, whether they're more intuitive or logical, more rational or feeling, and they vary their approach so that they're better understood and more persuasive.

But for some reason, when people create ads, they forget all about this. They create one ad for every audience they talk to. In short, we get lazy. We don't really try to imagine who these invisible people we're targeting are. What do they care about? What do they need? What are they worried about?

If your business only targets one kind of person, you have it easier. But if you target people who have multiple job titles, wouldn't it be more effective to target them separately and mention their job title in the ad? Of course it would! Don't be lazy.

Are you also targeting people who influence decision makers? Who are those people, and what do they care about most? Suppose you're selling ultrasound machines to hospitals. You might target the purchaser with an ad about its price and durability (they're concerned with budget). You target the physicians with an ad about how it's the state of the art and helps them get the diagnosis right (they want to do a good job, and their ego wants to know they have the best). You target nurses with an ad about how quick and easy it is use (they have so much to do, they want to know that using this machine won't hold them up).

Branding

Not all ads get clicks. Some of them aren't attention-grabbing enough, or you haven't hit on the message that resonates with your target yet.

But any ad can increase awareness of your company among your target market. If your company's logo or name is in the ad, you've incrementally made more people more aware. Numerous advertising and psychology studies have demonstrated the importance of people being aware of brands, and how it increases sales and people's affinity with the company. This is why Coca-Cola spends gazillions on animated polar bear ads. It's why real estate agents put their faces on bus stop benches. It's why politicians need insane amounts of cash to get elected. TV advertising is expensive! Familiarity helps you succeed.

A study by Buddy Media, a company that provides social media tools to eight of the world's top ten brands, found that the first place customers discovered a new brand was on Facebook. But Facebook rarely got any of the credit for sales or leads that resulted from that first impression.[9] Other studies where social media, Google ads, and natural Google search optimization were combined found that because social media familiarizes consumers with a brand, there were more Google searches for the brand and a higher click-through rates on the brand's Google ads.[10]

When you create each ad, think about the choice between branding or getting traffic, sales, or leads. You may be able to achieve both, or you might be focused on just one of them.

Branded logo ads, over time, create valuable familiarity, but ads designed to get people to take action are designed differently. Although the most interesting thing to other people is their own name, the least interesting is yours (unless you're famous)—and this applies to your company name and brand as well. If you lead with a logo (which about identity, as is your name), you may not get much action. Logos aren't great for action-oriented ads.

You get action by assuring people that you can fulfill their needs and wants. Talk about the benefits they'll experience. Tell them you want them to click or whatever other action you want them to take.

Metrics: Profits, Costs, Conversion Rate and Cost per Customer

The success of every advertising campaign will be evaluated with a metric that was selected for its ability to measure the campaign goal. Some ads focus on getting leads for salespeople. Some focus on getting sales. Some merely increase awareness of your company. The way each is measured and judged differs.

For example, you may be tasked with increasing profits (ROI), but not necessarily number of sales. Or it might be a combination. You might be given a specific cost per customer you can spend to acquire a customer or a specific cost per lead you generate.

If you want to get better results and score points with your higher ups, organize all your campaigns ahead of time in terms of their goal and key metric. Try to set a benchmark for the cost per lead or cost per click you anticipate. You may not be able to do this accurately in the beginning, but the more advertising you do within your niche, the better you can forecast.

Benchmarks

As we've already discussed, your approach can affect your metrics. If you're going for a lot of leads, you might be looking for the highest possible numbers in impressions, clicks, click-through rate (CTR), and conversion rate. One company I spoke to gets a 0.09% click-through rate on their ads, an astoundingly high number, but they are taking the high-volume approach and using marketing automation to nurture leads to a certain quality level before they ever reach the salespeople.

Your click-through rate probably won't be this high. I've been successful with CTRs as low as 0.03%. But if your CTR is lower than 0.025%, you may have a problem with your targeting or the message you're using. Still, there's no single correct CTR figure. If you want to target a really large number of people, your CTR is likely to be lower than if you target a small group of people who respond more to your super-customized ad.

The right benchmarks are different for every company. You may find you succeed in getting high-quality leads with low CTR and conversion rates. You might target an incredibly small niche and have a really long sales cycle, in which case your lead numbers will be small and your sales infrequent. If your average contract is worth $500,000, and it only takes you $1,000 of clicks to get one of these sales, is that a failure? Certainly not. And almost any results are better than not using LinkedIn advertising at all, because you might never get your company's name in front of some of these people with any other online ad network.

Again, approach this as a series of experiments. Over time, you will develop realistic averages for your metrics. When your company needs different results, you can take the actions you need to change the metrics. Is your sales force starving for leads? Increase the degree of incentivization by offering more for free. For example, offer more free and valuable information or more consultation, and you increase your click-through rate and conversion rate. If you need higher quality leads, reduce the incentives and raise the bar by including an off-putting minimum price in your ad copy.

Tracking

Another best practice in online advertising is tracking the behavior of ad viewers and potential customers on your website. LinkedIn offers data about people seeing and clicking your LinkedIn ads. If you use the lead collection feature of LinkedIn ads, you'll get that information too. But if you want to track what LinkedIn ad clickers do on your site and at what rate they fill out forms, you'll need to get that data from your website analytics. To do that, you can add tags and parameters to your URLs. We go into this more in Chapter 10.

Comparing Google, Facebook, and LinkedIn Ads

Google, Facebook, and LinkedIn are the three major sources of self-serve advertising traffic (they are open to everyone and don't require a company rep to place). They all have strengths and weaknesses, different targeting features, and different ad viewer behaviors, so the way you approach each is different. Expectations of results for each network should also be different.

Table 7.1 highlights the biggest differences. Note that these ad networks don't release this information. I was fortunate to be able to expand beyond data for my own clients to a huge amount of data on AdWords from Brad Geddes (author of two books on AdWords) and on Facebook from Dennis Yu of BlitzLocal. Some of it is estimated, or a range is given. The point here is simply to give you a broad comparison of these three ad networks. It's not perfect, but I believe it's more valuable than giving you no comparison at all.

Table 7.1   Thumbnail Sketch of the Differences in Major Online Advertising Networks

Ad Network	Google AdWords Search Network	Facebook Ads	LinkedIn Ads
Size of Audience	174 million U.S.	155 million U.S.	60 million U.S.
B2B or B2C	Either	Mostly B2C	Mostly B2B
Targeting Options	Mainly search keywords	Mainly interests, categories, and demographics	Mainly job title, industry, LinkedIn Groups
Click-Through Rate	1.73 – 3.31%	0.03 – 0.06%	0.05%
CPM	$5.67 – $20.42	$0.28	$0.75
CPC	$0.51 – $2.37	$0.40 – $0.93	$1.50 – $3.00
Impressions Per Click	100	2,000	2,000

Note that I highlight the differences in Table 7.1. There are certainly more ways to target people with LinkedIn and Facebook ads, but I've pointed out the most common and unique.

Targeting

How do you target the people you want to reach with online ads?

- Google AdWords has a lot of targeting options, but most of them target people who are searching for specific keywords. Google is about *what* people are searching for. These ads capitalize on fulfilling the demand expressed in people's searches.

- LinkedIn and Facebook ads give you a lot of options for slicing and dicing the people you want to target. LinkedIn and Facebook ads are about *who* you want to reach. You have to think about *who* you're targeting, and how you might identify those people with the targeting options you have available.

Social media advertising is challenging for many people. Those already experienced with Google ads have trouble getting out of the keyword mindset. The biggest rewards in Facebook advertising go to those who take the time to better understand their prospective buyer and test lots of precise interests to find the best way to reach them. You need to consider what magazines they read, TV shows they watch, and other things they've put into their Facebook profiles. You might look through your Facebook fans' profiles to see what kinds of things they're interested in, or use tools such as Quantcast and Infinigraph, which use data to discover the other interests of fans of your brand.

Targeting with LinkedIn advertising is a little more direct than Facebook. People aren't putting all those leisure and hobby items into their LinkedIn profiles because they're keeping it professional. On LinkedIn, your ad targeting options (see Figure 7.3) include the following:

- Continents, countries, states, and cities
- Company names and categories (by industry and company size)
- Specific job titles and categories of jobs (job function and seniority)
- LinkedIn Groups
- Gender
- Age

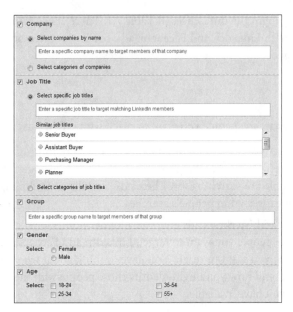

Figure 7.3   *Some of the ad targeting options for LinkedIn ads.*

These options can be combined in gazillions of ways, so you can target the exact people you want to reach. For example, to reach executive decision makers with your LinkedIn ads, you can target specific job titles such as CEO, President, Founder, EVP, and COO, and you can also test seniority options such as CXO, Director, Partner, and Owner. If you're a vendor, try specific job titles such as purchasing manager or project buyer. We'll go into even more detail on strategic ways to target people with ads in Chapter 10.

Cost

As you can see in Table 7.1 (shown earlier in this chapter), LinkedIn clicks are not the cheapest on a per-click basis. But every click is not equally valuable. If you want to target specific roles in a company, using LinkedIn is the best way to do it. That way, you have a better idea whether your advertising clicks are reaching the people you want to reach. The only thing that can approach this for B2B marketing is a few, very specific Google AdWords keywords. If you sell vinyl windows to contractors, for instance, advertising for the Google keywords "buy wholesale vinyl windows" is your sweet spot. But there are only so many "we're ready to buy" searches out there, and if you want to reach more of your future customers, you'll need more than those few Google ad keywords. The higher cost of LinkedIn ad clicks may be worth it—evaluate this via your cost per lead and cost per customer.

Conversion Rate

Conversion rate is the percentage of those who not only click yours ads but also take the action you want them to. If your ultimate goal is to generate business leads, then conversion rate is the percentage of people who click and then fill out a lead form.

A higher conversion rate and more leads are not always good, because you want *qualified* leads. You can create crazy incentives, discounts, and freebies ("get a free consult!") to get a higher quantity of leads, but these might lower your lead quality. Some companies use marketing automation software such as Eloqua to automatically nurture their leads through email, so they don't worry about low lead quality. They find that the lead nurturing system gets them enough sales to justify the large number of low-quality leads.

But if you have a smaller sales force and no marketing automation, you probably want to tone down the crazy incentives. You'll get fewer leads, but they'll be higher quality, and your sales force will close a higher percentage of them.

Are LinkedIn clicks more qualified than AdWords or Facebook ad clicks? Some businesses have found that LinkedIn provides a higher conversion rate and more qualified leads than AdWords does.[11] If you set up a CRM to track where people came from and whether these leads turned into sales, you can find out. The lead quality from each advertising network will vary with how easy it is to target your specific prospects on each advertising platform, and how thorough a job you do. We'll discuss the how-to of these in Chapters 8, 12, 13, and 14.

Ad Services Through LinkedIn Reps

Most of the advertising I discuss in this book is LinkedIn's self-service advertising platform. But LinkedIn also offers premium advertising services through their representatives, if you have a larger budget. If your advertising budget is less than $25,000 per month, for a minimum of three months, stick with the self-serve option. If you can afford them, the premium ads have significant advantages (see Figure 7.4). The display ads are bigger, as shown in Figure 7.5, so they'll get noticed and clicked more frequently, and you can add in polls and other content. You'll have a rep running the ads, doing the targeting for you, and reporting to you. Your time investment is less than it takes to create and optimize the self-serve ads.

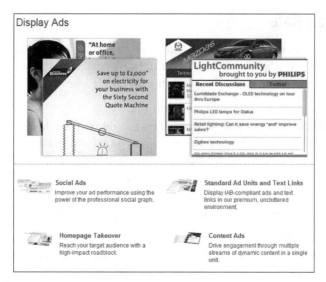

Figure 7.4   *Highlights of what's available for premium advertisers on LinkedIn.*

Figure 7.5   *An example of the larger display ad space available to premium LinkedIn advertisers.*

Summary

This chapter has summarized some of the history of advertising, both online and offline, and outlined wisdom that continues to be important. It also compared, in a broad way, how search and social advertising differ. Finally, it outlined general ways to apply these best practices to LinkedIn advertising. Chapter 8 discusses how inbound marketing strategies apply to LinkedIn advertising, and Chapters 9 and 10 look at both basic and advanced LinkedIn ad creation.

Endnotes

1. http://www.emarketer.com/PressRelease.aspx?R=1008788

2. "Time Warner to Shutter Pathfinder," CNET. April 26, 1999. http://news.cnet.com/2100-1023-224939.html

3. Stuart Elliot, "Banner Ads on Internet Attract Users," *The New York Times*, Dec 2, 1996. http://www.nytimes.com/1996/12/03/business/banner-ads-on-internet-attract-users.html

4. http://www.worldata.com/wdnet7/articles/the_history_of_Internet_Advertising.htm

5. Rex Briggs and Nigel Hollis, "Advertising on the Web: Is There Response Before Clickthrough?" *Journal of Advertising Research*, March-April 1997, pp. 33-45

6. Claude C. Hopkins, "Scientific Advertising," 1923. http://www.scientificadvertising.com/ScientificAdvertising.pdf

7. http://www.theconversationmanager.com/2011/10/07/social-network-ad-revenues-reach-10-billion-worldwide-2013/

8. "Kobe Gets Lessons From Hakeem Olajuwon," YouTube, October 9, 2009. http://www.youtube.com/watch?v=vww3lmLQQGM

9. Story told anecdotally at AllFacebook conference by Michael Jaindl of Buddy Media (July 2011)

10. http://www.comscore.com/Press_Events/Press_Releases/2009/10/GroupM_Search_and_comScore_Release_Study_on_the_Interplay_Between_Search_Marketing_and_Social_Media

11. http://www.seerinteractive.com/blog/using-linkedin-for-your-b2b-strategy

8

Win First with Strategy: Inbound Advertising and Marketing with LinkedIn

This book is separated into sections focused on specific roles and activities: advertising, marketing, and sales. For simplicity's sake, in this book, marketing includes all marketing functions except advertising. As you can see from reading the marketing chapters, on LinkedIn, marketing involves handling company pages, posting, improving profiles, coordinating created Groups, and creating and distributing content. Because digital advertising requires specific skills—and often that role is filled by someone with specific training while other marketing functions are performed by other people—I like to distinguish between advertising and marketing. You will certainly run across people in social media who consider what they do to be PR and marketing, but don't like to use advertising at all.

This chapter is part of the advertising section of the book, but it covers the overall inbound marketing strategy (inbound marketing is the entire flow of customers from their first awareness of the brand to becoming a qualified lead). We can't talk about advertising without placing it in that context.

Inbound marketing includes activities marketers do that impact the leads the sales department works with. People performing each role should read the entire book if time permits because the company can get better results if teams members understand how what everyone else is doing. Departmental siloes are one of the biggest challenges companies face: "I understand my role, but I don't really know or care what they do in that other department." The silo effect not only leads to fights over status and budget, but also means no one has the insights to help other departments getting better results for the entire company.

The point of this chapter for advertisers is that LinkedIn ads detached from your overall marketing and sales strategy are no more effective than an arm detached from your body. In fact, only a zombie arm can survive being detached, and chances are you aren't a zombie.[1] If your advertising efforts don't help marketing get attention where they need it (tell the right people about the new content marketing piece or get the right people to the LinkedIn company page) or bring in leads that sales can use, your advertising budget will probably be cut. In addition, because you need to be able to explain the value of your advertising efforts to your CEO and CFO, we also discuss goals and metrics in this chapter.

A survey of the industry suggests that LinkedIn advertising is relatively immature. It's used by fewer companies than Facebook ads, which are used less than AdWords ads. LinkedIn advertising revenues worldwide were only $154 million in 2011, out of the $32 *billion* online advertising industry.[2] Some advertisers have gotten results, some have gotten no results, and some have gotten stellar results.

How Does Inbound Marketing Dovetail with Advertising?

Inbound marketing is about attracting leads and buyers. It's a more passive approach than traditional interruptive advertising, telemarketing, or door-to-door sales. It centers around organic referral sources such as natural (unpaid) search, social media, and content marketing. But online advertising can also be the first point of awareness for prospects that might become leads into the sales funnel. Advertising that sits off to the side of your browsing experience (as LinkedIn advertising does) is certainly more passive than pop-up ads that cover your entire screen. This book primarily talks about this passive, more harmonious type of advertising.

The Sales Funnel: Advertising, Marketing, and Sales

How do advertising, marketing, and sales role players fit together? What do they have in common? In what order do prospects experience your LinkedIn advertising, Linked Group marketing, and contact from salespeople?

No doubt, content marketing materials can certainly be the first way prospective customers hear about your company, perhaps through SEO or nonpaid social media sharing. But usually when advertising is used, it's to reach new people, and sometimes it's used to project that content marketing material further out. It's the tip of the spear into the realm of those who aren't aware of you. For that reason, I put it first in the funnel. As shown in the Figure 8.1, here are some of the functions of each:

- **Advertising** can shape the consumer's perception of your brand. LinkedIn ads can grab attention for your brand or marketing efforts. They can even arouse interest when you use benefit-laden or goal-related messages. And they can drive people directly to specific content-marketing pieces.

- **Marketing** also affects the consumer's perception of the brand, educates and engages prospects, and increases their desire for your solution. You can use LinkedIn company pages, LinkedIn profiles, and content marketing to differentiate your company from your competitors.

- **Sales** can take qualified leads, create a human relationship, answer questions stimulated or unanswered by content marketing in LinkedIn Groups and elsewhere, and lead them to make that final buying decision. Sometimes a salesperson remains in touch with existing customers, or they may smoothly pass people off to an account manager. This sales communication can happen via many channels including LinkedIn's InMail, LinkedIn Groups, email, and phone.

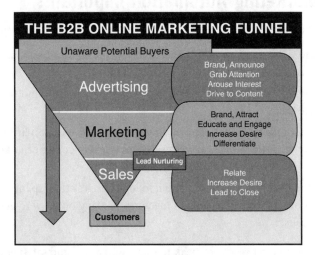

Figure 8.1   *A simplified view of how advertising, marketing, and sales fit into the B2B marketing sales funnel.*

Is there a difference between *lead generation*, *demand generation*, and *lead management*?

- Lead generation comes from a variety of tactics, including LinkedIn ads, marketing pieces, or salespeople networking with LinkedIn.

- Demand generation is the strategy by which you increase potential buyers' desire for your solution at every stage or level of the sales process—that includes LinkedIn advertising, marketing in LinkedIn Groups, as well as content marketing on LinkedIn, on other social channels, and with your blog.

- Lead management supports your demand generation strategy. Successful lead management keeps leads from leaking out of the funnel, ensuring everyone is addressed by marketing or makes it to sales. Managing leads can begin by exchanging LinkedIn messages with prospects or interacting in LinkedIn Groups, then move to the CRM and marketing automation software once you have their email address. Marketing automation uses lead-nurturing technology that enables demand generation and lead generation. It helps get the right content to people at the right stage of their buying process.[3] Just as a nurturer ensures that children get the right things for the right stage of their development, as we try to grow initial interest into a sale, we set up a system to send people the right information at the right time, moving them toward the next step.

Why Is Marketing Automation Important?

Marketing automation is a type of online software that helps you do the following:

- Get more out of all your LinkedIn leads—you can increase your overall response rates.

- Keep and nurture all leads—you've already spent money and time to acquire them.

- Save on LinkedIn advertising and marketing costs—there's little extra labor to set it up and get more results out of every content marketing piece.

- Save time—less labor from manual follow-ups, less time spent creating new content pieces, less time in meetings figuring out how to get bigger results.

Most customers aren't ready to speak to sales right away, and salespeople don't want to waste time with unqualified prospects. They're actually looking at the wrong product? Don't waste the salesperson's time. They're not ready? Let them think and experience lead nurturing emails until they are ready. They don't have the budget? There's no point in talking to them. Why should they talk to Sales? Use a process to properly qualify leads before they're sent to Sales.

A lead is not qualified until sales says they are, so sales helps you set the criteria for qualification, and you set up your marketing automation to score leads so that you know at what score they're qualified. You build into your marketing automation content that either persuades people or signals that they are now qualified.

Is marketing automation advertising, marketing, or sales? Marketing automation plays a part in all of these. Even if you already have a marketing and sales process, automating it can save time and reduce errors.

From the first contact, this software can track individual prospects and watch their behavior on the site. Then it can be modified by the salespeople who speak with the prospects—and all along, the system gives each of these leads a score. Leads are scored to figure out how ready they are to talk to sales (see the Lead Nurturing box in Figure 8.1). The higher the score, the more ready they are.

This lead scoring can and should be customized for each company. You might find that one particular blog post, video, or PDF creates much more qualified customers, so set it so that when they experience that content, it boosts their lead score higher than another piece of content. Or perhaps prospects who go to your Contact Us page (although they may not contact you yet) get a big lead score boost as well because they were thinking about contacting you again. Are people from LinkedIn Groups better prospects than from LinkedIn profile posts? Third-party data says so, but track it and find out for your company. Then reflect what you find in your lead scoring.

Marketing automation also can give feedback to the advertising and marketing folks about what's working and what's not. It can reshape your marketing priorities and process (forming it into a proven series that nurtures leads into customers). It can show where you're getting stuck in lead nurturing, leading you to brainstorm the next steps. It pushes you to get you more new customers from the same number of leads and grow your revenue. Marketing and sales need to agree on a lead score that indicates when it's time for sales to talk to the prospect as well as a handoff process. If sales encounters someone who's not quite ready, the lead can be re-entered into the lead-nurturing process rather than being lost completely.

There are numerous marketing automation companies, and they can help you with setup details and tutorials. Check out Marketo, Eloqua, and Aprimo, among others. Most of them dovetail with, rather than replace, Sales Force Automation (SFA) software such as Salesforce, ACT!, GoldMine, and Zoho. How important is this? Important enough to italicize: *Your salespeople need sales force automation, and your advertising and marketing folks need marketing automation.* The pricing is incidental compared to potential revenue increases. For many B2B companies, just one more sale a year from existing leads would more than cover it.

What if you don't take advantage of marketing automation? The risks are that your content marketing messages will be less relevant and effective than they could be. You might be excited about your content marketing but not sure why it's not working. You spent all this advertising money and time both networking and marketing to finally get their email into your system, so you don't want those leads to go to waste. Without marketing automation, people may find ways to ignore you, and you won't realize it. People will skip over blasé email subject lines and not respond. Your cost per sale will be high, because you won't be getting as much as you can from those LinkedIn leads. Your company won't be as compsetitive as it could be. Competitors who are using marketing automation may overtake you.

Strategies for LinkedIn Advertising

Let's talk about some of the strategies you can use with LinkedIn ads to achieve marketing and sales goals. In the next few chapters, we talk about how to create them and get advanced results.

Increasing Awareness of Your Company

No one can buy from your company if they don't know it exists. Companies buy pens with their logo on it. Politicians put out yard signs and create TV ads. The value of awareness is widely recognized. Therefore, an important aspect of LinkedIn ads is raising awareness among your best customer targets. Make sure you have a list of all the kinds of prospects you want to reach (job titles, personas, industries, and so on), and keep a list of these handy. You can use it as a checklist to track how much awareness you're creating, and to keep an eye out for segments you might not be reaching.

People need to see your logo, company name, and what you're all about, perhaps in the form of a slogan. Many ads will raise awareness of your company while accomplishing other goals. But some ads, focused on a particular objective, do less to increase awareness than others.

Watch for which ads are showing the most right now. People get tired of seeing ads and stop clicking them. Alternatively, you might add more effective, new ads to a campaign. Brand-awareness ads can seem boring to people and won't be clicked as much as other types of ads. If you've set ads to be optimized by click-through rate, LinkedIn shows the less-clicked ads less often. I recommend, if maintaining levels of brand awareness is critical to you, that you create specific campaigns for brand awareness so that these ads don't compete for clicks with ads for other objectives.

Advertising as a Part of Content Marketing

Did you create a great new white paper to engage prospects, position your company, or share great industry research? Is it part of a lead generation strategy? If so, how will people hear about it? You can use your existing email list and AdWords ads, certainly, but you may want to reach even more of your job title/ function/ industry prospects by advertising it on LinkedIn.

Did you create a valuable video or blog post? Again, if no one sees it, all the time and creativity you put into it is wasted. What's more, if it's a video with few views, it looks bad for your company. If it's a blog post that shows just a few Facebook likes, tweets, or LinkedIn shares, that also makes it look like either you're not reaching anyone or no one appreciates your content. Boost viewership and readership by driving more prospects to this content with LinkedIn ads.

Amplifying Media Coverage About Your Company

When your company is covered or interviewed on another website—say, a trade journal, a well-known blogger's site, or major mainstream media—you can create ads to send your prospects there. This might sound blasphemous, because you're paying to send people to someone else's website! However, the media coverage is only as valuable as which people see it. The website that covered you may or may not attract your prospects.

Don't assume your prospects are seeing the media coverage. Instead, create ads to send them to it. We'll cover more of the how-to of ad creation in the next few chapters, but start making a list of the publications you'd like coverage in, both mainstream and in your niche. You can create ads that target people who work at those companies.

You may need to do a little research to discover the parent company. For example, *Ad Age* and *BtoB* magazines are owned by Crain Communications. You can also target ads to job titles like editor in chief and journalist and industry categories under "Media" such as Broadcast Media, Publishing, Newspapers, and Online Media. If you're not sure you have all the best job titles for the media folks you want to reach, use Advanced People Search to find people at those companies and review the range of job titles they use, or check out their Company Pages and do the same. This will help you find less obvious job titles like columnist or contributor.

Segmentation

Segmentation is a fundamental part of all successful marketing. Segmentation involves dividing people up into groups and speaking to them about what they care about. You can't impact someone if you don't know what they care about, and you can't know what they care about if you don't know who they are.

Because you can target your advertisements to people in this segmented fashion, it makes sense to know what you should say to each group. CEOs and CFOs care about different things. They use different words. The same is true for many job functions. And when you target people by their job title, you can use that job title in the advertisement. For example, if you're a CEO and you see an ad that contains "Attention CEOs," you're more likely to pay attention to it and click it. In fact, it's never a bad idea for the executives of the companies you're targeting to be aware of your company and its value. At the very least, they will recognize the company when it's mentioned to them by someone else who you've reached at their company.

Prospects are also more impressed and more interested when you address their particular industry. If someone is a healthcare CFO, and you have a specific message targeting that job title, they are even more likely to respond than if your message is more general or, God forbid, all about your company.

Segmentation is powerful for the marketing and sales departments, too. If you don't have industry-specific or job-function-related marketing materials, creating them will help your company get better at serving its customers. Some of your salespeople may have wisdom and insight on these topics, if you just ask. This is definitely a meeting topic for advertising, marketing, and sales personnel to look at quarterly.

When you meet, you can make a grid of the top three to five industries, and the top three to give job titles that marketing and sales want to reach. (Use Table 8.1 as a worksheet.) These can include decision makers, influencers, financial people, and the people who use the solutions you sell. Fill in each square with the messages, benefits, and key points you want to convey to each group—what are their concerns, and how do you help them overcome their obstacles and meet their goals? This grid can also be used to generate ideas for content marketing.

Table 8.1   Industry and Job Title Message Brainstorming Grid

	Healthcare	Finance	Manufacturing	Retail
CEO				
CFO				
COO				
VP/Directors				
Solution Users				

Pre-Sales Persuasion

The goal of B2B advertising is to make things easier for the marketing and sales departments. The goal of the marketing department is to make things easier for sales. The goal of the sales department is to get sales so everyone else can make a living.

One thing that advertising and marketing can do to increase success for sales is to prepare prospects ahead of time. Clarify their concerns. Make them aware of why your company is great, and how your solutions fix their problems. Let them see other customers who've benefitted. Sales can deal with all kinds of variables and create customized solutions, but it's easier for them to do that when the prospect knows they have a problem and has confidence in your company.

What's more, if your competitors are doing effective pre-sale propaganda (I hate to call it that, but what else is it?) and you're not, your salespeople have a much steeper hill to climb. As one salesperson put it, "I have been in two different cycles this year already where the buyer was armed with a portfolio of misinformation. They dug their feet in because their people researched it on social media and the Internet," the sales rep wrote. "I didn't care so much that we lost, what I cared about was the clients' addiction to that information as if it were the truth."[4]

As you can see, the content marketing you and your competitors create can be viewed as the Bible-truth by prospect researchers who are pressed for time. People are easily convinced of the credibility of online sources these days, and may have nothing to compare it to. The marketing department needs to have its eyes open for competitor misinformation and develop strategies to combat it. Getting the word out to your prospect pool may require advertising.

Also, watch your competitors' content quality. While researching this book, I was very impressed by one company's content quality, and by comparison, their competitor lost my esteem because their content was much less helpful and substantial. Incorrectly or not, my view of their content quality affects my view of their entire company—just as a clean and well-dressed person seems more trustworthy than a dirty, smelly person. It's unfortunate, but human beings use cognitive shortcuts (stereotypes). If you do other things well at your company and want to get customers so you can help them, you're going to have to do content marketing, advertising, and sales well, too.

Even if your prices are relatively fixed, the only way to avoid cut-throat price wars (which slow undermine every industry and lead to layoffs and cutbacks)[5] is to increase your company's perceived value through better advertising, better content, and better relationships. To prevent your prospects from viewing you as a commodity, try to establish value your competitors can't undercut.

Existing Customers Versus New Customers

Many companies view advertising, marketing and sales simply as ways to get new customers. Their effect on or potential for existing customers is ignored. In some companies, salespeople remain involved in customer service as account managers. PR focuses on reporting company successes to the media. Marketing might handle an e-newsletter to existing customers to keep them up to date. As mentioned earlier in the section on using advertising to project the power of media coverage, your company's advertising folks can also help you reach existing customers.

Some of this happens automatically, because, for example, an advertisement to a LinkedIn Group that contains prospects probably also contains some existing customers. But you can also target by company. If you have customers that are medium- or large-sized companies, there might be some value for you in reaching more people in those companies. You might have contact with a few role players at those companies, and might reach them with an e-newsletter, but are other potential influencers in your customers' companies equally impressed by your company? Maybe not. To extend your influence, you can create advertisements about your company's media coverage or its developments to people with select job titles in your customers' companies.

Advertising Goals and Metrics

Let's discuss advertising goals and reporting. How do you measure whether your LinkedIn advertising is effective? How do you report on its effectiveness to others at your company? How do your executives know whether what you're doing with LinkedIn will continue to deserve a budget?

Marketing and advertising people need to be able to quantify their impact and spend or else they can't protect their budget or ask for a bigger one. What would 10% more or 10% less budget do to the company's profits? Strive to be able to answer this question by putting systems and software in place to quantify them.[6]

You need to be able to track and report on results, whether that's clicks, leads, sales, or even ROI. What's more, the different people you report to each have their own favorite metrics:

- Marketing might be impressed by the number of eyeballs you got their content in front of, or how many people clicked over, and how much time they spent on the content.
- Marketing and sales want to know the number of leads you're driving, and sales wants to know whether you're doing all you can to bring in *qualified* leads.

- Executives want to know how much revenue and profit you're driving, but may also be impressed by how many impressions and clicks your ads generate.

It's a good idea for advertising to report on all these metrics because different stakeholders have different concerns. And that means you also need clear ideas and buy-in on the priorities. If you have great lead nurturing going on, you can broaden your targeting and make your ad messages more appealing to everyone, increasing clicks even if they're less qualified. An increasing number of clicks may make salespeople worry about lead quality, but not if they have a clear understanding of the qualification and lead-nurturing system and believe it's working well.

How do you provide all of this? The biggest issue you face with having multiple analytics sources (from your LinkedIn ads, web analytics, and CRM, to name a few) is that once you print out all that data, it's probably too much for anyone but you to consume. Whether you're reporting to internal teams or to clients, even if they're impressed with a thick 20–100 page monthly report, very few people will read beyond the executive summary. So, talk to those you're reporting to about the most important metrics to them and what questions they want answered. Then design a monthly one-page executive summary, whether you choose to include detailed print-outs behind that or not.

Focusing on analytics and metrics also allows advertising to forecast not just spend but results. Know that there are people in your company whose job it is to cut unnecessary costs. They need to know why your cost is necessary—your job and your ad spend. Once you've tracked some results, you can forecast them.

How much revenue and profit do you believe your ads will drive in the next quarter? In the next year? If this number is bigger than the cost of your advertising activities (including your salary and so on), then it looks good. Just don't overestimate, because then you may be viewed as failing compared to your expectations later on.

Also, if you want to get in good with the cost-saving folks, offer to cut things that don't work. If you find there are ads or targets that don't work, be sure to communicate this and that you're cutting them. Explain what does work instead. You gain credibility with the CFO and CEO if you show you're managing a portfolio of advertising investments when allocating your marketing budget, rather than just indiscriminately spending in a fire-and-forget manner.

Summary

By now, you should understand where LinkedIn advertising fits into overall B2B marketing and sales strategy, what the major strategies are for LinkedIn advertising, the kind of goals and metrics you may choose to prioritize, and how to report on your results. Next, we can begin to look at advertising tactics in Chapters 9 and 10.

Endnotes

1. "Helping Hands," TV Tropes, http://tvtropes.org/pmwiki/pmwiki.php/Main/HelpingHands

2. Two charts from eMarketer in these two articles: Lauren Indvik, "Online Ad Spending to Surpass Print for First Time in 2012 [STUDY]," Mashable, January 19, 2012, http://mashable.com/2012/01/19/online-advertising-surpasses-print-2012/, and "Industry Stats & Data by eMarketer," Interactive Advertising Bureau, http://www.iab.net/insights_research/industry_data_and_landscape/1675

3. "How Demand Generation and Lead Management Work with Marketing Automation," *Marketing Automation Times*, December 20, 2011, http://marketingautomationtimes.com/2011/12/20/how-demand-generation-and-lead-management-work-with-marketing-automation/ and http://www.youtube.com/watch?feature=player_embedded&v=1RDQsatUk3U

4. Adele Revella, "B2B Marketers Won This Complex Sale," March 8, 2012, http://www.buyerpersona.com/2012/03/b2b-marketers-won-this-complex-sale.html

5. Kim and Mauborgne, *Blue Ocean Strategy: How to Create Uncontested Market Space and Make Competition Irrelevant*, Harvard Business Review Press, 2005.

6. "The Definitive Guide to Marketing Metrics and Marketing Analytics," Marketo, July 13, 2011. http://www.marketo.com/b2b-marketing-resources/best-practices/the-definitive-guide-to-marketing-metrics-and-marketing-analytics.php

9

B2B Advertising: How to Create and Optimize LinkedIn Ads

Do you want to reach LinkedIn's 1.3 million small business owners? Or its 12 million small business professionals? Or its 5.5 million high tech managers? Or its 2 million C-level executives? You can with LinkedIn advertising.

LinkedIn advertising is a powerful way to send your target audience a short message and get them to click into your marketing funnel. This chapter introduces you to LinkedIn ads. If you are new to online advertising, this chapter will be sufficient to get you started. If you have experience with Google AdWords, you'll find many similar concepts in LinkedIn ads (for example, limited lengths for ad messages and testing the response of the same audience to different ads). If you are experienced with Facebook advertising, you will see similarities to what you already do (targeting people based on who they are rather than, as AdWords does, what they're looking for right now). Table 9.1 compares the characteristics of ads on each network.

Table 9.1   A Comparison of Popular Online Self-Serve Advertisement Networks

Ad Network	Advertisements	Targeting	Account Organization	Reporting
LinkedIn	Small 50×50 image with text	*Who* people are (job titles, industries, and so on)	Multiple ad variations per campaign	Minimal
Facebook	Medium 99×72 image with text	*Who* people are (demographics, affinities, and so on)	Multiple ads in each campaign	Moderate
Google AdWords Search Network	Text-only ads	*What* people are searching for (mainly keyword targeting)	Multiple ads per ad group	Extensive
Google AdWords Display Network	Text or image ads, many sizes	*What* websites people use and who they are	Multiple ads per ad group	Extensive

The strength of self-serve LinkedIn advertising, and the main reason to use it over other advertising networks, is the capability to target people by job title, industry, company, and company size. In Facebook, you can target job titles by putting them into the precise interests section. There is also a workplaces section for company names, but a smaller percentage of users fill these out than on LinkedIn. Only about 16% of people on Facebook list their employer. This is one reason that Facebook is regarded as a great platform for business-to-consumer marketing, whereas LinkedIn is stronger as a business-to-business marketing platform.

Creating Your First Campaign

Go to LinkedIn ads (https://www.linkedin.com/ads/), and click New Ad Campaign, Start New. When building ads, LinkedIn asks you to create a campaign name and design your ad, which in my opinion is backward. It doesn't make sense to create an ad before choosing the target. Do you talk the same way to your boss as you do to your child? No, what you say and how you say it changes based on your audience. Ads must appeal to the people you target; otherwise, they probably won't get clicked.

LinkedIn forces you to create the ad first, but once you see the targeting options, don't be surprised if your ad ideas change. When you change your ad's targeting, you'll probably want to change the way your ad is written. For example, if you write your first ad to target a particular job title, but your targeting options include five more similar job titles that don't make sense to exclude from your targeting, you'll have to consider whether your ad copy should include all the job titles (and whether they'll fit within the description length), or you'll have to discover the one job title that every person in that audience will feel applies to them. For example, you might start with an ad to Chief Marketing Officers, but LinkedIn also suggests you target VP Marketing, SVP Marketing, EVP Marketing, Marketing Directors, and others. Now what should your ad say? I would go with "marketing execs."

Targeting Audiences

Let's choose how to target the people you're after. You are required to choose one geographic location, but you also have other options for selecting a LinkedIn audience (see Figure 9.1).

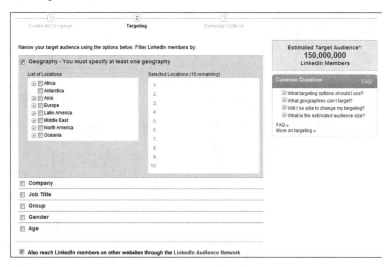

Figure 9.1   *An overview of LinkedIn advertising targeting categories.*

You can target all of the following:

- Continents, countries, states, provinces, and some cities
- Companies by their name or by category (includes industry and company size)
- People by specific job titles or by job category (includes job function and seniority)

- LinkedIn Groups that individuals are members of
- Gender
- Age groups (18–24, 25–34, 35–54, and 55+)

If you find that the city you want to target isn't included in LinkedIn's options, consider targeting LinkedIn Groups that have your target city in their name.

Because you don't yet know which segment will respond best to your ad, try several options. Even if your ads are relatively similar, you might want to try targeting the following with separate campaigns:

- Specific companies your targets work at
- Job titles
- LinkedIn Groups your targets are in

When you add more targeting criteria, such as both companies and job titles, the number of people your ads reach gets smaller. In Figure 9.2, you can see that the estimated audience size drops quickly with each additional option.

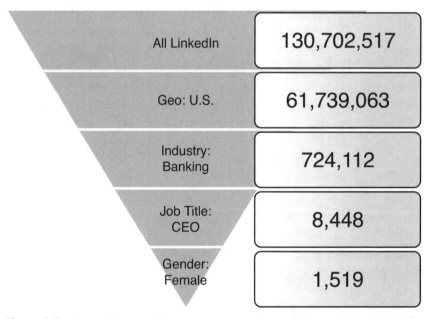

Figure 9.2 *A visualization of how your target audience decreases with each additional targeting criterion.*

A common mistake people make when first exposed to so many targeting options is to target too narrowly. Although LinkedIn does not run ads if the estimated target audience is less than 1,000, you might find target combinations that yield just 1,200 people, for example. Keep in mind that some people don't spend much time on LinkedIn, so such a narrowly focused ad can result in very few monthly clicks. This might work for you if you just want to increase the awareness of your brand among a specific group of people rather than get clicks or leads. Otherwise, stick to larger target audiences.

Using the LinkedIn Audience Network

Every LinkedIn ad-creation process gives you the option to show your ads on the LinkedIn Audience Network.[1] This network gives you the ability to show your ads outside of LinkedIn.com on partner websites.[2] If you want to place your ad campaign into this network of websites, your ads will show to the same segment of people you've targeted on LinkedIn itself (for example, based on job title or company).[3] There is speculation that this network of websites includes *The New York Times, BusinessWeek,* and CNBC, but the exact list has not been released publicly.[4]

It's a good idea to include the LinkedIn Audience Network when your targeting is very specific. Fewer people use LinkedIn than Facebook or AdWords, and they spend less time on LinkedIn per day, so there are fewer overall page views and ad views. Impression volume on LinkedIn.com (the number of times your ads are shown) is relatively low, and only a certain percentage of those ad views yields clicks. Therefore, to get a significant volume of clicks as an advertiser, you need thousands and thousands of impressions. The LinkedIn Audience Network helps boost that impression number and get you more clicks. However, if you target larger segments, you can and might want to opt out of the audience network.

Characteristics of LinkedIn Advertisements

Each LinkedIn ad is composed of four parts: a 50×50-pixel image, a headline, a description, and the landing page you want people to go to when they click (see Figure 9.3).

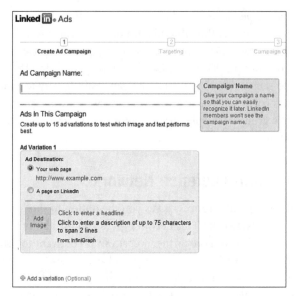

Figure 9.3   *Creating your ad's headline, image, description, and destination on LinkedIn.*

Note that you can choose a web page on your website or blog; you might also want to use ads to send people to your LinkedIn company page or LinkedIn Group. A drop-down list like the one in Figure 9.4 enables you to choose profiles or company pages. To send people to a Group, use the web address.

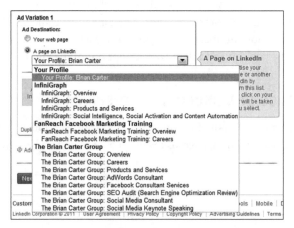

Figure 9.4   *Choosing LinkedIn pages you administer as a destination for your LinkedIn ad.*

Determining the Number of Ad Variations

When you first start advertising on LinkedIn, you can only guess what your audience might click. Creating multiple ad variations gives you more chances to succeed in getting that response from your audience. It also serves as a degree of market research because it teaches you about what they care about most.

You can create up to 15 ad variations per campaign, but that's too many ads for most campaigns. The amount of exposure your ad will get is limited by the size of the audience you target and how many pages they view on LinkedIn within a certain time period. Each ad needs a certain amount of exposure for you to get clicks and see how it's performing. To determine how many ads to run, first divide the size of the audience you're targeting by 2,000 to estimate your monthly clicks. Then figure you need at least five to ten clicks per ad to be somewhat confident how it's performing. How many ads is that? Divide the number of monthly clicks you expect by 5, 7, or 10, and that's the number of ads you should test. Alternatively, in summary, divide your audience size by 15,000 and create that many ads. (Note: This is just a rule of thumb. You certainly will want to get as much data as you can while testing, especially if you're optimizing at the lead conversion level, not just the CTR level.)

In general, I run three to five ads at a time and then check weekly to see what is working and what isn't. As you see what the top performing ideas are and which ones don't work, you'll learn more about the people you've targeted. We discuss optimizing your ads to get even better results in the next chapter.

Making Your Ads Fit Your Targets

Although we're just getting our feet wet in this chapter, start thinking about how your ads fit the people you're targeting. If you're targeting healthcare executives, think about their goals, priorities, and concerns. If you're targeting potential software users, how does your software solve the problems they face on a daily basis? The personas detailed in the next chapter give you even more ideas. We'll also look at customizing your ads for job titles, groups, and industries.

Calls to Action: Telling People What to Do

A fundamental lesson of direct marketing is that when you tell people what you want them to do, they're more likely to do it. In marketing, this is called a "call to action." Leaders know that people don't follow you if they don't know what you want. Parents know that you have to tell children several times before they do what you ask. The following phrases are examples of calls to action:

- Click here now.
- Check out our whitepaper.
- Watch this fascinating video.

Instructing people to click increases your click-through rate, which increases your chance of getting a lead. Although some search ad platforms like AdWords bar you from asking specifically for a click, the social ad platforms like LinkedIn and Facebook currently do not. This is a huge advantage, so use it while you can!

Campaign Options

As shown in Figure 9.5, the final screen of the ad-creation process gives you four more campaign options:

- Payment Method
- Daily Budget
- Lead Collection
- Show My Campaign

These campaign options are detailed in the following subsections.

Figure 9.5   *Filling in payment, budget, lead collection, and display details for your LinkedIn ad.*

Should You Pay with CPC or CPM?

You have two options for how you pay for your campaign: per click (CPC) or per thousand impressions (CPM). If you want to pay only when people click because you're focused on leads and results, choose CPC. If you want more awareness (more ad views) and don't care as much about clicks, choose CPM—but note that most experienced digital advertisers never use CPM.

If you choose CPC and don't get enough impressions, either you need a better ad that people respond to more, thus increasing your click-through rate, or you might try the CPM payment method to ensure that LinkedIn shows your ads more. If you choose CPM and find you're paying too much and want more clicks, switch to CPC so you're paying only for clicks.

Choose a Daily Budget

The minimum daily budget is $10. You can expect to pay $2 to $4 per click, so think about how much you can spend, and how many clicks you want per day or per month. Anywhere from 1% to 20% of your clicks will become leads, so your cost per lead could be anywhere from $100 to $400. In a recent campaign I ran, my cost per lead was only $48, but I would say about one-third were not qualified leads, so the real cost was more like $72 per lead. You need to think this way about your costs to ensure that you budget enough dollars to get the number of leads and sales you want.

Turn on Lead Collection

If you turn on lead collection, then when people click your ad, they will go to your website and will also see a special bar at the top from LinkedIn that enables these people to contact you and give you their email address. These leads will show up in the Leads section of your LinkedIn ads dashboard. Even cooler, you can contact these leads at no charge. The only reason not to turn on this feature is if you need people to contact you through your website rather than through LinkedIn. Your web analytics and CRM tracking setup may require as much, and leads collected in LinkedIn wouldn't be tracked the same way, which could throw off your lead nurturing, marketing automation, and sales force automation.

The "Show My Campaign" Options

You can choose whether to specify an end date or run continuously. I would only choose an end date if you are 100% sure of the end date. A campaign that's set to run continuously can be paused at any time. Managing to a strict budget requires frequent checking, because there's no way to set a total budget limit for a campaign, and it's difficult to estimate how much will be spent per day. The cost comes from clicks, and clicks may decrease from the same audience over time, because the same people are seeing the ad over and over again, and after a certain point, they've either already clicked it before or never will. When you refresh your ads with new variations, your clicks may go up again. If you need to manage your budget closely, you'll have to check the stats frequently.

What Kind of Results Should You Expect?

In your first few LinkedIn ad campaigns, you'll still be developing expectations about click-through rates, the volume of clicks, and lead quality. It might help you set these expectations by comparing some numbers for user behavior on other sites (see Table 9.2).

Table 9.2 Comparing Self-Serve Ad Networks

	LinkedIn	Google	Facebook	Twitter[5]
Estimated reach (% of global internet users)[6]	5%	50%	44%	10%
Share of daily page views	0.5%	5.5%	5.3%	0.4%
Page views per user	9	12	13	5
Active users	150 million[7]	1 billion[8]	850 million	100 million[9]
Average CTR	0.03%	1.0%	0.03%	N/A
Average CPC	$3.05	$2.50	$0.80[10]	N/A

Based on these comparisons, the LinkedIn audience is about one-tenth the size of Google or Facebook's, and much closer to the size of Twitter's. The LinkedIn Audience Network is a black box; it has not officially listed the members of this network, and it would require a huge number of audience-targeting tests to reverse engineer the number of page views available here.

Generally speaking, LinkedIn ads have a low CTR, more like Facebook ads or AdWords display ads than AdWords' search network. The CPC is high on LinkedIn—much higher than on Facebook, and higher than many of AdWords' search keywords. But companies who have used LinkedIn for B2B advertising believe it yields highly qualified leads. My personal take is that each ad network has strengths and weaknesses, so you should use them all. Each will contribute to your business. Over time, you'll figure out the right allocation of funds for each, based on what's possible to spend (you can only spend a certain amount of money without targeting beyond your best audience) and where you get the best results.

Your first three to five campaigns will help you set baselines. If you're looking for only the most targeted prospects, you may see a lower impression, click, and lead volume. On the other hand, if you have a good lead-nurturing solution, you can target wider and talk bigger—you know that fewer qualified prospects will develop over time. In Chapter 10, we discuss more advanced techniques to get even better results.

Endnotes

1. "Ads on the LinkedIn Audience Network," LinkedIn Help Center. http://help.linkedin.com/app/answers/detail/a_id/2363

2. "LinkedIn Launches the LinkedIn Audience Network," LinkedIn Press Center, September 15, 2008. http://press.linkedin.com/102/linkedin-launches-linkedin-audience-network

3. "LinkedIn announces 'Audience Network' for ads," Caroline McCarthy, CNET, September 15, 2008. http://news.cnet.com/8301-13577_3-10041420-36.html

4. LinkedIn Answer, http://www.linkedin.com/answers/using-linkedIn/ULI/728901-82584808

5. These stats are web-only. Note that Twitter has admitted that 50% of its users are "active," but 40% of these have not tweeted in the last month (http://www.huffingtonpost.com/2011/09/08/twitter-stats_n_954121.html). Estimates range on how many tweets are from mobile devices range from 40–55%. We may be able to double the Twitter reach and pageview numbers in this table.

6. In this table, the first three rows are drawn from Alexa.com, April 9, 2012.

7. About Us, LinkedIn Press Center. http://press.linkedin.com/about

8. Comscore put this number at 1 billion users in June 2011: http://www.comscoredatamine.com/2011/06/google-reaches-1-billion-global-visitors/

9. "Twitter Has 100 Million Active Users," Chris Taylor, September 8, 2011. http://mashable.com/2011/09/08/twitter-has-100-million-active-users/

10. The 2012 Facebook Ads Report, SocialFresh. http://socialfresh.com/facebook-advertising/

10

Advanced Strategies and Tactics for High-Impact LinkedIn Ads

Your Internet advertising is only as good as your ideas. Try to ignore the temptation of thinking you're a creative genius and are looking to develop that single "great idea." Lots of good ideas, combined with the discipline of testing, leads to better results faster. Fortunately, LinkedIn's ad platform gives us plenty of data about what works and what doesn't. It teaches us, like the Google AdWords and Facebook advertising platforms do, that most of our ideas are not as great as we thought. It teaches us that we have to tailor our message to the audience we're targeting, and that we should test the way we're targeting the people we want to reach.

My experience has been that when I create ads without trying at least three to five ideas, my results are not as reliably good. This chapter goes deeper into how you can create more and better LinkedIn ads to get more clicks, leads, and sales for your company.

Optimize Your Results by Creating Better Ads

Successful Internet advertisers *optimize*. They're always looking for "better." They ask "What can I do next to get better results?" They create, test, and improve. Internet advertising is not like media buying, where you acquire the ads once from a creative process, run them on many websites, and take whatever results you get. Internet advertising means going back to the creative and analytical process over and over again—correlating the targeting criteria and ad copy with better or worse results, and constantly improving by testing yet again (see Figure 10.1).

Figure 10.1   *The Facebook ad optimization cycle.*

Here's the process you'll repeat over and over to optimize ads and get better and better results:

1. Target your audience. Who are you trying to reach? How do you target them in LinkedIn?

2. Choose creative images and ad copy that will get the message across to this target. How can you get them to take action? What images will attract their attention and increase results without hurting your cause? (Some images grab attention and create curiosity—but too much—and you get clicks from the wrong people.) Create five to ten versions each of image, text, and headline so that you can find the best ideas and combinations.

3. Run the ads and wait for results.

4. Get the results, and run reports.

5. Analyze the data. Look at your key metric, whether that's CTR (click-through rate; how much did this audience respond to these ads?) or cost per lead (have you made this affordable yet?) Which creative ad worked best? Compare the ads with the best and worst responses—why do you think they responded that way? What does this teach you? Can you think of more ideas that are more like the best ads and less like the worst ones? Go back to step 1 and repeat the process.

Evaluating LinkedIn Ad Metrics

To evaluate the data that comes back from your LinkedIn ads, you first need to know what your key metrics are. When you put all your analytics sources together, you have access to dozens and dozens of metrics. Each goes up and down depending on what you're trying to achieve, so what's good or bad from each metric is not always clear. Sometimes in business we speak of having one key metric—and you certainly should know which one is most important to you—but because an entire sales funnel is usually involved (see the examples in Table 10.1), you can look at several key metrics along the way.

Table 10.1   Metrics for Each Phase of Marketing

Phase of Marketing	Metrics
Ad targeting	Estimated audience size
Awareness	Impressions, cost per thousand views (CPM)
Interested ad viewer	Clicks, CTR, cost per click (CPC)
Website traffic	Unique visitors
Effectiveness of website	Conversion rate (CR)
Interested prospects	Leads from website, cost per lead (CPL)
Qualified prospects	Lead score
Sales	Closing rate, cost per sale

Each ad will have clicks, impressions, CTR, and average cost per click (see Figure 10.2). Some ads, even within the same campaign, will have a better (higher) CTR but also a higher CPC. Which is more important to you? The CTR tells you how much the audience you targeted responded to the image and text, but the cost per click figures heavily into cost per lead and cost per sale. You'll care about which ad copy increases your conversion rate as well, so neither CTR nor CPC will be the key metrics.

Ad Variations						
Ad	Status	Clicks	Impressions ▲	CTR	Avg. CPC	Total Spent
Total for All Ad Variations		119	360296	0.033%	$2.73	$324.78
	Active Deactivate Hide	83	231077	0.036%	$2.72	$225.63
	Active Deactivate Hide	12	42972	0.028%	$2.79	$33.49
	Active Deactivate Hide	6	30730	0.020%	$2.66	$15.97
	Active Deactivate Hide	12	27653	0.043%	$2.79	$33.53
	Active Deactivate Hide	5	18587	0.027%	$2.79	$13.93

Figure 10.2 *A sample view of the metrics you'll see for your ad variations.*

Using Analytics to Get Deeper into Ad Quality

The advertising metrics on LinkedIn reveal only that people want to click your ads—and some ads are better at getting clicks than others. But are these ads giving you good prospects? Are the people who click also submitting their information on your website as leads? Are these leads high quality ones for Sales to talk to, or can they be nurtured into better leads through marketing automation? To get more information about the quality of the people you receive from ads, you need the capability to track what prospects are doing—from the first ad click all the way to the sale. Companies find out which campaigns work best by using some combination of web analytics (such as Google Analytics or Adobe SocialAnalytics), marketing automation (such as Eloqua or Marketo), and their customer relationship management or sales force automation software (such as Salesforce or Zoho). Regardless of how you set up your analytics, you need to track the individual results of each campaign or ad. It's best to track each ad, if you can, because you want to know whether a change in the headline, image, or body copy attracts more of the right leads and less of the wrong ones.

For example, Eloqua's social advertising expert, Elle Woulfe, explained their process this way:

"You can align your Eloqua campaigns with your LinkedIn campaigns so that there is a one-to-one relationship. Then you can see conversion all the way through the funnel from a specific advertising campaign. This data passes directly into the sales force automation system, so the salesperson can see details on which campaign caused the conversion. The rep can also use our tools to see the specific piece of content the prospect engaged with."

In other words, if you have the right tools (whatever company the tools come from), you can track all of this. You can determine which ads and which content got the results, and which ones didn't. Your sales reps can find out which ads and content someone responded to before they talk to them. If they know more specifically what a prospect responded to, that makes the first sales conversation much more productive—and first impressions count.

You can also track specific ads with web analytics. You can see how much time they spend on your website, and what percentage of them leave right away (bounce rate). Figure 10.3 shows the Google Analytics for the first week of LinkedIn advertising for a B2B business. The company, Imperium, provides market research quality-control services. We tested three main messages and saw very different results.

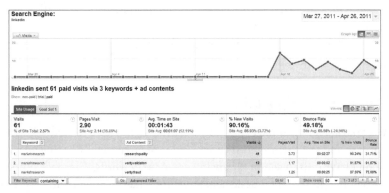

Figure 10.3 *Using Google Analytics and URL parameters to track how visitors from each LinkedIn ad behave on a website.*

Overall, the campaign brought in more than 90% new visitors, which is a good metric to examine when looking for new business. The bounce-rate and time-on-site metrics tell us that the people who clicked the first ad ("research quality," a message about increasing quality) were much more interested in what Imperium had to offer than those who clicked the research-validation or fraud-prevention messages. Chances are that what they were looking for on those topics was not exactly what Imperium offers.

Before you judge your time-on-site and bounce-rate numbers, however, consider this: If you send people to a page where they're intended to take one action and leave the site without going to another page, a high bounce rate is actually a good thing. High time-on-site values are not always desirable—maybe people are getting confused, or they're just window shoppers. Maybe the content they're viewing on your website is too interesting and not persuasive enough. If you're trying to speed up your sales cycle (getting people to buy sooner after they start shopping for what you offer) by targeting those most ready to buy, a high time-on-site number might be bad. The point is that you have to be careful how you interpret your analytics. The safest metrics to interpret are those closer to the conversion, such as cost per lead or cost per sale.

Get Better Results with Better Targeting

It's tough to test both ad creative (the image plus the text) and targeting at the same time. The math tells us that there are too many possible combinations. For example, if you have three headlines, five images, and three ad copy versions to test, that's already 45 potential combinations. You can only run 15 ad variations per LinkedIn ad campaign. If you're targeting dozens of LinkedIn Groups, at least several job titles, and who knows how many companies...let's say that's from 3 to 20 targets—and multiply that by the 15 ads...that's anywhere from 45 to 300 tests! You see my point—it's not really practical. So, before you test ad creative, you might want to test just the targeting.

The Power of Boring Ads

To test your targeting at the beginning of a campaign, create relatively boring ads on purpose and test them against several kinds of targeting. By boring ads, I mean they don't have calls to action, flashy images, or sexy words. They talk simply about what you offer, or present a basic benefit without adjectival flourishes. You can amplify their effect later, but just start with the simple message. For example, you could test the same boring ads in five to ten campaigns that target the following:

- A list of specific companies
- People with specific job titles at a company of a particular size
- A list of industries
- A list of relevant groups
- Any combination of this list

Testing boring ads will tell you which targeting settings produce an audience that's most responsive to what you offer. Then you can use those best targeting settings to continue on, testing more interesting ads. Instead, if you start with interesting ads but don't get amazing results, you may experience nagging doubts about whether it's your targeting that's holding you back.

Developing Your Targeting Strategy

Chapter 8 presented you with an industry/job title messaging grid. At first, creating such a grid can seem like a lot of work, but if you think ahead about what you want to say to the different audiences you write ads for, the ad creation will be quicker, and the results will be better. Then, you just need to add images to the chart, and you'll have all you need for that target-messaging brainstorm session (see Table 10.2).

Table 10.2 Ad Creative Brainstorming Grid		
	Headlines	Messages	Images
CEO			
CFO			
COO			
VP/Directors			
Solution Users			

In that brainstorming grid from Chapter 8, we looked at industries as well. You can put whatever you want down the left column. Make sure you include input from Marketing and Sales, which makes your job easier and you more effective. If you find you can't target some aspects of the people you want to reach, you can actually call that out in the ad headline or text. People who aren't in your target segment will see that and realize it's not for them.

Better Results When Targeting LinkedIn Groups

Remember that the average person who has a LinkedIn profile does not spend a great deal of time on LinkedIn. The people in Groups are usually the most active of those on LinkedIn, so they're a good place to start. However, Groups also can be open, so they accrue people who are marketing to the people you want to reach. The biggest offenders are HR people and, like yours truly, social media experts. That means if you set only Group-targeting in your ads, you might show your ads to the wrong people too. That decreases your results and can get you more "curiosity" clicks from people who'll never buy from you. The solution is to combine Group targeting with job title targeting.

For example, if I target the Groups that appear to be for Chief Marketing Officers, I get an estimated audience of 33,956 people. If I then narrow this down to those with relevant job titles (Chief Marketing Officer, Chief Sales Marketing Officer, Chief of Marketing), I get only 1,664 people. That's a big difference! It could be that many of those in the LinkedIn Groups would like to be CMOs or were CMOs once upon a time and now are not, but likely there are many other types of people in these Groups as well. I would run ads on that double target (CMO groups + CMO job titles) and also run the same ads in another campaign targeted to the Chief Marketing job titles *without* the Groups.

Let's look at CEOs as another example. Keep in mind that many solopreneurs call themselves CEOs, so let's narrow our CEOs to those in companies of more than 11 people (this reduces the number of CEOs from 668,995 to 92,573). Table 10.3 shows how many people we can target by choosing job titles only, related Groups only, or the combination of both.

Table 10.3   Various Ways to Target CEOs with LinkedIn Ads

CEO Job Titles Only	CEO Groups Only	Combination
Titles/Groups	CEO, Acting CEO, Interim CEO, Group CEO	Senior leadership group, CEO Club, CEO & Director's Network, CEO Women's Club, CXO Community, The LinkedIn CXO
Estimated audience size in North America	92,573	23,698

This tells us that there are 22,002 people in those CEO and CXO Groups who are not CEOs. Why is that? Many companies try to market to CEOs because CEOs have the most power; they are the biggest decision maker and not nearly the waste of time that a powerless solution user might be. Every Group, as mentioned previously, has hangers-on, marketers, HR people, and others. We would expect this phenomenon to be the worst in a CEO Group. This also means it may be one of the noisiest. CEO's are busy, and may be apt to spend less time in a noisy Group. The takeaway is that you might want to be skeptical of advertising to job-title-oriented Groups containing a low percentage of members with that actual job title.

A similar experiment with five Groups and 46 job titles for purchasers, buyers, and supply chain managers shows that 6,216 out of 22,219 Group members (28%) actually have those job titles. Compare this to 313,896 LinkedIn members who have those job titles but have not joined Groups named after their job. Only 2% of that number have joined those Groups. Certainly, these may be the 2% most active on LinkedIn, and we should target them. Again, we would also want to target their job titles without the Groups in a separate campaign.

Targeting All Relevant Job Titles

You could target thousands of job titles with LinkedIn advertising. Often, there are several ways to describe a job. Fortunately, LinkedIn suggests similar job titles while you enter them (see Figure 10.4).

Figure 10.4   *LinkedIn's ad platform suggests similar job titles for you.*

LinkedIn suggestions are certainly helpful, but they might not be enough. If this is your first time advertising into a new industry or trying to reach people with a certain position, you should research these companies and industries a bit to find more ideas. You can find information by using Google, Wikipedia, or even LinkedIn Answers. For example, let's say you're trying to reach the people at corporations who handle charity. If you search LinkedIn Answers for "corporate giving," you'll find a question about it, and an answer that suggests "titles usually include such key words as corporate giving, strategic philanthropy, social responsibility, corporate responsibility, corporate citizenship, public affairs, and community affairs."

You can also use Indeed.com, which is really a job search engine, to find job titles. If you enter "purchasing" with no geographic location, you discover "buyer" and "supply chain." Revise your search to "purchasing buyer supply" and scroll through the results to find more ideas, such as "supervisor of purchasing," which was not in LinkedIn's suggestions.

The AdWords keyword tool is also an option, but it's more likely to show you search terms including the job titles you put in than the synonyms you're looking for.

Persona-Based Advertising

One of the biggest problems in advertising and marketing is understanding an audience you've never met. How can you communicate effectively with someone you don't know? It's like trying to be a therapist to someone who never talks. You can research, you can look at your advertising performance results for different messages, and you can get ideas from salespeople who actually talk to good prospects and customers. Your job is to gather as much information and understand as much as you can to make the people real, three-dimensional human beings. What are their problems? Tendencies? Preferences? Hang-ups? Fears? How do they think? What do they need and, more importantly, what do they want?

Buyer personas are detailed profiles of real buyers, examples of real people you need to influence. Personas may contain surprising ideas not obvious from your targets' job descriptions.[1] They're based on your own specific research, interviews with customers and prospects, as well as interviews with your own company's salespeople who've hopefully talked to many of them. You want information that may not be available to your competitors. Good personas contain insights that help you create marketing with a real competitive advantage. The alternative is to create ads based on guesses about your prospects—and then you might quickly be bested by a competitor who rolls out ads and marketing that more accurately address the prospects' needs, obstacles, and buying criteria.

A March 2012 Marketing Sherpa survey found that 41% of B2B firms had established buyer personas, while 47% had not.[2] This is a strategy that a large number of B2B companies find valid, but not every company has adopted. Even more interesting are the most effective ways to develop buyer personas. The marketers surveyed said that they got the best information by interviewing prospects and customers, and the worst by monitoring social media. Second best was interviewing Sales, and second worst was keyword research. Clearly, you have to get out of your cubicle and talk to customers and salespeople if you want to understand these very real human beings you're trying to market to.

I found something similar when I was learning to do effective Facebook advertising. Coming from a search background, I was too dependent on keywords research and analytics. Because social media advertising is about targeting *who* audiences are, we need to understand *who they are as people* before we can write effective advertisements to them.

How many of your buyers have you actually talked to? This is a danger for startup businesses who are calibrating their offerings and marketing while their sales force is talking to potential buyers. Sales is getting critical and sometimes fascinating feedback from these real people: Are those in charge of advertising and marketing getting that information? What about when the market or industry trends change? When buyer needs change? When laws change? Consider updating your personas at least annually.

A mistake, when first starting with personas, is just making stuff up. If your personas are not based in reality, your message will be too bland and not persuasive. Your leads will be fewer in number and less in quality. Sales will have to work harder and will like you less.

One-on-one interviews and anonymous surveys are better than focus groups, which are notorious for delivering answers polluted by temporary conformity and trying to please the interviewer. People are more likely to confide the truth one-on-one, and have no way of impressing anyone with an anonymous survey.

Here are some of the questions you need to answer to round out your buyer personas:

- What are the objectives or problems they devote their time to most?
- What worries them most?
- What problem could you solve that would make the biggest impact to their quarter or their year?
- How do they measure success, if they can measure it? What's the metric? And what's the number?
- What triggers them to look for a solution?
- How do they narrow down solutions? Which ones do they eliminate and why?
- How do they make their decisions?

Once you've answered these questions, you'll write much more effective and relevant advertisements. You can also download freely available buyer persona templates from BuyerPersona.com.

One caveat on buyer personas is, like focus group results, the information comes from the buyer's mouths. You can confirm or disprove each idea by watching how prospects respond to ads, content marketing, and sales interactions. Over time, use the analytics from your website, marketing automation, and sales force automation, along with discussions with salespeople, to discern if any of the buyer persona information might be inaccurate.

Relevance: Know Your Audience

In bygone eras, advertising reached larger audiences (via magazines, radio shows, or TV shows that claimed a demographic similar to your consumer's) because there were no other advertising vehicles. Advertisers attempted, despite the diverse nature of these audiences, to reach out to specific types of consumers with messages that impacted them and pushed them closer to a buying decision. Even branding advertising, which creates or enhances a product or company's image, often positions the brand in a way that's favorable for more sales. Advertising professionals have always been more effective when their messages were relevant to the audience's needs and desires. After all, your product or service is meant to help a specific group in a specific way. If you can reach them and convince them it will help, you should get the business results you want.

The fracturing of media—with the growth of so many cable TV stations and shows, satellite radio, and heavily used websites—has increased our ability to reach more unique types of consumers. People are no longer all grouped together. Their preferences and behavior have spread them out and made them easier to target by their association with their favorite media. Internet marketing and advertising capitalizes on these opportunities to target audiences more specifically. Google's keyword-targeted search ads, whereby the advertiser can reach someone who's looking for exactly what the business offers, were the first major step in that direction. Improving Google display ad opportunities, along with highly customizable Facebook and LinkedIn audience targeting, are pushing advertising relevance and response further than ever been before.

Now we need ways to organize these specific consumer profiles and to think about how to create messages that resonate with each. Buyer personas are one such method. Marketing automation also helps identify the most effective content pieces and where gaps might require additional content.

Advertising Copy for Job Titles

If you target CEOs, do you have a real buyer persona for that CEO? Perhaps you will develop one. You can combine this with generalized messages that fit what you know CEOs generally care about. The same goes for CMOs and CFOs. Here are some examples:

- To CEOs: "We help you boost your ROI."
- To CMOs: "We help you measure and prove the effectiveness of your marketing."
- To CFOs: "We help you reduce your costs."
- To purchasers: "We help you make the right purchasing decision and save money."
- To software users: "Our tools are easy to learn, highly effective, and we have live chat help available online."

This information will already be part of good personas, but if you're still developing your personas, the job title shortcut can be used temporarily.

Industry-Specific Advertising

Specific terminology is key. If you show ads to healthcare executives, do you think they'll pay more attention to one that mentions healthcare or one that doesn't? Specificity precipitates responses. You want them to say to themselves, "Oh, that's for me. This company is helpful to my industry."

And if you understand the concerns of someone in an industry, be sure to mention them! For example, which job title in a healthcare company cares most about the word HIPPA? The COO? Legal? Mention it to them. Most job roles correspond to specific fears or worries—it's their job to pay attention to certain problem areas. They have to know everything about those topics to prevent disaster. Therefore, if your ad mentions that kind of key jargon, they have to at least look at the ad.

How to Get Better Ideas

Better advertising performance comes from better ideas. As we've discussed, segmentation and personalization are key, but without creativity and inspiration, your competitors will outperform you.

You need a combination of analytics and creativity. Take it from me—I spent several years championing process and analytics because they created great AdWords ROI. I was aware of another breed of advertising professional that preferred "The Big Idea"—a big TV commercial concept or a viral video. However, to me, if it didn't achieve business results according to your analytics, it was pointless. It seemed that those who were more creatively focused dismissed analytics, ROI, and optimization. I've learned, though, through social marketing, that inspiration is indispensible. Advertising success has always been determined by unique ideas. Search advertising certainly can perform very well with a minimum of personalization and creativity, but social advertising does not. Those funny Old Spice ads from 2010 that went from TV to viral video are a great example of twenty-first century hybrid success—profitable creativity that went viral socially—because they led to an increase of $3.5 million in revenue.

So how do you get better ideas? This section focuses on some processes for generating better images, ad copy, headlines, and landing pages.

Image Ideas

Images for self-serve LinkedIn ads are challenging. They're only 50×50 pixels. So small! You might zoom in on one part of a larger image. You'll need high contrast, or people won't be able to tell what your image is. To get more ideas, try the Google Image search and choose images that are exactly 50×50. If you don't see that option, look in the left column and scroll down until you see sizes, click Exactly..., type in the dimensions, and click Search. Now you can try a number of searches in your niche to see what kinds of images exist at this size. The idea is not to steal anyone's images, but to use Google Images as a brainstorming tool.

The first thing that becomes clear from perusing Google Images is that logos, flags, and faces make sense at that size. You can also symbolize many concepts, such as money with a dollar sign or whatever currency you're using. Or you can take the icon approach—simple and highly symbolic—because icons can fit into that small space and are clearly identifiable. What concepts are you selling that you can turn into symbols or icons? What about road signs such as stop, yield, slow, merge, or go? How about a fork in the road to symbolize making a decision?

With symbols, though, don't assume people will understand. People may rush visually over the ad and not make the connection. Use your headline and copy to tie the whole idea together.

Headline Ideas

The headline allows just 25 characters, or room for about four words. That's not a lot of space, so you've got to make it count. Here are some ideas on how to get the most out of your headlines:

- **Call out the audience.** For example, my headline, if I'm targeting the CEO job title, might be "Hey, CEOs!" This gets the attention of the people I'm targeting, which is the first order of the day.
- **Summarize what your company is.** If I'm advertising the social media content insight system InfiniGraph, I might use the headline "Social Intelligence Now."
- **Talk about how the audience will benefit.** Why should they care? Using the previous example, I could target agencies or new business directors by saying, "Win Your Next Big Pitch," and then use the description (body copy) to explain how InfiniGraph helps them stand out from the competition and get more business.
- **Summarize the content you're promoting.** If you're trying to get more people to see your new content marketing video, PDF, or info-graphic, tease them! For example, "Weird Infographic."
- **Use a keyword.** This isn't Google AdWords, but if you know your audience well enough, then you know the critical words that get their attention (such as HIPPA, JACHO, NACHO, profits, ROI, or risk). You should test using those words in your headline.

Both the headline and the image play a key role in grabbing attention. These self-serve ads aren't very big, so you can't ignore the need to be interesting. If your CTR is low, you might not be grabbing attention effectively. If you can get attention and clicks by conveying benefits and why prospects should click, then you've succeeded. Ultimately, you want good customers, but you can't get there without grabbing attention and getting a click. That's a lot to achieve with a 25-character headline, 50×50 image, and 75-character description, so brainstorm and test as much as you can.

Ad Copy (Description) Ideas

The description (body copy) under the headline allows only 75 characters. That's space for just 10 or 11 words, on average. Your job here is to take up where your headline left off and complete the job of the ad. Here are the things you want your ad to do overall, some of which the headline may or may not have taken care of:

- **Verify relevance.** When people glance past ads, they wonder, "Is this ad really for me? Should I pay attention to it? Or is it another example of a website showing me the wrong ad?" This goes back to calling out the audience by job title, geography, age, or other targeting factors, or mentioning those keywords or benefits your target audience cares about most.

- **Grab attention.** Sometimes calling out the audience isn't enough to put that sparkle of excitement in their eye. Can you be different somehow? Can you use a weird word or idea that doesn't hurt your brand's image?

- **Make them care.** As a potential customer, I want to know how you're going to help me, and how much. How are you going to make my life or work better? This is where you mention your company's benefits to the target customer. You can also use information from personas here, and stimulate their emotions appropriately. (Is this target audience fear motivated? If so, mention the thing they're afraid of.)

- **Get them to click.** Sometimes raising their curiosity or mentioning benefits is enough to get you a good CTR. Other times, you need to actually tell people what to do: "Click now to...." Tell them why to click, if you have the space. This technique is so effective that Google AdWords banned it many years ago, but Facebook and LinkedIn still allow you to use it.

Again, 75 characters isn't much space, so you may only be able to use one or two of these ideas per ad. This is another reason for creating at least four to five ads per campaign. You'll find out which of the previous tactics works best for that audience.

Segmented Landing Pages

Once your audience clicks the ad—which was written so specifically and effectively—are you sending them to a landing page that continues to affirm those ideas and get them to take action? Or are you sending them to the home page, which may create a disconnect between the ad and where they are now? Is it obvious to these people now what to do next?

One of the biggest mistakes I see companies make in online marketing is not imagining every step of the process their customers are going through. At every step, there's a chance people could drop out, leave, and go do something else. As your customer proceeds from advertisement to website into the lead and sales process, is their experience more like a waterslide or an obstacle course? You'll get more customers if it's as easy as a waterside.

Supplementing with Facebook and AdWords Ads

Some companies might get everything they need out of LinkedIn, but most will want more clicks as well as the branding and credibility that comes from "being everywhere." I recommend that most companies consider diversifying their advertising across LinkedIn, Google, Facebook, and Twitter.

As you saw at the beginning of the chapter, each advertising platform has strengths and weaknesses. You may get the targeting you want with LinkedIn ads but not the volume. You might get higher volume but less qualified leads from Facebook ads. And you can get buying-intent-indicative leads from Google search ads.

Lastly, be sure to test Google's remarketing ads. You set a cookie on your website so that anyone who has been to your site will see these display ads as they surf the Web. You don't want them to forget about you. Because many companies have longer sales cycles, and not every prospect becomes a lead right away, this gives you the chance to remind people to come back and make a decision. You already paid to raise their awareness of you, and they wouldn't have clicked if they weren't at least a little bit curious. If you can get them to click again on remarketing, there's a good chance their original interest has grown, and this time they may contact you and become a lead. The simple way to figure out if you should use remarketing is ask yourself, "Do I want another chance to speak to the people who've already been to my website?" In most cases, the answer is yes.

Endnotes

1. "Nothing useful about these buyer personas," Adele Revella, BuyerPersona Institute Blog, April 6, 2011. http://www.buyerpersona.com/2011/04/nothing-useful-about-these-buyer-personas.html

2. "Marketing Research Chart: Top Tactics in Developing Buyer Personae," Marketing Sherpa, March 6, 2012. http://www.marketingsherpa.com/article.php?ident=32126

11

Best Practices: Traditional and Modern Sales

Salespeople are critical to most businesses. It's the rare business that thrives on marketing alone (think Amazon. com) and doesn't require any salespeople. Even in the case of Amazon, CEO Jeff Bezos had to sell the viability of his business to investors, Wall Street, and the media. It's worth $25 billion now, but Amazon was not profitable for 6 years.[1] Telling everyone "don't stop believing" (think Journey) took some serious salesmanship. And it turned out he was right. But most businesses still require salespeople, either as customer service in retail stores or as expert consultants who help businesses purchase multimillion-dollar solutions.

This chapter summarizes traditional sales and how or if certain aspects have been changed by the Internet and LinkedIn. It seems the percentage of companies using the newer approach—combining LinkedIn and other Internet lead sources with lead nurturing, marketing automation, and sales force automation—is small.

These companies may exemplify what more companies will adopt, but I don't want to make any assumptions. To get a broader sense of the sales landscape and its history, I spoke with salespeople with multiple decades of experience via phone and LinkedIn. They gave me their perspectives on what works best now in sales, how that's different than it was in the past, and how it's the same. I also profiled companies that are improving their lead quality for salespeople. It seemed appropriate to this book's topic to speak to people on LinkedIn. I was impressed by how many salespeople with more than 20 years of experience were available and responded. The salespeople on LinkedIn these days are not just newbies to sales. You'll find these veterans' perspectives throughout this chapter.

Sales All-Time Best Practices

What is sales all about, and what aspects of it are timeless? Despite all the technological improvements, some things have not changed:

- **You still have to talk to people.** Marketing never completely replaces the need for human contact at some stage of some purchases. Sure, you can buy a book or a candy bar without talking to an expert. But would you buy a Ferrari from a robot salesperson? Would you invest $5 million of your company's money in a business solution after simply reading a website and a PDF?

  One salesperson I interviewed was Patrick K. Hollister, a B2B sales professional in San Francisco, California. Patrick is Regional Sales Manager at Panasonic Electronic Components. He has 21 years experience in sales and marketing, 16 years of those in sales specifically, and 15 years of sales management experience. He told me, "People still buy from people they like. Companies who've outsourced their sales team and call centers are finding that out on a daily basis." This quote illustrates that relationships are also still important. Buyers want to be able to ask questions and get personalized answers.

- **You still have to get purchasers to make a decision to buy.** Even when people think everything looks right and that making the purchase is the right decision, they still want to hear that you think it's the right decision, too. They want to hear the benefits again and hear your positivity when they make that final decision. Reassurance is a factor. As Alex Baldwin famously put it in the classic dark film about salespeople *Glengarry Glen Ross*: "Mitch and Murray paid good money for these leads.... The leads are weak? *You're* weak.... Only one thing counts: Get them to sign on the line, which is dotted."[2]

- **You have to know your customers.** Just as in good marketing, you have to get to know the buyer or you can't answer their questions,

convince them, or reassure them. People want to be seen and understood. The psychological needs of human buyers have not disappeared
with the advent of computers or the Internet.

The History of Sales

In earliest history, selling was difficult, because travel was on foot, by sea, or by
animal. Ecological and geographic barriers often prevented trade between certain
regions. First there was barter, then there was money. Marketplaces grew up in
certain cities.

In America, we've seen Yankee Peddlers, gypsies, snake oil salesmen, door-to-door
salesmen, telemarketers, and email spammers. There can be a fine line between
our Horatio Alger–istic *Pursuit of Happyness* sales archetype (good guys diligently
working their way up from nothing) and the lying con men of *Boiler Room*.

It's funny that so many of history's salesperson types are disliked for being aggressive. I'm sure that not every salesperson was this way, but the archetype is someone who does something *to* buyers, rather than works *with* them to find the right
solution.

Types of Sales

There are more than one kind of sales, and this book is concerned with a very specific type of sales.

Inside Sales Versus Outside Sales

Outside sales (or field sales) involves travel, visits to an office, golf outings, din-
ing at restaurants, and other in-person activities. Inside salespeople sell with the
phone or Web without traveling to see customers and prospects in person, and
they may play a support role for the outside salespeople. This book doesn't distinguish between the importance of the two. Once you get leads from LinkedIn and
other sources, if outside sales visits are required, so be it. However, many expensive
services and products are sold these days via conference calls and web demos. Your
company might not even have outside sales—it might use LinkedIn to get leads
and then inside sales closes the deal.

Complex Sales

Complex sales is an interesting term because there's no one definition everyone
agrees on. Complex sales involve the following:

- Multiple decision makers
- Multiple phases of discovering customer needs
- Difficulty defining the needs and constraints of each stakeholder (and sometimes conflicts between them) on the buyer side
- Extensive purchasing authorizations
- Money coming from multiple sources
- Customization of the solution and pricing required by the salesperson

Sound familiar? Many B2B sales that start with LinkedIn are complex sales. Complex sales have longer sales cycles (the time it takes from becoming aware of a need or solution until the actual purchase and implementation). Complex sales can take many months not only to close (sign) but also to launch (start the service).[3] They can be expensive. What's the solution? Marketing via LinkedIn Groups and your website, plus lead nurturing via email, can help prepare prospects so that the sales process is a quicker, smoother, and more profitable.

When you have a long sales cycle, marketing can indirectly keep it moving. Your prospects are busy people, too; the ball may be in their court. All action may have halted. Seeing marketing pieces on LinkedIn that reaffirm your company's value can prod the prospect to take the next step. Lead-nurturing automation can send specific emails to prospects at specific phases of their buying process.

Part of the complex sales process is mapping out who the stakeholders are, and the role and persona of each. This map of buyers guides salespeople, marketers, and advertisers. *The New Strategic Selling*, one of the most important sales books of the last two decades, delineated these types of buyers.[4] They include the following:

- The User Buyer, who will be involved in using your solution day-to-day
- The Economic Buyer, who makes the final decision on purchasing
- The Technical Buyer, who uses a set of specifications to screen vendors like you and asks difficult questions to ensure your solution fits their needs
- The Coach, who is a friendly contact inside the company you're selling to, who wants the sale to succeed, helps the salesperson navigate though the company, and validates the salesperson in front of others

When starting to sell into a target company, the salesperson's first contact could be with any of the preceding types of buyers. That buyer might first see an advertisement or marketing piece on LinkedIn, and then contact the salesperson. Or they might serendipitously meet the salesperson at an event.

Those involved in LinkedIn advertising and marketing can tailor their approach to prepare these buyers ahead of time. You can think about what you want to say to each person. For example, the "technical" type of buyer may be more interested in checking items off a list to make sure your solution fits their needs, whereas the user buyer wants to know how easy your solution will be to work with on a daily basis. That's why sales feedback to advertising and marketing is so important. If sales can provide sufficiently detailed information about buyers, such as their types, their personas, their concerns, and job titles, then advertising and marketing can create much more relevant and powerful ads and marketing pieces. Marketing can create an infographic that addresses technical buyers' typical questions, and then you can distribute that via LinkedIn Groups, put it on your website, integrate it into your marketing automation, and draw people to it with LinkedIn ads.

LinkedIn's biggest strength for B2B business is lead generation via advertising and marketing. Salespeople might find leads with LinkedIn or just contact qualified leads that originally came from LinkedIn. "Because of social media," says Bay Area marketer Julia Stege, "I have increased my number of leads. These leads are of a superior quality because they are already familiar with my essence and my approach due to my exposure online. In terms of how the actual sales process goes once we talk, I still do sales calls over the phone and all goes similarly as before."

Consultative Sales

Many sales situations require you to adopt the position of expert and trusted consultant. You must act like a consultant before your can "sell." You come alongside the buyer, uncover their needs, and help them figure out the best solution. This is a fairly common description of B2B marketing and sales. You explain the value of the services and products your company offers, and perhaps customize a solution before selling it. That's why it's so important that salespeople are as expert in both the offering *and* the prospect as the marketer who creates an infographic and delivers it on LinkedIn. Salespeople need to be as much of an expert on customers as the LinkedIn advertiser who sees words and phrases prospects respond to or don't.

The opposite of a consultative sales is transactional sales, where the buyers usually do their own research, and by the time they talk to a salesperson, they may be primarily concerned with price. They don't want consultation. They are "just looking." Transactional buyers want to find a good price and be done with it. They may not plan to buy anything from you in the future. But, the consultative buyers want help and advice, especially if they're looking for a long-term relationship with multiple purchases.

As I was told by 26-year sales and marketing pro, Babette Ten Haken, "Buyers can find anything they want to online based on information, high-level drilldown research, social media presence, and branding. By the time they contact sellers, the buyer has already made their buying decision, and now it's down to a beauty contest, if you are lucky. Salespeople can no longer churn and burn through leads lists, hoping to get lucky. You have to do your homework, research companies, determine trigger events which may tip the scales in terms of your company, and enter the buying cycle at the beginning of the business development process. Waiting around to sell when you either are called upon or can get an appointment—and then determining pain points—has gone the way of the dinosaur." This illustrates the importance of quality content marketing and a robust LinkedIn presence.

Most complex sales are consultative because the customization involved requires human ingenuity. The needs-discovery process requires skillful questioning. In my work, I often recommend an entire Internet marketing strategy. Or, depending on the situation, I might convince a prospect, even though they came to me about Facebook ads, that LinkedIn ads or AdWords ads would better reach their audience and achieve their goals. Creating a comprehensive strategy, or knowing a service is the wrong one for them, requires all my 12 years of experience in numerous marketing and advertising channels, consulting with businesses, the feedback they've given me, the successes and failures I've seen, and the missing gaps I've encountered. That's the human ingenuity sales needs to deal with leads from LinkedIn.

Even a good salesperson at Best Buy with just 3 months of training will listen to your needs and help you decide which computer is the best fit. Both require consultation—questioning and advising. The consultative-versus-transactional distinction is not about whether the customer cares about price, but whether expertise and relationship are required for salespeople to help them.

The Internet has made more sales more transactional, thus reducing the need for salespeople, as Babette alluded to previously. Amazon.com is the obvious example. Imagine how many salespeople would be needed to help sell all those books in person—or all the shoes that Zappos sells online. Now you just buy books online without help. Amazon has automated the process of saying, "Hey, if you like that, you might also like this." You can buy two sizes of shoes from Zappos and send back, at their cost, the pair that doesn't fit. Even so, consultative sales will never go away. As long as we have complicated buying situations and major purchases where the wrong buying decision can end someone's job, we'll have salespeople. But because transactional sales are being automated, the salesperson's role is shifting toward the consultative end.[5]

"Social media will continue to help sales evolve from mere pursuit, in terms of cold calling and mass emailing, to positioning," says James Gingerich, who is Senior Partner Account Manager at Sybase and has 27 years experience in sales. "Through a combination of LinkedIn, Twitter, Google+, Facebook, and even YouTube, the clarity and consistency of one's message will draw higher quality prospects to you. In the Internet age, a prospector will now have to research where his prospects hang out and then apply creativity to draw their attention to the real value of his message. Selling will change from something you do *to* someone and become more of a process you go through *with* someone after they have already indicated through social media that they are in fact a prospect." This means that although your lead may come from LinkedIn, some of the persuasion may have come from sales previously via automated emails that drip out the appropriate content marketing to better qualify and condition that prospect before sales even talks to them.

Patrick K. Hollister is Regional Sales Manager at Panasonic Electronic Components and has 21 years experience in sales and marketing. He said, "The Internet has made the job easier, but you are only as good as the sales tools that are created for you. I still love building relationships and driving or flying to customers. This part has not really changed. Salesforce has made it easier for managers to manage the funnel and staff. LinkedIn has made business development less difficult. Skype is not used at all, and my cell phone bill is at an all-time high." A lot of the people I know love Skype, but Patrick is indicating that many of the buyers he talks to are not using it. It's always good to approach people with a communication method they're comfortable and familiar with—or at least give them the option. LinkedIn can plug into any part of that, and certainly if the prospect is an avid LinkedIn user, the salesperson should use LinkedIn messages to communicate with them more. But if the prospect hardly ever uses LinkedIn and consistently asks the salesperson for phone calls, it doesn't make sense to push LinkedIn on them.

The Shift to Inbound Marketing

There has been a shift from interruptive (outbound) to permission-based (inbound) marketing. The Internet has proven to be powerful in several phases of the sales process. Many companies have attracted sales and leads through "inbound" Internet marketing such as LinkedIn, Facebook, Twitter, Pinterest, Google, and YouTube. Search engine optimization creates better search engine rankings for companies on the keywords that fit the services and products they offer. Some companies rely entirely on these inbound strategies, and they can create attractive margins.

As William T. Cooper, CEO of ChristiaNet (an Internet marketing company specializing in Christian advertising) told me, "Sales have gone from in-person to inbound. In the past 10 years, we have met in person less than one client in a hundred for fairly high ticket Internet marketing services."

Some marketers make a distinction between paid, earned, and owned media. Paid media requires a cash outlay, as in LinkedIn advertising. Earned media can be the journalistic coverage that comes from PR, or leads you earn from the quality of the content marketing you distribute in LinkedIn Groups. Owned media refers to direct mail lists or email lists where you "own" the list. We might put Facebook fans and LinkedIn company followers under a new category called "rented media," especially given Facebook's recent moves to charge big companies to guarantee the visibility of their posts to their own fans. Search equity, in the form of stable keyword rankings, also falls somewhere between earned and owned, because the rankings often come from the links other sites create based on the value of your content marketing. All of these can play a part in inbound marketing, and the margins come from the strategies with one-time investments of cash or labor that lead to long-term web traffic.

At the same time, many interruptive outbound opportunities have been blocked. The national Do Not Call list seeks to combat telemarketing, which was once a source of big business for some companies. Answering machines made it possible for people to screen calls, and now most cell phones feature caller ID, and people don't have to answer calls from unknown callers. What's more, these aggressive and interruptive tactics can carry a scarlet-letter perception that diminishes people's esteem for the brand. Even the most relevant forms of advertising such as the Google AdWords search network are viewed by some with disdain.

All of these new opportunities and obstacles have created a shift toward inbound marketing, which is described in detail in the next chapter. MarketingSherpa's "2012 B2B Benchmark Report" found that the biggest growth areas were in inbound tactics and that planned budget cuts were more severe for interruptive tactics.[6] For example, the biggest planned growth areas were website optimization, social media, and webinars. Those being cut by the most companies were print advertising, tradeshows, and direct mail. By no means do companies need to cease all outbound/interruptive activities—in fact, you might call Google AdWords an interruptive marketing method, and it's effective and rising in popularity—but not adopting new and proven inbound marketing processes such as LinkedIn and content marketing would be irresponsible and foolhardy.

What this means to the salesperson is that leads can come from anywhere, and these leads come in all different shapes and sizes. Some are more qualified than others, so without clear qualification criteria and effective lead nurturing, salespeople will waste time and get frustrated. If a LinkedIn ad is too interesting and doesn't tell the whole truth, it might generate tons of low-quality leads for salespeople to sort through. Certainly, your LinkedIn ads person should only be doing that if your lead-nurturing and lead-scoring processes are strong. But overall, these tools create new opportunities for more leads and more qualified prospects.

This new world of inbound and social marketing also means you can use social media to track prospects and customers throughout their career. No longer does a job change mean that sales has lost a customer or prospect. LinkedIn tells you they switched companies, and that even gives you an excuse to message them and strike up a new conversation that might lead to an opportunity! You can map the prospect's organization more quickly and accurately with LinkedIn. If that's not enough and you love org charts, the website TheOfficialBoard will blow your mind. It launched in 2009 and now contains the org charts for 30,000 of the world's largest corporations—and it's up to date. I'm looking at it right now and it says 50,615 contacts have been updated, added, or deleted in the last 10 weeks. You can take these people from TheOfficialBoard or LinkedIn and get their phone numbers from Jigsaw. What more do you need? Imagine showing these tools to a salesperson from 1985–their brain would explode.

Sales management has also developed best practices.[7] Here are some best practices that have a big impact on individual salespeople's effectiveness but are beyond the scope of this book (definitely use other resources to check these off your list):

- Aligning sales goals with organizational goals.
- Establishing strong leadership.
- Maintaining sales knowledge, sharing in effective meetings. What are sales, marketing, and advertising learning about prospects? How can knowledge from one department make the others more effective?
- Using customer relationship management and sales force automation tools. (How these fit into your LinkedIn advertising, marketing, and sales processes are touched on in this book, but you'll probably need additional training and help from those vendors.)

But others' best practices can be applied when you do prospecting and sales with LinkedIn. The following can all improve your results:

- **Define your prospect qualification criteria.** Work with marketing and sales to make sure everyone's on the same page about these.
- **Investigate businesses before contacting them.** Use TheOfficialBoard, their company's LinkedIn page, Wikipedia, and company profile sites such as Hoovers, Dun & Bradstreet, and The Vault.
- **Research the industry.** Check out IBISWorld and FirstResearch.
- **Network with new prospects.** See Chapter 5 for marketers and see Chapter 13 for salespeople.
- **Address customer needs in content marketing.** When you help marketing better understand the prospects you speak to, they can distribute content on LinkedIn and other places to help you address concerns and persuade prospects before you ever talk to them.

- **Refine presentations based on marketing automation data.**
  Marketing will discover how people respond to content marketing and
  can give you information that might help you better tailor your sales
  conversations.

You learn more about specific ways to get better results through teamwork in
Chapter 14.

Best Practices in Twenty-first Century Sales

The role of sales professionals has shifted toward consultative and complex sales.
And sources such as LinkedIn continue to offer more and more advances that
increase the number and quality of leads that sales can service. So what characterizes the best sales professionals and sales organizations today? What are the best
practices? Sales, as a discipline, is replete with myth and anecdote, so I was happy
to discover a "Good To Great" style survey of sales best practices from the company Miller Heiman.

Miller Heiman, founded by and based on the work of two strategic selling greats,
has conducted an annual Sales Best Practices study since 2003. They survey more
than 1,000 salespeople across companies and then compare the answers of those
in the top 5%—10% best performing organizations to see what stands out. Their
findings in the last couple years are similar. Here, from their 2012 study of 1,227
respondents, are the 12 key best practices of the better performing salespeople and
sales organizations. To clarify who is who, I've rewritten the list to the sales professional. If you're a best practices sales organization, then...

- Your value proposition to customers is clear, and you assume that your
  customer knows their wants and needs better than your organization
  does.
- You have a standardized process for qualifying opportunities.
- You are highly effective at allocating the right resource to pursue large
  deals.
- You clearly understand your customers' issues before proposing a
  solution.
- You collaborate across departments to manage key/strategic accounts
  (the customers with the highest value to your organization).
- Your top executives have relationships with your strategic accounts,
  and you're always thinking about how your customers perceive you.
- You have a highly effective process for ramping new hires up to
  full productivity (new hires receive support and coaching by sales
  managers).

- When your organization loses a high-performing salesperson, your executives understand why. Also, the top motivator in such decisions is not always pay.

- Your sales performance metrics are aligned with your business objectives.

- Your sales management team is highly confident in the data available from your CRM. That system is an effective tool in the sales process, and the discipline of use among your salespeople is high.

- You leverage the best practices of your top performing salespeople to improve everyone else. You make top performers mentors if they like that role, and you get them to document what they do that makes them so effective.

- Your sales force spends enough time with customers to truly know them.[8]

These were from the 2012 survey. Miller Heiman's 2011 survey also found that the best organizations used social media to identify decision makers. Of the most effective sales organizations, 52% used social media in this way (versus 15% of the less effective companies).[9] If this doesn't argue for LinkedIn as a sales research tool, I don't know what would!

In 2006, the survey found that top salespeople are 30% more likely to rely on a well-defined approach to determining which clients they should target. These top salespeople are more curious, not more pushy, than less effective salespeople. They enjoy learning, both to improve themselves and to better understand their customers. They are persistent, but they don't badger.[10]

Miller Heiman's best practices for getting big deals revealed a four-step process:

1. **Research.** Do your homework up front to understand the customer's business, which you can do via LinkedIn, Hoovers, the target's corporate blog, and other resources mentioned earlier.

2. **Reach.** Reach the people in the target company who can actually buy or influence the buying of your solution. Again, LinkedIn can help with this, as can Jigsaw.

3. **Pinpoint.** Pinpoint the source of power. This means finding the economic buyer. This person may not be the first person you talk to, but until they are involved, you aren't close to a deal.

4. **Team up.** Work with a "friendly" at the target company; this is the coach type referred to previously when mapping stakeholders. This person can brief you on the company's inner workings. This person

wants your solution and finds you to be credible. This person can also make you look smart to the other buyers.[11]

These solid sales practices are confirmed and expanded by insights from other surveys and echoed by LinkedIn professionals. AchieveGlobal, a workforce development and training company (which has 560 employees on LinkedIn), released a 44-page report in 2011 called "A Survey of Sales Effectiveness: Global Research on What Drives Sales Success."[12] Here are some of the most important revelations from that study:

- Many respondents indicated similar problems: Their sales organization didn't use metrics and dashboards effectively, salespeople weren't following the sales process, and their sales force automation tools weren't making selling easier. The most effective salespeople worked in organizations that didn't have these three issues. This highlights the critical role of sales managers and executives in providing the most effective training and tools. Incentives for sticking to the sales process might increase effectiveness.

- Outside field salespeople identified different problem areas than sales managers and inside salespeople did. Outside sales may need more support or a different type of support than they're currently receiving.

- Salespeople who received more coaching and training also closed bigger deals. Also, regardless of whether the salesperson is a high or low performer, there is a strong correlation between performance and coaching and training. More coaching and training meant increased sales revenue and deal size, whereas less coaching and training meant decreased revenues. Make sure Sales is trained on all the techniques mentioned in this book, as well as other sales best practices outside of social media.

- Regardless of their success, sales professionals indicated they did best and were most confident with establishing relationships with new prospects, but had the most trouble with a preceding phase: developing new business. Fortunately, LinkedIn and inbound marketing fill this gap.

The difference in opinion between highest and lowest performing salespeople is fascinating when these groups were asked, "What factors most contribute to your success?" The results are organized for comparison purposes in Table 11.1.

Table 11.1 What Tasks Do Top Sales Performers Emphasize?

Highest Performing and Best Trained Salespeople Success Contributors	Lowest Performing and Least Trained Salespeople's Success Contributors
Setting goals	Building a network of contacts
Using social media for networking and prospecting	Identifying all stakeholders involved with an account
Prospecting continuously to keep the pipeline full (which agrees with Miller Heiman's prioritizing the top of the funnel over the middle)	Aggressively pursuing leads
Having an in-depth knowledge of the customer's industry	Configuring the solution to meet the client's needs
Uncovering client needs	Crafting agreements that balance the needs of the customer and the selling organization
Requesting client feedback	Acting as the customer's advocate and taking responsibility for meeting their needs
Creating a call strategy before meeting the customer	
Articulating a business case that shows how a solution will financially benefit the client	
Communicating solutions through engaging presentations and proposals	
Effectively using closing skills to gain commitment	
Maintaining high ethical standards	

Top sales performers focus on strategy and process. They look for new prospects, listen, understand, and plan. Lesser performing salespeople are focused on tactics that certainly play a part in successful sales, but perhaps should not be the highest priorities. This is an important point: Don't get lost in the details of something like social media to the extent that you miss bigger strategic best practices. For example, a low performing salesperson might InMail prospects impersonally and repeatedly, whereas the higher performing salesperson would be more strategic about what to InMail, when to InMail it, and how their messages fit into the prospect's needs.

Note that use of social media for leads is one of the top performers' key success contributors. Says Chicago sales trainer Sarah Houston, "Social media is a great tool because it now allows people to put a name with a face, and it publicizes a person's credentials. It also expands the network of people that you can access on a massive level. It also allows access to people that may not necessarily be in your geographic area." As Sarah indicates, even the first time you connect with a prospect, LinkedIn conveys your credibility quicker than was possible before.

Judy Freeman, a D.C. professional with 20 years of sales experience, said, · "LinkedIn is an excellent tool to connect with colleagues, customers, and networking associates. It is helpful for getting background information on people who I don't know and finding out where former associates are today. So, LinkedIn is a research tool for me. I use Skype instead of phone meetings with partners and clients. For me, it enhances the communication because I can see them and read their body language. Specifically, I can tell if they are 'thinking' or 'perplexed.' This helps me to clarify and pace our conversation." You'll notice that Skype works for some salespeople and not others. This will vary by both industry and prospect. You might be selling to people in "high tech" who love using Skype, or you might be talking to someone who prefers the phone. Be sensitive to your industry and to each prospect's preferences.

How LinkedIn Changes Sales...or Doesn't

I've alluded to some of the ways LinkedIn can help salespeople with some of the activities most critical to their success. However, it's best to let salespeople put it in their own words. As I've mentioned, I dialogued with dozens of sales professionals on LinkedIn about how the Internet and LinkedIn specifically have altered or improved their approach, as well as what things have not changed about sales. Here are some of the questions and answers that resulted from that dialogue (edited for spelling and grammar).

Why Is Social Media Valuable to Sales?

"What social media did is open flood gates of leads, if used properly. And if you are a salesperson like I am, you have to work these leads to change them to actual sales. Social media just increased the canvas of the painting around us. Even if you Skype them by video, you still have to have that personal touch and meet them face-to-face, especially when they are local. I don't think that the benefits of face-to-face will ever change or be replaced no matter how much we are sophisticated in using our social media tools."

—Sahar Andrade, VP of Technology and SMM at National Association of African Americans in HR.

"Your focus should be on your impression count. How many impressions do you have in your marketplace? They create the top of mind awareness of who you are and what you offer. Social networks offer the opportunity to build your brand and create a reputation that helps create the referrals, both business and personal, that will drive you forward. Think of it as mass marketing, one on one. Make every word, headshot, and thought count as if it were your 'last lasting impression.'"

—Michael B. Manthey of 50 Below Sales & Marketing in Duluth, Minnesota, 25 years sales experience.

How Do You Prospect on LinkedIn?

"I think that LinkedIn Signal is a good tool to use for business prospecting. With Signal, I have learned to listen to the conversations that have some relevance to my business interest. You may join these conversations, ask questions, and contribute your knowledge. By participating in the just-mentioned activities, you just might be able to answer some real business needs in relation to what your company provides. Finally, link to Twitter from your LinkedIn business profile. If you are active on Twitter, a business prospect may desire to view your business summary on your LinkedIn account. Inviting a Twitter prospect to view your business profile on LinkedIn invites transparency and can add legitimacy and trust to your business endeavors."

—Edward Jamison Jr., Business-to-Business Sales/Territory Manager with United Health in Greenville, South Carolina.

What Hasn't Changed with LinkedIn and the Internet?

"I have yet to see a sales model—a successful one, that is—not requiring the salesperson to call on the telephone. Social media has, however, provided two important elements to the sales model that must be taken into account. The first element is that social media provides a safe, commitment-less environment for the prospect to see who the salesperson is and also what the product/service is. It is unprecedented and supplies the prospect with a massive amount of information. The danger for the salesperson is that there may be *too* much information, and it tones down the "discovery" connection for the prospect. The amount of information should be an open discussion between marketing and sales. (Isn't it always?) The second is that it provides the salesperson an opportunity to truly differentiate him or herself from the competition. Regardless of the product or service, a blog will give the prospect the chance to see the salesperson as a reference and an authority. Twitter and Facebook can also be used in this manner. Ultimately, it will lead to sales based on the salesperson and not the product or service. It provides many more leads, but there have always been great lead sources. The true value of the platform is, and always will be, dependent on the salesperson."

—Nery Leal, 25 years in sales, now a SMB sales consultant in Connecticut.

"It's great in that it broadens a person's connectivity. It still does require conversations and meetings. People buy from people and not from companies or brands. Years ago many people speculated that social media would wipe out the need for people to actually meet. Ultimately what I see is that Director-level-and-under people are using social media while executives are still focused on people, partners, and process. That's not a bad thing, and I don't believe that will ever change because they understand that it takes collaboration to achieve top- and bottom-line priorities. Collaboration can be facilitated by social media, but it stills comes down to people."

—Jason Croyle, an analyst who works with marketing and sales leadership at MECLABS.

How Do You Create Value and Differentiate Yourself on LinkedIn?

"With LinkedIn, as with life...find where you can bring benefit. Whether for a current client or not; be the one that shapes expectations, helps others, and is known as a thought leader."

—Michael B. Manthey, 25 years of sales experience, now a consultant in Minnesota.

What Do You Use for Prospecting on LinkedIn?

"Advanced People Search coupled with Groups and InMail should work fairly well, but you need to be careful that you are not being invasive."

—Jay Sigler, CEO at IT Assurance, 15 years in sales and entrepreneurship.

Endnotes

1. "The Institutional Yes: An Interview with Jeff Bezos by Julia Kirby and Thomas A. Stewart," Harvard Business Review, October 2007, http://hbr.org/2007/10/the-institutional-yes/ar/pr, and "Amazon Posts A Profit," *CNNMoney*, January 22, 2002, http://money.cnn.com/2002/01/22/technology/amazon/

2. Alec Baldwin speech (fictional, but a great composite) from the movie *Glengarry Glen Ross*, http://www.youtube.com/watch?v=zCf46yHIzSo

3. LinkedIn Answers discussion on the definition of "complex sale," http://www.linkedin.com/answers/marketing-sales/sales/ sales-techniques/MAR_SLS_STC/273705-5861039

4. Heiman, S. and D. Sanchez. *The New Strategic Selling.* New York: Warner Books, Inc., 1998

5. "Transactional vs. Consultative Selling: Knowing the Difference Makes All the Difference," John Tabita, January 29, 2012, SitePoint. com, http://www.sitepoint.com/transactional-vs-consultative-selling- knowing-the-difference-makes-all-the-difference/

6. "2012 B2B Marketing Benchmark Report," MarketingSherpa, August 2011, http://www.meclabs.com/training/publications/benchmark- report/2012-b2b-marketing/overview?9641

7. "Sales Process Mapping: Best Practices For Sales Management," The Sales Management Association, 2008, http://www.slideshare.net/ TheSalesMgtAssoc/sales-process-mapping-best-practices-for-sales- management-514222

8. "2012 Executive Summary of Miller Heiman Sales Best Practices Study," Miller Heiman, http://www.millerheiman.com/research_ center/sales_best_practices_study/index.html

9. "2011 Executive Summary of Miller Heiman Sales Best Practices Study," Miller Heiman, http://store.millerheiman.com/kc/abstract.aspx ?itemid=0000000000000737

10. "Seven Myths and Misperceptions About Top Performing Sales People," Miller Heiman, 2006

11. "The Art and Science of Big Deals: A Four-Part Strategy," Miller Heiman, 2006, http://store.millerheiman.com/kc/abstract.aspx?ite mid=0000000000000427

12. "A Survey of Sales Effectiveness," AchieveGlobal, 2011, http://www. achieveglobal.com/resources/files/AG__SurveyofSalesEffectiveness.pdf

12

Salespeople and Social Sales

If you're a salesperson in a company that uses inbound marketing and social media, should you just sit back and wait for the leads? Maybe. Or can you use social media to find leads and create new sales opportunities? Yes, you can!

There's a famous saying: "Dial for dollars." It's something sales managers used to say to encourage salespeople to make more cold calls. Pick up the phone and call someone who doesn't know you and doesn't care about what you offer. It's hard, but do it, because that's how you get the dollars. Well, unfortunately, that's not so true anymore. Telemarketing is much less effective than it used to be. In this chapter, we discuss why that is and how you can now use social media to "network for dollars" instead.

Less Interruption, More Discovery

There has been a huge shift from outbound marketing to inbound marketing. Outbound marketing is also called "interruption marketing" because it more aggressively invades the prospect's world. Inbound marketing is called "permission marketing" because it focuses more on being found and only giving information to people when they request it. Table 12.1 gives some common examples of outbound and inbound marketing.

Table 12.1   Common Examples of Outbound and Inbound Marketing

Outbound Marketing "Reach and Interruption"	Inbound Marketing "Findability and Permission"
Trade shows	Search engine optimization
Telemarketing	Search engine advertising
Print advertising	Social media
Direct mail	Opt-in email marketing
TV & radio advertising	

There has also been a shift in consumer perception. People are fed up with the dinner-time telemarketing calls. People bought answering machines and started screening their calls. There's a national "Do Not Call" list. Most people with smartphones use caller ID, and some people don't answer calls from unfamiliar numbers.

Using search engines has become commonplace. People know they can go online and find out where to get whatever they need: books, marketing, car repair, or haircuts. Today, many purchases begin with people looking for something online. That's the essence of inbound marketing: Set your company up to be found by consumers who want what you have. Less purchases come from interruptive marketing, and more from inbound marketing.

Neither type of marketing is good or bad. We need both. I recommend both to my clients. I use both to market my services.

Some people have gone too far toward inbound marketing. For example, I don't think we should put email spam in the same category as TV ads, but Wikipedia's editors do.[1] Some people have fallen so in love with inbound marketing, and so dislike asking for a sale, that they want to completely eliminate the sales department.

But demonize all interruption marketing at your peril, because it is sometimes welcome and effective. There are many products you'd never buy if you hadn't discovered them through an interruptive advertisement. Interruption has a place.

And so do salespeople who enjoy talking to qualified prospects and can take them through the sales process, close them, and secure the revenue for your company. Without interruptive marketing and salespeople, you'll miss out on a portion of your sales. Think of some prospects as "swing consumers"—not unlike "swing voters." Presidential elections can hinge on who gets the voters who aren't sure. The company who captures the prospects who aren't sure has an advantage over its competitors.

When you combine both inbound and outbound marketing, you take advantage of their complementary strengths. In Figure 12.1's sales funnel, both inbound (marketing) and outbound (advertising and sales) play necessary roles. Inbound marketing reduces the labor and time costs associated with the beginning of the funnel. Marketing automation services provide lead nurturing to make sure they're qualified (needy and ready) by the time they reach the sales department. Put your salespeople on the portion of the job they excel at. If they receive leads that are more qualified, they close a higher percentage of their sales, and subsequently, they are happier.

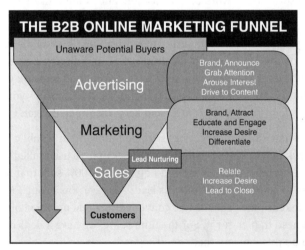

Figure 12.1 *A complete funnel showing how advertising, marketing, and sales functions can secure new customers. Advertising is outbound. What marketing does may be mostly inbound. After lead nurturing or scoring, the sales department can close the sale.*

What Is "Social Sales"?

What salespeople can do in the social media era is "network for dollars," or perform "Social Sales." Networking means building relationships, whether with someone the salesperson has found on their own or someone that came through an inbound lead-generation process.

There's a challenge in that the average business person is skeptical of strangers as well as too busy to talk to random people on the phone. Time is our most precious commodity in the twenty-first century. No one wants to get stuck with someone who's wasting their time.

Online interactions are easier to create. Your prospects know that social media interactions, even with strangers, take seconds. There's no commitment. It's not a big risk to their time. But people still have their guard up. If you start out too direct ("Hey, have you seen what our company offers?"), then you're leading with your chin, and they'll knock you out. The relationship won't develop. You might as well go back and do telemarketing with Dial America.

Here's what one project manager said about social networking compared to cold calling: "In general, I believe social networking is much more productive. But you must take care to build your reputation and not just use the social web as a sales farm. To be successful, you must establish your personal value by contributing real [quality] content. This then establishes a brand reputation for yourself and sales leads will follow. It takes work and dedication, and is not a short-term strategy."[2]

The importance of Social Sales differs for each organization. It may not help your company if your buyers are primarily price-driven or all your competitors are made aware of all RFPs (requests for proposal). But if discovering new clients and opportunities makes sense for you, Social Sales could increase your revenue. If price is not the primary factor in your niche, the relationships you create with prospects can help you get more sales and keep customers longer.

Han Mo of Teleperformance (China) said the following in a public LinkedIn Answer: "Back in late 2010, I required all salespeople to use LinkedIn to generate sales leads. After more than a year of doing it, I am 100% sure that this is the most effective way to generate qualified sales leads. To give you a rough number, 1 out of every 8 LinkedIn messages can be converted to a real qualified opportunity. Of course, you need to plan for it. For the time being, we have a dedicated LinkedIn specialist to do this job, and that's good so far."[3]

In some cases, salespeople do double-duty as account managers or customer service representatives. In that case, the relationship you build through "bonding" (that is, finding mutual interests and developing relationship; see Figure 12.2) helps prevent mistakes or service delays from becoming contract-ending events. A real relationship, because you talk more often, can also help you find more opportunities with the same clients.

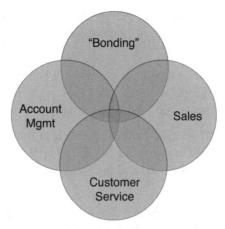

Figure 12.2 *Depending on your company organization, the same people doing sales may do account management and customer service. Or account managers may do upselling of existing customers. The bonding that happens in social media can enhance your effectiveness in these other roles.*

What Motivates Salespeople?

What motivates salespeople? One small poll of salespeople on LinkedIn found that regardless of gender, the top motivation was "compensation or incentives." The second was "making progress or winning." The other two choices, recognition and the thrill of the chase, were much less popular.[4]

In this section, we talk about how salespeople's motivation is affected by lead quality. We also look at which salespeople have the right kind of motivation to succeed at Social Sales.

Lead Quality Issues

When it comes to following up on leads, we want our salespeople to do their work, but we don't want them wasting their time on bad leads. We know that salespeople can blame the leads when they themselves are not doing a good job. However, let's assume that you've hired people who fall somewhere between competent and great; therefore, it's more likely that the quality of a lead is the issue.

I had an AdWords client at a used medical device company whose lead volume I had increased dramatically. They asked me to lower their ad spend so they could get fewer leads. I was shocked. However, they explained to me that their sales-people weren't really "working" the leads. They had so many leads coming in, the sales department was just looking for those who were going to buy right away. If they just took orders, they'd make a lot more money. They weren't being patient with the other leads.

This illustrates the tension between how many leads you have and how qualified they are. Because salespeople are usually paid more when they close more sales, they know that their time is best used on the most qualified leads.

Marketing Sherpa's 2011 B2B Summit reported that only 27% of B2B inquiries were sufficiently qualified to go to sales and that, overall, only 20% of B2B leads will buy, but 61% of companies send all their leads directly to sales.[5]

Marketing Sherpa's 2012 B2B Benchmark Report surveyed 1,745 B2B marketers, and found that 68% had not identified their sales and marketing funnel.[6] That means thinking about what a good lead is and how you might score leads (give them a grade for how qualified they are) and nurture them (staying in touch until they're qualified) before passing them off to sales. Lead nurturing requires an automated service (it's not cost-effective to have humans do it), and is beyond the scope of this book, but marketers should compare vendors such as Eloqua, Genoo, and Zoho to find one that fits their business. Alternatively, your version of lead nurturing may just be repeated marketing campaigns to your prospect base, and a CRM such as Salesforce can track those and score people based on whether they responded or not.

The sales and marketing departments should sit down and define what makes a good sales lead. Think about the customers who have bought from you, and how you help them. Here are some questions that should be asked:

- What does our target customer need?
- What corporate initiatives might cause them to look for our services?
- What information do we need in order to determine whether we should follow up on the lead? What questions need to be answered? What information is required from prospects?
- What are the job titles of buyers and of those who influence the purchasing decision?
- What does the ideal sales opportunity look like?
- What's the target customer's budget and timeframe for purchasing?

The answers to these questions will direct how marketing works and how you score leads.

LinkedIn Social Sales

Another factor in Social Sales is that not all salespeople are going to be excited about this kind of sales. An old sales adage is "ability * motivation = performance." Therefore, those among your sales force who love relationship building will excel at this. I wouldn't push every salesperson to do this sort of work. Also, because a learning curve is involved in social networking, sales networkers won't be as effective in the beginning. If a salesperson feels that the learning curve cuts too much into the sales that they might make spending their time elsewhere, they may abandon LinkedIn before they get results with it. They'll have to either believe there's a light at the end of the tunnel or feel so drawn to social media activity that their enjoyment offsets the time taken by the learning curve.

Here's what one Director of Sales said about investing time in LinkedIn: "I have been contacted several times over the past 12 months and increasingly see LinkedIn as a route to new business or targeting the people I really want to deal with. Finding the more I put in to LinkedIn as a sales resource, the more I get out. I try to spend at least 10 minutes a day looking for target companies, for people, and at who has been looking at my profile!"[7]

Endnotes

1. http://en.wikipedia.org/wiki/Interruption_marketing

2. Gary Gertz in a LinkedIn Answer: http://www.linkedin.com/answers/marketing-sales/sales/sales-techniques/MAR_SLS_STC/394092-2322797?searchIdx=1&sik=1325787350184&goback=%2E asr_1_1325787350184

3. "Salespeople: Have You Networked Your Way to New Leads, RFP's, and Sales with LinkedIn?" LinkedIn Answers, February 2012. http://www.linkedin.com/answers/marketing-sales/sales/lead-generation/MAR_SLS_LGN/964047-12218765

4. http://sales20network.com/blog/?p=1133

5. "2012 B2B Marketing Benchmark Report," MarketingSherpa, August 2011. http://www.meclabs.com/training/publications/benchmark-report/2012-b2b-marketing/overview?9641

6. http://www.slideshare.net/B2BLeadRoundtable/how-marketers-are-transforming-mounting-pressure-challenges-into-revenues

7. Chris J. Griffin of Westbrook International, U.K., in a LinkedIn Answer.

13

Social Sales Prospecting and Making Contact

For the Sales professional, LinkedIn has many benefits, both direct and indirect. Other parts of this book discuss how advertising and marketing people can bring in a higher volume of leads, as well as better qualified leads for Sales to follow up on. But LinkedIn is also a great source of information about the company you want to sell into, its structure, and its people.

Here are some of the ways LinkedIn can help you do Social Sales:

- *Find new potential customers by prospecting*

- *Warm up cold calls with introductions by people you're already connected to*

- *Discover which people from the target company are using LinkedIn*

- *Learn about people you might contact ahead of time so you can use that information to create rapport during the call*

- *Find Groups your prospects are in so you can get into the conversation and create commonalities*

Modern sales tend to be consultative, strategic, and complex. You need to map out the multiple stakeholders in the company, gather info from them, and gain their trust. But before we get to that, let's talk about prospecting.

Finding New Customers with LinkedIn

Not all of your business will come from advertising and marketing. You may discover sales yourself. You may be assigned to a geographic region, or simply be involved in new business development for your company. In addition to the methods we discussed in the last chapter (Advanced Search, Groups, and Answers), there are a couple more places salespeople can find new potential customers: in the newsfeed and from existing connections.

Newsfeed and Recommendations

Many people completely ignore the newsfeed, but you can filter it by new connections. If you see that one of your connections has just connected to someone you'd like to connect with, now is a good time to get an introduction! The worst thing about introductions is that sometimes people connect with someone but forget who they are a year later. Fresh connections are top of mind.

Similarly, you can filter the newsfeed by recommendations. If someone just gave or received a recommendation, there's a lot of positivity in that relationship, and the chance of your introduction succeeding is even higher.

Your Connections

The people you've connected to directly on LinkedIn are called *first-degree connections*. This is your immediate network. The people who are connections of your first-degree connections are *second-degree connections* to you. For example, you may have a coworker in HR who is your first-degree connection on LinkedIn, and he or she has a first-degree connection who might make a good prospect. But because you have not directly connected with that prospect on LinkedIn, so that person is a second-degree connection to you. We talk about how you can turn second-degree connections into first-degree connections later in this chapter. There are also third-degree connections, but beyond that LinkedIn doesn't number them.

Are you starting to think about *Six Degrees of Separation*? There was a game Kevin Bacon created as part of a charity effort that popularized the idea that we are only six people away from an introduction to anyone in the world—which still has not been proven. However, the point is that you can leverage your connections to increase your connections.

LinkedIn Groups and Answers

We discussed how the Marketing team can use LinkedIn Groups and Answers in
Chapter 5, but these are also good places for sales-networkers to find prospects and
start relationships. Answering a question from a prospect can demonstrate your
company's relevance, value, and expertise. Discussions in Groups can start a conversation. You can even use LinkedIn Answers yourself to ask questions that might
draw prospects out of the woodwork. Ask them about their challenges. Once you
identify prospects this way, use the six-step relationship-building process from this
chapter to move toward an opportunity.

Advanced Search

Advanced Search is one of the most exciting aspects of LinkedIn, but also one
that should be used with care. LinkedIn's Advanced Search allows you to search
LinkedIn for anyone, on many criteria, even if you don't know them. You might
need to request an introduction or send a cordial InMail. If there's such a thing as
cold calling on LinkedIn, this is it.

Check out Figure 13.1 for all the criteria you can use when searching for people on
LinkedIn.

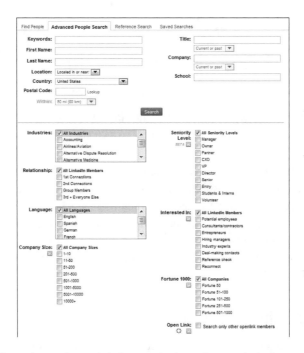

Figure 13.1   *Advanced Search helps you find people in LinkedIn by 17 different
criteria.*

When you start doing Advanced Searches, you'll find that you need to return to your definition of a high-quality lead. Who are the buyers in companies you sell to? What's their job title? Seniority level? How big is their company? Are they in specific industries?

It can take some trial and error to build a good search based on multiple criteria, so you'd better save that work. In the upper-right corner, click the green plus button to save your search (see Figure 13.2).

Figure 13.2 *As you build your search, watch the number of results, and make sure you save your search before moving on to another activity.*

How do you know when you've narrowed down your search properly? Realistically, how many prospects would be good customers for your business? In B2B, often a company finds a sweet spot when there are 5,000 or fewer target companies to go after. However, this is certainly not the case if you sell copier paper—there are millions of prospects! But how many buying decision makers are there? You can narrow down a search by putting "purchaser" or "buyer" in the keyword or title field.

Mapping Out the Target Company

If you're following up on a lead from your company's advertising or marketing campaigns, you may need to network your way through a company to find the economic buyer (final decision maker) who will use the solution you're selling and who might have influence over the purchasing decision. You can go to the company's LinkedIn page and take a look at its employees. You can also go to www. theofficialboard.com if you're targeting one of the 30,000 biggest corporations in the world.

Reaching Decision Makers and Other Stakeholders

The first thing to do is look at the LinkedIn company page and see which of the company's employees you have as first-degree connections. If you find people in the target company who are willing to help you, a positive conversation that demonstrates how you'll help their company (and serve their interests) could lead to LinkedIn introductions to other folks in the company, or their phone numbers. Even if you get the phone numbers directly from the last person you talked to, or from Jigsaw, you can use LinkedIn to look each person up and get to know a bit about before calling. You could get a formal LinkedIn introduction, and then call the next day. Even if your new targets haven't yet accepted your introduction or replied, if you have their phone number, you can call them and they'll at least recognize you. You can also find employees in LinkedIn Groups. Strike up a conversation if they've posted.

It might freak out some of the people you contact if they find out you used Jigsaw (www.data.com) to get their phone number. They might think it too forward. But then again, they might not ask how you got their number. And if you're really looking for a win-win situation, and you're respectful, it's not like you're a spammer, is it? You're a salesperson who's looking to help everyone involved. "Is this a good time? If not, when would be?" Each salesperson has his or her own level of aggressiveness. Perhaps the least intrusive approach would be the formal LinkedIn introduction or a mailpiece (yes, actually sending someone a letter).

The Six Steps of Relationship Building

The steps you take in building a relationship online—from the first to the last—can take many forms. If you haven't done a lot of social networking, you may benefit from the following model, which details the six steps of online relationship building (see Figure 13.3).

Following is a description of each step:

1. **Listen**—Read anything you can find from this person: their posts in Groups, LinkedIn profile posts, tweets, and blog posts. Try to understand where they're coming from, what their goals and values are, what their problems are, and how they think.

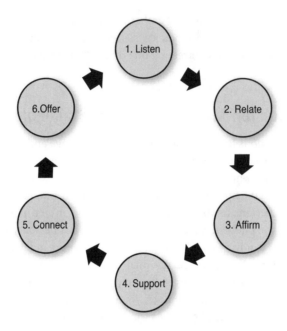

Figure 13.3 *The six steps of online relationship building*

2. **Relate**—In all this reading, you may discover mutual interests. Are they a fan of the same sports team? Do they like a TV show you like? Do you share specific opinions on how to business should be done?

3. **Affirm**—Contact them in some form (see the "More Ways to Contact New Prospects" section, later in this chapter) in regard to your passion about a mutual interest. This kind of contact can begin publicly with a tweet, a response to one of their LinkedIn questions or Group posts, or you might comment favorably on their blog. This step also could make use of the "Get Introduced by a Connection" feature you'll see on people's LinkedIn profiles (discussed later in this chapter).

4. **Support**—If you get an acknowledgment or favorable response, then a couple days later you can send the contact something useful about their interest. This might be a link to content on your blog or a site that has info about your company, but it could be anywhere on the Web. In fact, if it's not your website, even better. Too much self-interest at this point is bad. Your goal is to make a connection, not get an immediate sale. You're going for friendly and generous here. Think Ned Flanders from *The Simpsons*. This person may realize you do sales, even if that's not in your job title. Because you're on social media, they may have their eyes wide open, watching out for the

insensitive telemarketer-gone-to-Twitter sort of hard sales guy. You're trying to make a connection that's not specifically business, because this prospect may or may not be ready to buy. If they're not ready to buy, why should they get to know you? Ah, because you have a mutual interest and seem like a nice person. If you can side-step the pressure to buy or sell at the outset, you can start a relationship that hopefully will continue until the prospect realizes they need to buy from you. On the other hand, if you're doing a hard sale, and they're not ready to buy and they have no emotional connection with you, it's too easy for them to just ignore you. They'll make the decision to turn off to you, and you may never be able to turn that situation around. This sales approach isn't different from taking someone out golfing or entertaining clients; you're sharing something not specifically business to create a relationship. It's just online and a bit nerdier.

5. **Connect**—Connect on as many networks as possible with them. Follow them on Twitter, request a connection on LinkedIn, keep commenting on their blog posts. Save Facebook for last, because some people think it's weird when you request a Facebook friendship before you've had some personal interaction. But some Facebook profiles allow you to like or comment on posts, even if you're not a friend yet (sometimes it's because they're a friend of a friend). Liking people's posts makes them like you. Does all this make you seem like an e-stalker? The more familiar someone is with social media, the more normal this seems. Now when someone connects with me on LinkedIn and Twitter, I think, "Oh, this person understands social media and is diligent." If you are getting to know someone remotely, it just makes sense to be in touch with them in all these ways; if you aren't thorough like this, you may end up with someone who several months later says, "Hey, why aren't you following me on Twitter? Why don't you don't like me or what I have to say?" and actually is somewhat offended.

6. **Offer**—After you have a bond and some time together (2–3 weeks), ask how you can help. It's kind of like dating, isn't it? You might need to repeat step 4 (sharing) before you feel it's time. Just don't do it so often and so forcefully that you seem like a stalker. The purpose of step 6 is to open up a conversation to discover their needs, which can lead to how you might help. You don't have to mechanically do this by saying, "How can I help you?" That might seem forced and out of place. Here are some other ways to phrase this:

   • "I'm curious, what's your biggest obstacle in your current position?"

   • "What's working best for you in your work right now?"

- "What's not working for you in your work these days?"

- "How's your work going? Any persistent challenges?"

- "Have you worked with a [whatever you are] before? How did it go?"

These questions are a lot more subtle than "Have you seen what my company offers?" This is important because the shift in the relationship can be a big shock. Going from being social media buddies to the start of an informal needs analysis is a big change, so the key is to make the change comfortable. We're easing through this process in a way that seems natural and puts higher value on the human side of the equation. Emphasizing the human side ultimately pays off on the business side.

If you're the extroverted type, let me give you a different slant on sales. My type of sales is very introverted, because I grew up shy. I'm better at computers than hanging out with people. But over time, I found more comfortable and enjoyable ways to relate to people. My favorite was asking questions. I found customers and partners for myself and companies I worked for, but didn't see myself as a salesperson. Because I didn't go to school for business or get specific mentoring in sales, I was insecure about my way of doing it. I didn't realize there was more than one good way to do sales. I just thought I was too gutless to do it the forceful way.

Eventually I found a sales mentor who said, "It doesn't matter what you say about your solution or company if the prospect isn't ready." They need a burning desire. They must feel they need help right now. If you can use questions to get them to describe their problem and dwell in the discomfort, this increases the desire to make a change now. Your questions help them sell themselves. At that point, you make an offer and try to close the deal. The other approach, where the salesperson does most of the talking from the beginning, is risky. You don't get a lot of information back from the potential customer. You shut your prospect down. They may judge you while you're talking. After your long speech, they may not even give you much when they do talk.

As I said at the beginning of this section, this relationship-building process is not set in stone. The main point of showing you the process is to put some flesh on the bones of what online networking looks like. You may follow it mechanically at first. Over time, try to develop a sense of how fast you should move, and experiment with different approaches. Spend some time looking for cues from prospects about their level of interest and openness. Calibrate your approach based on whatever cues you see. There are a lot of variables in the relationship-building process. For example, you might have occasion to meet the prospect in person right after step 3.

More Ways to Contact New Prospects

Step 6 is where we try to bridge into a sales conversation. If that's done publicly, it can feel even weirder to a prospect. This phase of online relationship building requires something a bit more private. For this phase, we'll use the LinkedIn inbox (for InMail and Introductions), or perhaps we'll contact them via email or phone after we get their information from Jigsaw.

Introductions

When you want to connect to a friend of a friend, in LinkedIn terms, that's a first-degree connection who has a first-degree connection you're not connected to. You can ask your friend to introduce you. To do this, go to the profile of the people you want to connect with and click Get Introduced Through a Connection. A window will pop up, as shown in Figure 13.4, to walk you through the process of choosing who you'll ask to introduce you.

Figure 13.4   *The Introduction Request pop up. Choose someone to introduce you and then craft a message to that person about why you want to be introduced.*

One aspect of Advanced People Search is that you can specify only people who are more open to InMail. Instead of leaving the Interested In selection on All LinkedIn Members, choose people who have said they are interested in specific types of contact. For example, if you're selling, you might want to select only people who are interested in "consultants/contractors" and "deal-making contacts."

InMail

InMail provides private messaging on LinkedIn. If you don't have a relationship with someone, you can use InMail to contact them directly. Much of LinkedIn is free, but other features like this require you pay. LinkedIn says that "professionals are 30 times more likely to open LinkedIn InMail than email, because they view InMail as originating from a trusted source." In fact, you get a Feedback score from LinkedIn InMail about how many positive responses you receive, and if you don't get a response within 7 days, LinkedIn will credit your account with a new InMail.

To get the most out of InMail, think like an email marketer. Emails have to have compelling subject lines, or be from someone you're close to, to get opened. Tell people why they should bother to open it and read it. Start the email by acknowledging the value of their time, then get to the point. Tell them what you'd like to do next—whether that's to connect, to discuss something, or to get on a webinar. As discussed earlier, remember that moving too fast in social media can turn people off.

Jigsaw (Data.com)

Some LinkedIn users report getting results with InMail, but here's a counterpoint: Jeff Stevenson at Good Pay Low Rates in Flagstaff, Arizona, said in a public LinkedIn Answer, "I use LinkedIn to find the people I want to contact. Then I use Jigsaw to find their phone numbers and emails. I have never had anyone answer an InMail I have sent." If you find the same, consider Jigsaw.

Jigsaw is a business contact directory that was purchased by Salesforce in 2010. (They renamed it Data.com, but many people still refer to it by the old name.) It's a crowdsourced directory of business professionals. People like you join it and contribute business contact information. You get credit if you add people or update a bad phone number or address. You can use those credits, or buy credits, to get contact info for people you've found on LinkedIn. Some people think this approach is too aggressive, and some salespeople will not publicly admit they use Jigsaw. But clearly, it can be an effective tool.

More Real-world Experiences with LinkedIn Social Sales

The six steps of relationship building exist because, if your goal is to sell on LinkedIn, you can't succeed by starting with an email pitching your products or services. It doesn't work, and it burns bridges faster than you can build them. Sales professional Pat McGraw agrees. He reports the following on what he sees his peers doing:

"Hundreds of salespeople have peppered me with invitations to connect over the past 12–18 months. The 'best practice' appears to be (a) join a group, and then (b) send an invitation to everyone in the group. Then, if I accept the invitation, based on historical performance, about 50% come up with a completely pointless pitch that shows they have no idea what I do and the other 50% never speak to me again. Just for the record, I prefer the silent types."

I'm sure as a sales professional, he doesn't want salespeople to be completely quiet—but you get his point. The hit-and-run approach is a turn-off in social media.

A more relational approach comes from Beth Avery, Director of Sales at Contexo Media and Dorland Health:

"I'll either find a way to interact with them in a group, or email them outside of LinkedIn using 'LinkedIn' as my subject line. The best way to start a conversation, especially if you found them on LinkedIn, is to let them know why you're reaching out. For example, 'Jim, I saw your profile on LinkedIn, and I thought it was interesting the way you answered XYZ question in the ABC group. What are your thoughts on 123?' You're starting a genuine conversation, you're introducing yourself as a peer, and there will be time to 'sell' later. Would you likely get a response to the note above? Yes. Would you likely get a response if you pitched your product in the email? No."

Robert Madison, Business Development Manager at Spiral 16, a market research company in Overland, Kansas, chimed in and added the following:

"Beth Avery has the right idea. I can personally verify that I've tried both methods she's described (and then some!) and, as it turns out, genuine interaction and authenticity will win the day, 90+ percent of the time. It takes more work, but if sales were easy, more people would do it."

And to round out our discussion, we have some input from a sales guy who has found that sometimes an older technology is the best way to start: "Pick up the phone! It's the most natural and human way to connect," says Jason Croyle, a sales and marketing researcher at MECLABS. He continues:

"I reach out to the person and share that I found them on Linked In because I was researching their company and thought that we could provide value to each other. I share what I know that value is and strike up a real in-depth conversation or schedule a better time to talk. I always admit my resource and that it's random, along with my dial attempt. I don't use persuasion—clarity and honest always trump this and hype. Intros through LinkedIn are a mixed bag. There are too many open networkers that connect people together and honestly they don't abide by the open networking principles of helping people to connect. When I do write them, I utilize content from my organization that is fresh and relevant to their rank, role, and function within their organization. The success rate is in the double figures, but it's my last resort if picking up the phone doesn't work. Honestly, you'd be surprised at how many VP and C-Level executives would rather talk to you than fire banter back and forth electronically. Even the younger generation of executives is more apt to discuss with you over the phone than they are to engage in electronic communications. Social media is great for building networks, finding new people to connect with, and syndicating content. It's not the end-all-be-all of marketing. It must be integrated in an optimized fashion to existing marketing and sales efforts."

What about prospects you connect with that don't work out? Or LinkedIn Groups where you don't immediately find business? Jeff Lee has some great thoughts on this topic. Jeff has 10 years experience as a Sales Director and was also Head of Vendor Relations for ACS Ltd, a medium-sized business in the Business Supplies and Equipment industry in the U.K.

"As with any form of 'first contact,' honesty is the best policy. Be open and let people know you want to sell something, *but* match what you are selling with a well researched need on the part of your potential client. I would be (have been) very disappointed after several conversations with a peer group member I thought was genuinely interested in developing their own networks and contributing to others, only for them to disappear into the woodwork after their pitch was spurned. There is nothing wrong with wanting to sell something, and whilst keeping your eyes on the prize should be forefront in all salespersons, there is also a secondary position of growing strong potential client networks. If a potential client says no and you have a product or service they need or use, why walk away? Work with them in their networks, contribute to their lives, for free. At some point that 'no' will change, and you will end up with a client that's as difficult to lose as they were to win. However, it takes all sorts, and this type of client should form a part of your overall client base."

As you can see, there are a variety of ways to succeed with social sales, but the common elements are building real relationships and being respectful, honest, and helpful.

14

How Advertising, Marketing, and Sales Employees Work Together for Extraordinary B2B Results

How can your company get the best possible results from LinkedIn and inbound marketing? This book provides help for three major job functions: advertising, marketing, and sales. It also speaks to executives and sales managers about objectives, obstacles, and management practices.

Siloization is a well-known problem. Each department or employee might attempt to fulfill its own objectives in a vacuum, with no concern for how others might be impeded. In some companies there's no incentive to help other departments. There may be a fear of being seen to obstruct other departments; however, it may not be sufficiently clear when one department is impeding the progress of another. If your marketing automation, sales force automation, and analytics aren't set up correctly, and if executives don't receive accurate reporting, it's tough to verify what's really going on.

There are usually at least some individuals who recognize the value of interdepartmental cooperation for both themselves and the company. And some companies are highly cooperative and collaborative. Good teamwork can come from expectations set by leadership, or the character of your employees, or both. It can be sustained by instituting collaborative processes and applying those processes with discipline. The advice in this chapter can't fix teamwork issues that are rooted in leadership or hiring practices, so your mileage will vary. But for companies and employees who do want the benefits of greater cooperation, this chapter offers a map to that promised land.

Collaborating around LinkedIn and marketing automation tools could become a rallying point for your organization. If you've historically had trouble getting Sales and Marketing to work together constructively, maybe you can now. These new tools include analytics—you'll get measurable facts to work with—so you can shift to a quantified discussion. What works or doesn't work can be proven. Removing that subjectivity may resolve a lot of arguments and help you move forward toward better results.

The Benefits of Teamwork

This chapter outlines the types of collaboration necessary for your organization to get superior results. The benefits are:

- Every department gets better results.
- Your company becomes more competitive in the marketplace.
- You drive more revenue.
- You close better deals with customers you're more likely to satisfy.
- You enjoy status as a thought leader and innovator in your industry.

Every employee can share in the fruits of a vital company, whether though better pay or greater job security.

You might use LinkedIn for group communication, but this may duplicate a communication solution you already have. Your company probably already collaborates via face-to-face meetings and email. Maybe you use Skype for remote workers, Chatter inside of Salesforce, or Yammer. If not, you might create one or more LinkedIn Groups for this purpose. Still, not everyone adopts such solutions—and if email is already working for you, I'd just stick with that. Good collaboration isn't highly inconvenient for anyone.

Seven Topics for Team Collaboration

Throughout this book, we've discussed a number of topics, strategies, and tools that require input from multiple departments. Here are the most important LinkedIn topics for interdepartmental collaboration:

- Content marketing personas, content, and objectives
- LinkedIn ad targeting, messages, and objectives
- Coordinating networking activities in LinkedIn Groups
- Messages posted on employee profiles
- Marketing automation and lead nurturing
- Lead quality criteria and lead scoring
- Sales topics of discussion with prospects, obstacles, and solutions

Naturally, a marketing or PR department will discuss its progress with LinkedIn content marketing internally, and salespeople will discuss sales problems and LinkedIn prospecting issues with each other and their sales manager. But this is only the first step. How can Marketing's content pieces prevent some of the problems that salespeople confront? Salespeople need to inform the content creators in Marketing of obstacles during the sales process. What new content marketing needs to be created? Sales and Marketing can figure this out together. What if the marketing is overselling the company's offerings and creating dissonances during the sales process? Sales is telling the truth to people who are suddenly disillusioned about the company. Interdepartmental discussion is critical.

One size doesn't fit all. LinkedIn advertising and marketing may be handled by the same department in some companies. In a very large company, collaborative teamwork between every advertising, marketing, and sales employee may be impractical—instead, a discussion among managers may be required. Managers of each department can gather information, issues and questions to discuss with one another and relay the insights and action items back to their departments.

For Advertising People: How to Mesh with Sales and Marketing

Advertising may be the front line for your company. If you're the one doing the advertising, you need to know how your company should be portrayed, what the branding guidelines are, and how you should position the company compared to your competitors. You need to know what degree of control you have over messaging—for example, does every piece of copy need to be approved by someone else, or are you trusted to experiment with ad copy and images, given certain parameters?

The Marketing department may have specific content pieces they want to promote via LinkedIn ads. They may have specific audiences in mind for each content piece. Sales may want to begin to develop leads from new audiences, industries, or companies that you could target with your LinkedIn ads. Go back to the segmentation chart in Chapter 9 and work with Marketing and Sales to fill out the details.

Find out from Sales what obstacles they're running into during the selling process. Are there messages or ideas they'd like prospects to understand sooner? Are they dealing with misconceptions they need your help to combat? Create LinkedIn ads to condition prospects in a way that solves these problems. Are they aware of competitor advertising that's creating problems for them; if so, how can you help fight back?

Be sure to give Marketing and Sales executive summaries of what you find in your advertising tests. For each audience or job title or industry, what messages are working and what aren't? If you're able to track which ads are bringing in the strongest leads, what messages have those prospects seen before they get to Sales?

Make sure the Sales team knows the history of perceptions you've given prospects. One expert I interviewed was sales and marketing expert and keynote speaker Garrison Wynn. As he put it, "The salesperson needs to know the information that was used to educate the potential customer before they speak to them." Sales can use the phrases that worked best in the ads and won't be blindsided with questions about ideas used in advertising.

For Marketing People: How to Mesh with Advertising and Sales

As content creators and LinkedIn Group leaders, marketers are in a powerful position to grab attention, persuade prospects, position the company relative to its competitors, and even plant seeds of doubt that your company can assuage but your competition cannot. You pick up the torch from Advertising and pass it to Sales.

You can also use a chart like the segmentation table in Chapter 9 to map your content pieces to specific job functions and industries. Because Sales needs to close any prospects you persuade through content marketing, make sure you, Advertising, and Sales are on the same page in regard to objectives and audience mindset. Are there any persistent or stubborn issues they have with prospects that a new content marketing piece might fix? Create it! Post your content pieces in LinkedIn Groups that are used by the job functions and industries you're targeting.

Watch out for overselling. It's tempting to make your company, service, or product sound even better than it is. Remember that when you do this, you may increase leads, but you also bring in prospects who now have misconceptions that salespeople have to deal with. Accuracy and clarity are important. Author and Sales expert Garrison Wynn says, "Salespeople sometimes realize that the customers they're speaking with didn't understand all the details of the product—or had a misconception. The customer can then think the salesperson came under false pretenses. Marketing people may try to appeal to prospects at a broad level, but that customer had a specific need—the customer assumed your product or service would solve *all* their problems, but in fact, that need isn't included in what your company offers. If the marketing information isn't clear enough, the customer can be confused about what the deliverable is."

The Marketing or PR department may be tasked with coordinating the company's "brand army." That means organizing the employees who have volunteered as social media representatives on LinkedIn and elsewhere. When you launch a new piece of content marketing, you not only need to coordinate with advertising, but also let the brand army know so that they can post it on LinkedIn, tweet it on Twitter, and wherever else they may be designated to pass it on.

Marketing or PR may also be in charge of leading LinkedIn Group activity. That includes any Groups you've created and grown yourself, as well as how the entire company contributes to Groups where more than one of your employees is a member. It's a no-brainer that a marketing person would post a new content piece to company-owned Groups, but what about others Groups? Let's say there's another Group that several people from your company participate in. Who should post the new content piece there? Probably Marketing should, unless it's a Group that only salespeople have penetrated. Do you have specific goals for your participation in each Group? Often, participation is enough, but different employees may be developing specific relationships—make sure everyone in your company is on the same page. Watch out for having too aggressive a corporate presence in smaller or less active Groups, or people may perceive it as simply a Group your advertise in—this can turn everyone else off or perhaps annoy the Group's owner. Take turns amongst employees posting and interacting in these smaller Groups.

As part of the Marketing department, you may also be heavily involved in the setup of the marketing automation system. You help map which content pieces go with which phases of the sales cycle. And do different audiences and job titles need to see different content? Match the content pieces that live on your website with the audiences you're trying to reach and the corresponding LinkedIn Groups they frequent. What issues are most likely to delay prospects and what content might help move it along? As you figure out this map, convey it to Sales so they are certain which pieces of content they might InMail to prospects on LinkedIn.

Also, you must team up with Sales on one of the most difficult of all collaborative issues: lead scoring. The worst approach is to generate a huge number of leads of dubious quality, dump them into the Sales department, and expect them to sort everything out. When their first 50 leads turn out to be the wrong sort of people, or people who aren't ready to buy, salespeople get disgruntled with Marketing. Rather than build up resentment and perpetuate an us-versus-them mentality, use marketing automation and lead scoring to make the handoff more effective.

Marketing must understand that not all leads are of equal quality. Your marketing activities can bring in a larger number of less qualified leads, or a smaller number of more qualified leads. You can use lead nurturing to develop unqualified leads. Be accountable for that. The job of Sales is to help you define what makes a lead qualified and give you feedback on the scoring and lead-nurturing system's effectiveness over time. Executives also need to understand that Marketing should not be punished or rewarded based on the number of leads they drive but the number of *high-quality* leads.

Everyone has ownership and accountability within marketing automation, sales force automation, and CRMs. The goals are as follows:

- Bring Advertising, Marketing, and Sales together for greater results.
- Generate more leads *and* better qualified leads.
- Improve accountability among all employees and departments.
- Drive more revenue for less cost.

The last point is your executive team's favorite. The whole point of marketing and sales alignment is to increase revenues and drive more revenue from the same number of leads and the same advertising and marketing budget. When departments aren't on the same page, it doesn't matter how justified each department feels or what great reasoning they have about how it's the other department's fault. Do what you can to help each other drive more revenue, and you'll create a happier company, better jobs and fresher breath.

For Salespeople: How to Mesh with Marketing and Advertising

As the other sections of this chapter outline, you as a salesperson need to supply those in advertising and marketing with the following information:

- Who your prospects are. Provide a three-dimensional picture that can help Marketing create personas to communicate with on LinkedIn and elsewhere.

- Companies you're currently marketing to that might be stimulated by specific LinkedIn ads.

- New industries, job functions, and companies you want to reach.

- Ideas about the company's unique advantages it can use to create a difference in the customer's mind.

- Phrases and questions you find work to get prospects' attention, interest them, reassure them, and increase their urgency to act.

- Details about misconceptions that prospects bring to the sales process, so Advertising and Marketing can undo or change these misconceptions.

- Information about what's working (or not) in the LinkedIn Groups you participate in.

- Insight about the messages that prospects in various job functions, industries, and companies need to hear.

- What makes a lead (prospect) "qualified" to you.

This last point is one of the most important ones for the Sales department to help create and improve. Who do you want as a lead? Who's a good lead? Where do they work? What industries and companies? What job functions? What makes for a good or bad lead? What signals to you that a lead is ready to talk to Sales? What issues make a lead unready for Sales? Marketing will tie that into the marketing automation, lead nurturing, and lead scoring, how they create content marketing, and what LinkedIn Groups they disperse the content to. Advertising will use that to improve the targeting and messages in their LinkedIn ads. Then you'll need to let Advertising and Marketing know when you're still getting unqualified leads and how those leads are unqualified so that they can tweak the settings. If certain stubborn issues need to be addressed before sales conversations, a new content marketing piece can be designed.

15

The LinkedIn Advantage: Five Organizational Shifts That Support B2B Success

How can LinkedIn open up new opportunities, drive revenue, and create a competitive edge for your company? This chapter is for those of you who hold a leadership role—including executives, VPs, directors, and managers. You're at the top of your company. You set the tone, the mission, and the objectives for those below you. You decide what defines success and failure. You know what kind of employees you want. You shape corporate culture and processes—what your "way" is.

Naturally, as a leader, how much you understand, accept, and are interested in social media has a huge effect on your organization. If the Marketing department embraces it, but Sales does not, you have a problem. Only you can resolve those kinds of misalignments. This book teaches you how to get great results from LinkedIn, but excellent results come from teams that are excited to work together to make things happen. If one team doesn't care, doesn't prioritize, and won't give or accept feedback, the results will be lackluster. The leveraging of social media, and LinkedIn in particular, must be clearly supported from the top-down.

The Internet Changes Quickly and Often

LinkedIn and other social media sites represent big opportunities for your company—or threats from competitors who use them better than your company does. It's important to recognize new technological opportunities that can improve revenue and decrease costs, and take advantage of them quickly. The pace of innovation has quickened. Big opportunities come and go quicker.

One day Twitter is not taken seriously, and then Dell announced it made millions of dollars using Twitter.[1] The online shoes company Zappos had 400+ employees using Twitter in 2008,[2] and in 2011 the company was acquired by Amazon for $928 million.[3] YouTube was once just considered an entertainment site, and then suddenly it played a major role in the election of the first African American U.S. President.[4] Facebook is considered just for college kids, and then a blog post shows how three businesses are making profits from Facebook.[5] Some people think LinkedIn is just a boring online resume site, but some companies are driving business and closing deals from it.

Companies who have waited years to use Google ads start out paying several times more per click as they would have if they'd started earlier. These days, a year of due diligence can cost your company big bucks in lost opportunities and competitive disadvantages. While you're just learning how to get results, your competition is already at the top of the learning curve and getting good results. How many competitors do you want ahead of you because you chose to wait?

Adopting New Opportunities at the Right Time

These days, you need to constantly ask yourself questions like: "Is it now time for us to start using this or that social site or tool? Is it time for us to use it more? Are companies gaining traction and getting results there, even if it's in other industries? Is anyone in our industry using that site in an above-average way? Are we already behind?"

When you realize it's time to take your company's usage of a social website to the next level, you need to take the following five steps:

1. **Assess each opportunity's benefits.** What is good about each of these social sites? Read what the big blogs like Mashable and Techcrunch have to say about them. What have other companies gained by using each of them? Look for case studies.

2. **Anticipate the costs.** How many employees do companies like yours have working on each of these sites? Look at the salaries and job descriptions for these employees on Indeed.com. How much labor time is involved for each? Multiply that by an hourly rate from the salaries. Has an advertising budget critical to the success of companies using these sites? Add up these costs for each site.

3. **Quantify the learning curve.** Will employees require training? Find training providers and count the costs. Anticipate how much time it will take employees to both grasp the concepts and learn while implementing them.

4. **Select your key opportunities.** Which pay-offs are most important to your company? Correlate the benefits of each site to your corporate objectives. Which tech opportunities appear to have the most promising ROI for you? Choose the best one or two sites to invest most of your social marketing time on.

5. **Create a plan and implement it.** Get training. Get a consultant to help design your strategy. Create timelines. Divide responsibilities. Get to work.

You can also use this process to go granular on specific aspects of social sites. For example, if you decide it's time to do more with LinkedIn, is the biggest opportunity for you the company profile? LinkedIn Groups? Ads? Salespeople networking with new prospects? And how do the biggest opportunities on LinkedIn fit into what your people are already doing? Does LinkedIn replace some of their older tools? What kind of support do they need in the transition? Be systematic about how you move forward with social marketing and sales.

How Much Change Are We Talking About?

I'm not one of those social media gurus who thinks that social media should change the entire corporation (and there are definitely a few gurus who are quite visible that do think this). Sure, there are ways social media affects everyone in your company. But should every employee be on Twitter, representing the company by tweeting? Should every employee be posting in LinkedIn Groups or blogging? That presents risks. Not every employee wants to participate in social media. Some are better than others at written communication, some are brilliant at branding and marketing, and some are great at what they do for your company but might be liabilities in relating directly to the public.

Some of your people and some of your processes may need to shift. How much your company changes is up to you and the executive team. But change is not easy.

Big changes can lead to employees leaving for other companies that still do things the way they're comfortable with. You can't teach an old dog new tricks—unless it really wants to learn them. Therefore, navigating these changes might not be easy.

The speed of change is one of the most important aspects. How agile is your organization? How much can you get people to change the way they're doing things? Certainly, people who can't or won't change can be a liability these days, but you must be sensitive to how your employees handle the stress of changing. No one likes to go from feeling competent in their job to feeling incompetent. Think like a coach. Make sure your employees understand you support them through the growing pains. Affirm their effort, find out what they're having trouble with, and get them outside help (training or consulting) if necessary.

Critical Shifts for Your Organization

Here are the five critical shifts your company needs to make to increase B2B success and leverage LinkedIn:

1. Create quality content marketing and iterate based on analytics.

2. Create and leverage cross-silo feedback loops.

3. Foster salespeople who are relational and analytical.

4. Raise and deploy your brand army.

5. Empower adaptation and innovation.

Create Quality Content Marketing and Iterate Based on Analytics

As discussed in Chapter 5, prospects need information, and relationships are easiest to build when you have something to talk about. These content pieces can achieve multiple marketing and sales objectives.

Thousands of companies create and distribute content marketing pieces. And your prospects are receiving them. If they receive content from your competition, you may lose the propaganda war. Your competitors are planting seeds of doubt by emphasizing their strengths and your weaknesses, making it easier for their salespeople and harder for yours. This makes it clear that your company needs to do content marketing, too.

But your company also needs to do it well. You need high-quality content that people like, share, and respond to. You need to be able to answer yes to all of the following questions:

- Does this content look good? Does it represent the company well?
- Does it grab attention? Does it do so while maintaining a respectable image?
- Does it sound credible? Is it based in reality?
- Is it stimulating? What proportion of the people who see it also like and share it via social media?
- Does it get results? What proportion of the people who view or read it also contact your company?

The quality of your content, which might be a prospect's first impression of your company, must be high. If your content looks bad, people will think worse of your company—just as, right or wrong, we assume a sloppily dressed person is a disorganized worker. Make sure you keep an eye on the level of quality your competition is putting out, as well as what the best content marketing anywhere is.

How do you find and monitor the best content out there? And how do you get ideas for new content? Several types of tools are available that monitor social media. One type involves listening for conversation: Radian6, one of the best known social monitoring solutions (and now a Salesforce tool since they acquired the company), helps you find people who are talking about your company. That's great for customer service or gauging people's sentiment about your brand, but not useful for content marketing.

The more helpful tool for content marketing is Infinigraph (of which, I must disclose, I am VP of Marketing and Customer Success). You can enter a company name into Infinigraph's discovery engine, it will find the social media audience for that company, and then show you what other companies that audience interacts with. It finds the social media content that this audience is interacting with the most. That content is proven to stimulate interaction and viral sharing. You can actually repost that content, or use it as an idea generator for your own original content. In this way, you can finally measure the effectiveness of content. You can create new content and constantly learn what your audience responds to and what it ignores.

Create and Leverage Cross-Silo Feedback Loops

Encourage your employees to talk to each other. Team-building exercises are often seen as forced and dumb. Read Chapter 14 in this book on how teams can work together on LinkedIn. The whole should be greater than sum, and it is with successful teams. There are many entire books on team building and breaking out of siloes, including Patrick Lencioni's *The Five Dysfunctions of a Team*. The following tips will help your team get the most out of LinkedIn:

- **Buy and assign this book to all department members.** Make sure everyone in your Advertising, Marketing, and Sales departments reads this book. At the very least, they need to read the parts about how these roles should interact to get the best results. Ask them how they are making these changes. Ask them what obstacle they foresee and how they'll overcome them. If they don't see obstacles, they aren't taking the change seriously.

- **Focus on results and hold people accountable.** Know what metrics or key performance indicators (KPIs) you care about most from each department. Communicate that clearly, and hold them accountable to those results on a monthly basis. Keep asking about progress on those specific metrics. Keep them focused on those metrics. Watch for team members who are focused on metrics you care less about, and have a frank conversation with them about why they think certain metrics more important. You might learn something, or uncover a gap in your company's process for attaining the results you want.

- **Encourage both criticism and praise.** A culture of nonconfrontation is a dishonest one that lacks the feedback needed for improvement. If team members are not capable of both constructive criticism and praise, they are missing half the skills needed for teamwork. Suggest that people criticize privately and praise publicly. Wrap every criticism in twice as much praise. If someone can't take criticism privately, they may be too insecure to improve their teamwork. Watch for passive-aggressive team members who are talented at backhanded compliments. Privately make them aware of what they're doing and let them know that it's emotionally inappropriate, not helpful to the team, and needs to change if they want to stay on the team.

Foster Salespeople Who Are Relational and Analytical

Salespeople need to embrace consultative sales plus learn to convey rapport online. They should accept salesforce automation and customer relationship management software. They must participate in criticizing and collaborating to improve the implementation of these softwares. You want them to understand how advertising and marketing contribute to your success. They need to grasp how lead nurturing improves your results and your bottom line. Make sure their compensation incentivizes them to work with Advertising and Marketing as a team player.

Raise and Deploy Your Brand Army

Both the marketing and sales sections of this book discuss how a number of your employees may connect with prospects and peers as representatives of your company. This could be just a handful of people, or it could be more than 400, as was the case for Zappos. Gone are the days when your company had one public relations representative to speak to the media, or when only the CEO spoke for a company. And you can't get these days back, unless you bar all your employees from ever putting their employer in their social media profiles, even LinkedIn. Employees are now much more visible, which is both good and bad.

Here is what you must do to take advantage of this opportunity and avoid potential bad consequences. Refer to best practice #14 in Chapter 2 and check off the following three items:

- Create a social media policy.
- Identify the best social media representatives.
- Meet with these social media reps regularly.

There is also more discussion of the "volunteer brand army" in Chapters 5, 6, and 14. We recommend your brand army be organized and maintained by the Marketing team.

Empower Adaptation and Innovation

Change is a scary word. Instead, let's say "adapt and innovate." *Adaptation* is a no-brainer, because we don't want to be a Darwinian punch line. And when market conditions change, or powerful new tools become available, you'd better adjust, right? *Innovation* sounds fun and smart, like something Steve Jobs would approve of. The right changes can rocket your company ahead of the competition. You've likely already guided your company through other changes before.

Don't want to change yet again? Hoping that ignorance won't have too great a consequence for your company is not a good strategy. Come to terms with the new reality. Get familiar with what's new. Learn from your employees. It was Henry Ford who supposedly stated that because he didn't know everything, he made sure he hired people who knew what he didn't know. You don't have to know everything about LinkedIn or marketing automation or sales force automation—you can delegate that and just keep tabs on the results. If you know what results you want and what strategies your people are using to try to achieve them, you'll be able to tell if things are working or not pretty quickly.

The wrong changes are harmful. How do you know which course is the right one when the opportunities are new and the path isn't clear? It's prudent to wait until there are some case studies demonstrating positive results. Before that point, there is chaos—and merely promise—not true proof of viability. I prudently waited with Facebook marketing. I didn't adopt it until early 2010, even though others had been using it throughout 2009. One of my clients wanted a competitive advantage, so they pushed me into it. Soon after, I worked with a number of companies that achieved profits from Facebook marketing. Then I systematized what worked and began to teach it. In that first year, I saw many companies drag their feet on adopting it while their competitors began to reap the benefits. Not every client benefitted from it, and not every company has used it well. Those who have done best availed themselves of training, read blog posts, and did a lot of experimenting. Those who did worst did everything by the seat of their pants with no training, and did not try very many tactics.

The same process is now repeating itself for LinkedIn marketing. A few pioneers are getting great results, but the vast majority is underutilizing it. Those who adopt it now, learn the best practices, and experiment diligently will reap the greatest rewards soonest.

Endnotes

1. "Dell Tweets Up $3 Million In Revenue, While Twitter Still Searches For Profit," Clay Dillow, *Fast Company*, June 12, 2009. http://www. fastcompany.com/blog/clay-dillow/culture-buffet/dell-tweets-3-million-revenue-while-twitter-still-searches-profit

2. "Twitter Marketing, An Interview With Zappos CEO, Tony Hsieh," Brian Carter, *The Inquisitr*, August 28, 2008. http://www.inquisitr. com/2694/twitter-marketing-an-interview-with-zappos-ceo-tony-hsieh/

3. "Amazon buying shoe seller Zappos for $928 million, Nicole Maestri and Alexandria Sage," Reuters, July 29, 2009. http://www.reuters.com/ article/2009/07/23/us-amazon-zappos-idUSTRE56L6TQ20090723

4. "How Obama's Internet Campaign Changed Politics," Claire Cain Miller, *The New York Times*, November 7, 2008. http://bits.blogs. nytimes.com/2008/11/07/how-obamas-internet-campaign-changed-politics/

5. "Facebook Marketing ROI: 3 Case Studies," Brian Carter, SearchEngineJournal.com, March 2, 2011. http://www. searchenginejournal.com/facebook-marketing-roi-3-case-studies/28254/

16

Social Prospects: The Future of B2B Social Media

What's the future of B2B social media and B2B marketing? How can we prepare for it? How can we be better prepared than our competitors? The answers to these questions are the focus of this chapter.

People are fascinated by the future. Sci-fi authors and tarot cards readers make money telling the future. And when I speak, I usually get at least one forward-looking question from the crowd. Futurists, authors, and speakers who attempt to anticipate the future play an important role. It's as if human beings and nations are hurtling forward at a dangerous pace, and we want to know whether we're about to hit a wall or need to make a turn. Leaders want to know the future, so that they can lead people in the best and safest direction.

In technology, I think it's tough to make predictions more than five years ahead. Did anyone in 2007 see Facebook becoming the biggest social network in the world? Did anyone in 1999 see Google becoming the top search engine for more than a decade? Could we have foreseen how big Apple's iResurgence would be? Of course it seems obvious now, but I don't recall anyone who saw advances coming this soon. The key is to see the trends early enough to profit from them.

In 2008 and 2009, when experts were asked what the next big thing would be next year, most said "mobile marketing." Mobile has finally materialized to a degree, thanks to the popularity of the iPhone, but futurists were overly excited about mobile for years. So we need to be cautious about all predictions, and perhaps invest our time and money in them marginally and experimentally, but not heavily.

So how far ahead can I predict? I think if my predictions in this chapter hold true for three years, that would be a big success. Sure, some things don't change—we still drive cars while listening to the radio and we still watch a lot of TV. But I want to look at more specific questions: Will the leading online marketing platform be Google or Facebook or someone else? Should we shift half our search marketing efforts over to social? What things are more affected by short-term trends? We look at the answers to these questions in this chapter. First, though, what's the big lesson from all these changes?

Ride Every Wave of Opportunity

Ever since the Industrial Revolution, new technologies continually emerge. Every advance—radio, TV, the Internet—has created and destroyed companies. Ford's assembly line, Goodyear's telemarketing, Microsoft's operating system, Netflix's Internet/mail hybrid, Google's search advertising, and Facebook's people data have all created huge companies from nothing. Their competitors ignored these advances at their peril. New technological opportunities come faster and faster. There might be a new strategy or tactic for your company to adopt every year. You should watch for new opportunities, embrace the ones that seem most viable, and quickly begin to use them while watching the analytics to guide you toward increasing effectiveness.

You should ride each new wave of opportunity. Just like waves in the ocean, it's bad to catch them too early or too late. Early adopters, such as Robert Scoble and Guy Kawasaki, are praised for embracing platforms like Twitter, Friendfeed, and Google Plus, but not all online opportunities create equal ROI. You should see some evidence of value and profit before you adopt them. And yet, you need to discern those opportunities as early as possible to get ahead of your competitors. Right now, it is still a great time to begin to learn how to get B2B results for your company on LinkedIn. You don't want to wait until it's much more competitive.

The future is only important to the degree that you can capitalize on it now. Let's go back to the mobile example. Should you have created a mobile website in 2008?

Accessing websites via mobile wasn't nearly that common then as it was just a couple years later (mobile data traffic has doubled each year since then).[1] Should you create a mobile app now? Maybe. But do we really want every company in the world to have a mobile app? I don't. When I go to a website that I don't go to every day and it interrupts me to download an app, I get annoyed and skip it. If your users react that way, it hurts your brand, and maybe your future. So, it's a bad move to be too aggressive about adopting futuristic changes without stopping to think how it affects your users.

At what point in time was it obvious that you should jump on Google marketing? I would say that, as early as 2003 or 2004, it was obvious to those who knew the Internet marketing landscape. When was it obvious you should at least test various aspects of Facebook marketing and advertising? I would say that happened in mid to late 2011, once we began to see companies profiting from Facebook, and as we saw its use by the mainstream. Pinterest has grown quickly in the last year—faster than most sites, and much faster into the mainstream than Twitter did. You have to watch for explosive trends, and be ready to start experimenting with them faster. At this point, LinkedIn Groups and Ads are very strong options, but the best tactics may use some other part of LinkedIn in the future. Jump on these while they're hot.

Online Marketing Trends

Let's take a look at some of the main trends and conflicts in Internet marketing, and how they will affect the future of your business.

The Shift from Desktop to Mobile

Is mobile usage growing so fast that it will outpace desktop computer usage? Morgan Stanley thinks so. They've said mobile is becoming popular faster than desktop Internet did, and that there will be more mobile users than desktop ones in 2014.[2] This sounds doable when you consider that mobile happens on more than smartphones. Yes, if it were just phones, we would have valid complaints about the experience and how productive we could be on those little screens. But mobile includes tablets, iPhones, Kindles, and Nooks.

It's hard to believe that we won't still prefer desktop computing for some uses, but what if our mobile computer also becomes a projector with a virtual keyboard? This is pretty futuristic and even more flexible and useful than Corning's vision of ubiquitous glass touchscreens.[3] If our mobile device becomes capable of acting like a computer as well, then all computers will go mobile. As someone who has done a lot of video processing on my laptop and knows how highly CPU-intensive these activities (and others, such as graphics) are, I still think we'll have some desktop computers around for many years. But going predominantly mobile for most uses is believable.

Does a shift to mobile affect how we market? To some degree, it does already:

- If you run Google AdWords ads, it's recommended to create separate campaigns for mobile so that they function optimally. Mobile usage has gained enough traction to make this a default best practice for most AdWords accounts.

- If you run live events, having a hashtag for Twitter and using Twitter and text messaging make sense for coordinating both educational experiences and live networking events. You should have at least one LinkedIn Group, and you can create one or more subgroups to coordinate activities at your live events.

- Does your website work equally well on mobile browsers? Don't dismiss your mobile users just because the percentage is low. What if a decision maker checks out your website on his mobile and it doesn't work? Could that lose a deal for you? It might. The perception of your brand's quality can be impacted by this.

We will only shift to mobile when it doesn't limit what we need to do. I've adapted to using NBA mobile instead of going to NBA.com because it allows me to do 90% of what I can do at the website. But LinkedIn's iPhone app doesn't let me do all the marketing functions I need to, so I rarely use it.

Rise of Content Marketing

As we discussed in Chapter 5, 60% of companies are increasing their investment in content marketing. We could go so far as to say that companies are becoming publishers. Thought leadership through content differentiates and positions your company. Strong content persuades and wins prospects to your side before they finalize their decision—perhaps even changes the criteria they use for their decision. It's a strategy outlined for marketers in Chapter 5.

And yet, every strategy is enacted well by some companies, poorly by others, and completely neglected by still others. Will your company embrace content marketing, invest in it, distribute it via LinkedIn, and measure its effect to improve its results? Will you figure out what it takes to be one of the best content-marketing brands in your niche? Will your brand have the best content in your niche on LinkedIn? If not, perhaps your brand belongs to the past—not the future.

B2B Email Versus Social Media

In marketing, it helps to have a list of people we can reach over and over. B2B marketers are moving beyond the monthly e-newsletter to more specific offerings or to more sophisticated lead-nurturing systems that tie in with their content marketing, CRM, and analytics. They also are segmenting their emails by personas and behavior. Emails are still a fundamental part of B2B and don't appear to be going anywhere. After all, when you give access to a white paper, do you ask for an email or a Facebook like? For most B2B marketers, it's the email, and LinkedIn is just another way to get people to go to a website and give you their email. As we've discussed, LinkedIn can also help you create a Group, a community of people you can reach over and over again—the social version of an email list.

Are Facebook fans better than your followers and Group members on LinkedIn? The value of Facebook fans took a hit in 2012. Facebook admitted at their first-ever Facebook Marketing Conference that the average page reaches only about 16% of its fans. One of the fundamental risks involved in using Facebook for your permission-based marketing is that you don't really own the Facebook page; if you accidentally violate one of the terms of service and the page is taken away, or some other *force majeure* were to happen, your permission-based list would be gone. What if Facebook becomes the next MySpace? It's a good idea to grow your lists in multiple places: email, Facebook, LinkedIn, and others, just to make sure your eggs aren't all in one basket.

Certainly, you could argue that the capability to show socially enabled advertisements to your fans is a big advantage because it makes a Facebook fan base worthwhile. And you don't have to choose either email or Facebook overall; you just need to choose what actions you want people to take in order to get your content. You could use Facebook Connect to get their email *and* other Facebook profile data, which is the best of both worlds. You can use LinkedIn ads and Groups to get traffic to that opt-in page. No matter what changes in the future, if you use whatever website is hot right now (Facebook or LinkedIn) to get traffic and emails, you own the list and can move on to the next social platform safely.

Social SEO

For years, social media activity, likes, and shares have indirectly affected search engine optimization. For example, links on Twitter have some enhancing effect on search rankings, and Google used to have access to Twitter's API. As Google switches its emphasis from Google Plus as a Facebook competitor to Google Plus as a search-ranking quality validator (called "Search Plus Your World"), participation in Google Plus is required, whether you like it or not.[4]

The real question over time is, will Google find that the Google Plus user base skews its results in the wrong direction, and be forced to go back to measuring activity on other social networks? My guess is they will, or they will secretly still use that information. I can't prove it, but it looks to me like Google focused on quality search results early on, then took a break while they focused on corporate earnings, and now they're working hard to get to the next level of quality. If they aren't just talking a good game for Wall Street, if they really want social activity to improve the quality of their search results, they're going to need the social signals that come from the bigger players in social media, such as Facebook, Twitter, LinkedIn, and Pinterest. This is purely my opinion, but I think their position is untenable unless people suddenly start really enjoying Google Plus. They'll either have to admit they don't have the social data they need and resume drawing from other social websites, or their search quality will suffer and they leave themselves open to competition in search from others—maybe even Facebook.

What this means is that you should do search for search, and social for social. If a social website isn't that attractive for users, don't invest in it simply out of fear of Google.

Search versus Social

Will the use of search decline with the rise of social media? Will Facebook and LinkedIn destroy Google? I've looked at available data from Alexa and Compete, and I've asked people I know who have access to many websites' analytics. We have not seen a decline in search usage overall, despite people using social media more in 2011 and 2012. Google has had the greatest search share for years, and it has not declined.[5]

My observation is that search and social are two very different behaviors, or usage modes:

- When I know what I want, I Google it. If I have a question, I might ask my social media friends, but even with a network of thousands, I find that sometimes none of them have been in the situation I'm in. When I Google, I'm accessing the collective wisdom of many millions of people.

- When I want to see something novel or unexpected, I go to social media. When I want to share an idea or piece of content quickly, I go to social media. Blogging takes a lot longer, and isn't worth the extra time if all I want to do is share a photo.

I don't believe social media will take away from search. Facebook may improve its search functionality and tie that in with all our social connections, but then

Facebook becomes a search and social site. Search itself doesn't go away as an activity.

Even if somehow Google activity were to diminish significantly, there's reason to think that B2B marketing would stick with Google Search marketing longer than B2C would. Nearly two-thirds of B2B marketers like their search ROI, and 96% planned to maintain or increase their search marketing and advertising spend in 2012.[6]

Will Facebook improve its search functionality and attempt to steal share of search from Google? Facebook has all the social data Google Plus wishes it did (to become a higher quality version of Google's "Search Plus Your World"). Facebook has a partnership with Bing for web search results. And soon Facebook will have all the pressure of Wall Street asking them for another big win. In my opinion, all Facebook would have to do is create search that is "good enough," and make web search more predominant in their user experience. Then they could use a growing number of web searches to place Google-like keyword-related ads. If Facebook's ad platform allowed you to target search-keywords, Facebook could steal a lot more of Google's multibillion dollar ad revenue. Why? Because companies believe, so far, that search-keywords more quickly generate revenue and business results than Facebook's or LinkedIn's people-oriented ads. You should always invest your advertising dollars to get business results, and perhaps to increase brand awareness. Therefore, watch Facebook to see if they become more capable of both.

B2B Marketing Spend

Where is spending going? According to a Forrester research, B2B interactive marketing (search marketing, display advertising, mobile marketing, email marketing, and social media) spending is expected to grow at a 14.4% CAGR, to 5.7 billion in 2016. Despite the relatively low growth, B2B is projected to boost mobile marketing investments, from $129 million in 2011, to $639 million in 2016—a 38% CAGR over the next five years.[7]

From what I've seen, this is believable. B2B marketers may lag conservatively after B2C in spending their marketing budgets online, but those online budgets have continued to increase year after year. What's more, faith in many traditional offline marketing channels has decreased. In 2011, according to Marketing Sherpa, the channels that most B2B marketers were planning to spend less on were print advertising, tradeshows, direct mail, and telemarketing.[8]

Should you be a bit less conservative? I have nothing to lose, so I'll say yes. If you can do so without being offensive, going a bit more cutting edge will differentiate you. If my experience with B2B companies is a good gauge, your sense of what's cutting edge is a bit off. Try to move into new channels faster, and experiment more, while holding firmly to your identity. Unless your marketing is boring. You should remain professional, but in this attention economy, one of the least forgivable sins is being boring.

People Trends

To plan for the future, we need to think about how our business is affected by where people are spending their time, trends in the workplaces, generational shifts, and technology shifts.

Work as a State of Mind and Not a Place

People are answering work emails in the evening from home. (I do myself, and I hear stories about people who do—do you?) People are participating in continuing education and keeping up with current events, trends, and news from mobile devices, at all times of day. Fewer people think that the workday ends at 5 p.m. In fact, if you have insomnia, you might be working at 3 a.m.! Setting B2B ads to turn off at 5 p.m. (as some want to do with Google AdWords) doesn't make much sense to me. Even if you have data that shows conversions happen during the day, are you certain people didn't first start their research phase in their "off hours"? If you aren't visible then, you might not make it onto their shortlist of companies.

For some companies, social media fans are more interactive on the weekend. In an analysis I did with InfiniGraph, we found that Chanel's fans were most responsive on Saturdays, but they tend to post most on Thursdays. Every company is different, but not all know which days are most favorable or have adjusted their posting schedule to match. You can use a content-scheduling tool such as HootSuite or InfiniGraph to ensure that, even if you take the weekend off, you're at least putting something out there for people to interact with. Do you need someone monitoring the responses? Yes, if you can manage it. But you can also put in your policies, just like a customer service availability schedule, that your responses may be slower on weekends.

More people are working remotely. I do a lot of remote work, both consulting and webinars. Everyone I talk to wants to know where I am geographically. Therefore, I've naturally developed a bit of a spiel about it: "I'm from Ohio, I met my wife in California, and we still have a house in San Diego we rent out, but I moved to South Carolina for an agency job, and it was so nice here that when I went solo we didn't want to leave!" People want to connect with you, and they love regional details. If they want more, I'll describe the view from our porch. I recently met Ekaterina Walter (on the phone, of course), Intel's Social Media Strategist, and we bonded over our choice of remote work in beautiful parts of the country—it helps you stay positive while working harder. Although this remote work phenomenon may be strange for some managers, it has grown more and more important to some people, so get used to it!

When you research companies you're targeting via LinkedIn, check where the person in the position you want to reach is located. The company you're going after may be in San Francisco, but what if the role player you need the most is located in Portland? You end up over-targeting the wrong city.

Gen Y and Gen Z

Generational definitions are not well agreed upon. Gen Y was born roughly between 1980 and 2000, and Gen Z was born roughly between 1995 and 2015. They both share a deep integration of their lives with technology—the comfort and familiarity with technology of digital natives. They multitask and are optimistic and entrepreneurial. Gen Z is a bit young to have developed careers yet.

Gen Y loves to learn and has asked for more career development in their jobs.[9] This suggests an increase in the educational segment of your content marketing, as you market to them in the future. They care about social responsibility, so they'll welcome you emphasizing any aspect of this in your own company's mission or as examples in your content. Gen Y learned from technology to be flexible. Interfaces and devices change frequently. New websites become available. They also have the adaptability of young brains. And they perceive older generations as inflexible. If you have Gen Y employees in your Marketing or Sales departments, prepare to allow them to try new things frequently. The good news is that their flexibility fits with an analytics-driven culture. As you see what works and what doesn't, give them feedback, and they may have an easier time switching to changed and recently proven methods than Gen X or Boomers would.

However, they may also need more psychological support as they develop their careers, because the self-esteem culture they were raised in is not always compatible with work environments influenced by Gen X'ers and Boomers.[10] Because Gen X'ers and Boomers don't need or expect as much affirmation, they may not immediately give it. This also means your marketing, if it targets Gen Y age businesspeople, might need to be a lot more positive and affirming. I was amazed by one finding, that saying someone was "nice" could actually be considered an insult by Gen Y because they were all told they were gorgeous geniuses.[11] Gen Y is also more entrepreneurial, so support services for entrepreneurs may experience a boom over the next decade.[12] This could translate into LinkedIn ad targeting of young people with a CEO title and company size under 10.

Fighting for Attention

People are using more devices, and there are more websites and more TV stations. In the course of a day, a person might pay attention to TV, email, a web portal, Facebook, a search engine, Pinterest, smartphone apps, smartphone games, video games, and online music. Today, so far (and it's only 2 p.m. right now), I have been on 22 different websites on my desktop computer (during which I've listened to about three hours of music), four websites on my iPhone, and before the day is over I'll watch a few hours of sports (while my wife watches "TV" on her iPad). We may watch *Portlandia* on Netflix through our Wii, I'll text two or three people, and play two or three games on my iPhone. I am Gen X, but more like Gen Y in my content consumption and device usage.

Gen Y has been called many names, most of which I can print here, including Gen M for *multitasking*. Although many question the wisdom or effectiveness of multitasking, there's no question they do it more than previous generations. The 2011 Cisco Connected World Technology Report revealed that one-third of college students felt Internet access was as important as food, water, air, and shelter. More than half of college students, and six out of ten of another group of 20-somethings, felt they couldn't live without the Internet. Stunning! Most get their news primarily from their laptop. Also, 40% would be willing to accept lower paying jobs if that meant flexibility with device choice (bringing their own phones or getting to choose what kind), social media access, and mobility.[13]

Even if multitasking declines as they age, you can expect some of these habits to continue and be stronger than they ever were for Boomers or Gen X. That means you have more competition than ever. In my marketing experience, companies consistently underestimate how much they need to focus on grabbing attention. You may never be as interesting as a smartphone game or a fan's team playing an important game, but you need to be more interesting than an encyclopedia—you should be as interesting as Mashable or a magazine on the rack in an airport newsstand.

There's a continuum, from relatively boring to relatively risqué, with the *Wall Street Journal* on one end, *USA Today* in the middle, and *Cosmopolitan* and *FHM* on the other. As a professional B2B business, you probably want to stay on the *WSJ* side, but move a little closer to the middle. I would never recommend you do anything to lose credibility, but you should at least occasionally ask yourself whether your brand is too boring. If you get less social marketing results than you'd like, and you never think about how to grab people's attention, maybe that's why!

Have you noticed how many blog headlines are attention-grabbers? Some go so far as to recommend you come up with a great headline before you write the blog post. The same goes for white papers. If no one pays attention to the ad or the blog post headline, no one will click, no one will read—and you won't get many leads.

What I love about *USA Today*, even though an elitist would look down their nose at me for it (and if you're an elitist, I look down my nose at you), is it's written at a fifth-grade reading level. It's eminently accessible. Even if you have an I.Q. of 140, you may be distributing that IQ among several activities, so truly smart people will never hate you for keeping things clear and simple.

Summary

This chapter gives you a glance at some of the principles of change management and the trends we're experiencing, plus how these principles and trends affect social marketing and sales, particularly on LinkedIn. Naturally, how you implement these insights will depend on your corporate goals and culture, and your resources and team. Change is the only constant, yet some things never change. The key is figuring out which is which is which! Keep your eye on your analytics and your ear to the ground. I hope this chapter and this book has been helpful to your company, and I would love to hear about how. Thanks for reading!

Endnotes

1. "Cisco Visual Networking Index Forecast Projects 18-Fold Growth in Global Mobile Internet Data Traffic From 2011 to 2016," Cisco Newsroom, February 14, 2012. http://newsroom.cisco.com/press-release-content?articleId=668380&type=webcontent

2. "Mobile Explosion Will Surpass Desktop: Morgan Stanley," Steve Rosenbaum, Huffington Post, April 24, 2010. http://www.huffingtonpost.com/steve-rosenbaum/mobile-explosion-will-sur_b_550772.html

3. "Is This the Future Of Touchscreen Tech? New Video Will Blow Your Mind," Samantha Murphy, Mashable, February 3, 2012. http://mashable.com/2012/02/03/day-of-glass/

4. "The Future of B2B Search: Start Preparing for Social SEO Now," Brad Neelan, Search Engine Land, February 15, 2012. http://searchengineland.com/the-future-of-b2b-search-start-preparing-for-social-seo-now-110763

5. As you might expect when Wall Street is involved and companies such as Yahoo! and Microsoft who struggle with search share are worried about their stock price, some strange ways of counting "searches" emerge (like counting slideshow article views as searches) to try make these bedfellows look better compared to Google, and we've had to create crazy terminology such as "explicit core searches" to

stay focused on real search numbers. If you feel like wasting a couple hours trying to understand the details, see these articles: http://searchengineland.com/time-to-end-the-bullshit-search-engine-share-figures-44100 and http://searchengineland.com/comscores-new-core-search-figures-48762

6. "Search Still Half of All Digital Spending," Christopher Hosford, BtoBonline.com, February 13, 2012. http://www.btobonline.com/article/20120213/SEARCH09/302139959/search-still-half-of-all-digital-spending. "B2B Marketers Focus on Seo and PPC," Kathy Crossett, MarketingForecast.com, February 21, 2012. http://www.marketingforecast.com/archives/16872

7. "Forrester: B2B Interactive Marketing Spend Forecast Lower," Marketing Profs, November 21, 2011. http://www.marketingprofs.com/charts/2011/6432/forrester-b2b-interactive-marketing-spend-forecast-lower#ixzz1sVRmNC56

8. 2011 B2B Benchmark Report, Marketing Sherpa, 2011. http://bit.ly/msherpabwb2011

9. "Most Bang for Your Buck: Five Principles on Retaining Generation Y Managers," http://thegenyblogger.wordpress.com/2011/07/22/most-bang-for-your-buck-five-principles-on-retaining-generation-y-managers/

10. "Is Generation Y suffering from a Self Esteem Overdose?" Coffee With Caesar, April 9, 2012. http://coffeewithcaesar.com/is-generation-y-suffering-from-a-self-esteen-overdose/

11. "Narcissistic and Entitled to Everything! Does Gen Y Have Too Much Self-Esteem?" Aspen Education. http://www.aspeneducation.com/article-entitlement.html

12. "Poll: Gen Y Loves Entrepreneurship, Needs Help." CBS News, November 11, 2011. http://www.cbsnews.com/8301-505143_162-57322961/poll-gen-y-loves-entrepreneurship-needs-help/

13. Cisco Connected World Technology Report, 2011. http://www.cisco.com/en/US/netsol/ns1120/index.html

Index

W

X-Y-Z

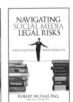

BRIAN CARTER

FREE
Online Edition

Safari
Books Online

Your purchase of *LinkedIn for Business* includes access to a free online edition for 45 days through the **Safari Books Online** subscription service. Nearly every Que book is available online through **Safari Books Online**, along with thousands of books and videos from publishers such as Addison-Wesley Professional, Cisco Press, Exam Cram, IBM Press, O'Reilly Media, Prentice Hall, Sams, and VMware Press.

Safari Books Online is a digital library providing searchable, on-demand access to thousands of technology, digital media, and professional development books and videos from leading publishers. With one monthly or yearly subscription price, you get unlimited access to learning tools and information on topics including mobile app and software development, tips and tricks on using your favorite gadgets, networking, project management, graphic design, and much more.

Activate your FREE Online Edition at
informit.com/safarifree

STEP 1: Enter the coupon code: MZZDWFA.

STEP 2: New Safari users, complete the brief registration form.
Safari subscribers, just log in.

If you have difficulty registering on Safari or accessing the online edition,
please e-mail customer-service@safaribooksonline.com